Praise for
NLP at Work

"This book may help you to understand life more clearly."
Paul Smith, fashion designer

"The definitive volume on the topic... an excellent introduction... a clear, thoughtful structure. The style of writing is realistic and practical and it is easy to become immersed in the book."
Personnel Today

"A jargon-free approach, featuring exercises, examples and action tips to show how to use NLP techniques, to accelerate learning and enhance creativity, communication and influence."
People Management

"Should be on the bookshelf of any NLP student."
Training Management

"NLP at Work outlines NLP in a business setting. Understanding how your behaviour influences the responses of those you deal with can be the key to modifying attitudes and establishing rapport."
The Guardian

"The clearest book on NLP that I have come across. It is easy to read, relevant and insightful."
Management Training

"Recommended heartily for its good visual presentation, jargon-reduced descriptions and lots of fine examples of NLP at work in the workplace. It's a great place to start."
NLP World

The business agenda at the start of the twenty-first century focuses on working with change and developing people's potential and performance. The *People Skills for Professionals* series brings this leading theme to life with a practical range of self-development and human resource guides for anyone who wants to get the best from their people.

Other titles in the Series

LEADING YOUR TEAM
How to Involve and Inspire Teams
Second edition
Andrew Leigh and Michael Maynard

THE NEW NEGOTIATING EDGE
The Behavioral Approach for
Results and Relationships
Gavin Kennedy

MANAGING TRANSITIONS
Making the Most of Change
William Bridges

COACHING FOR PERFORMANCE
GROWing Human Potential
and Purpose
Fourth edition
John Whitmore

MEDIATION FOR MANAGERS
Getting Beyond Conflict to Performance
John Crawley and Katherine Graham

NLP at Work

The essence of excellence

Third edition

Sue Knight

NICHOLAS BREALEY
PUBLISHING

LONDON · BOSTON

This third edition first published in 2009 by Nicholas Brealey Publishing
An imprint of John Murray Press

An Hachette company

1

First edition published in 1995

British Library Cataloguing-in-Publication Data
A catalogue record for this book is available from the British Library.

ISBN 978-1-85788-529-3
eBook (UK) ISBN 978-1-85788-446-3
eBook (US) ISBN 978-1-47364-485-4

Printed and bound by CPI Group (UK) Ltd, Croydon, CR0 4YY

John Murray Press policy is to use papers that are natural, renewable and recyclable products
and made from wood grown in sustainable forests. The logging and manufacturing processes
are expected to conform to the environmental regulations of the country of origin.

Nicholas Brealey Publishing
John Murray Press
Carmelite House
50 Victoria Embankment
London, EC4Y 0DZ, UK
Tel: 020 3122 6000

Nicholas Brealey Publishing
Hachette Book Group
Market Place Center, 53
State Street
Boston, MA 02109, USA

Tel: (617) 263 1834

www.nicholasbrealey.com
www.sueknight.com

Contents

Preface to the Third Edition

It is over a decade since I wrote the first edition of *NLP at Work*. It has traveled the world since then and is available in 14 languages. I have followed in its footsteps: to the US, Turkey, Madagascar, Denmark, Sweden, Finland, Portugal, Belgium, France, Canada, Australia and, most especially today, India.

The title *NLP at Work* is deliberately ambiguous. NLP works in all contexts: in business as in the home, in relationships with others as much as in relationships with oneself, in the world of marketing, IT and finance just as in the arts, sports and leisure. I pioneered the use of NLP in business, and writing the first edition of this book was instrumental in this, as I sought to make it accessible to people in business as well as in life as a whole. It has long since achieved this goal.

In the 20 years since I first heard the term Neuro Linguistic Programming, it has become the core of my work and my life. I could not have predicted the way my life would unfold when I stumbled across it. I am lucky to do what I love, celebrating excellence through my training, talks, coaching and writing. I have studied and learnt from many models of excellence, both famous, such as Brian Keenan, Heston Blumenthal and Paul Boateng, and not so famous, such as the father of one of the SOS children's villages, home to many children orphaned or abandoned in India, and an 82-year-old cycling veteran who is still winning races and cycling 200 miles a week no matter what the weather. I coach many leaders in business and, more importantly, I learn from them all.

WHAT IS NEW?

Every chapter in this latest edition has a new slant to it. The chapter on metaphor includes more ways of eliciting and working with metaphor as the language for change. The section on modeling includes more cross-cultural examples and nonverbal ways of modeling excellence. The significance, purpose and application of clean questioning are included alongside precision questions so that each enhances the other. And I incorporate something that has been present in the way NLP has been taught for years and yet is so obvious that it has often been overlooked: humor and provocative therapy. I have also written new material on how we represent time and how we can use that representation to enrich our experience in the present.

I am aware that many NLP trainers use *NLP at Work* as their course material, as do I. To help with this, I have included more summary checklists with steps for students in the chapters on outcomes and perceptual positions. Over the years NLP has been misunderstood and misused, specifically through an overemphasis on technique. We have looked too much at the finger rather than what the finger is pointing at. To redress the balance, I have simplified some of the original chapters on techniques.

However, the main reason for a third edition is that what I wrote in both the first and second editions I now view and use with the seasoning of age, faith and experience. I have appreciated applications and nuances that were limited by my immaturity when I wrote that first draft all those years ago. And the world has changed. The only things that are certain are uncertainty and mortality, and NLP has been a means for me to learn to live with both. If I were to prioritize the learning I encourage in my students, it is the ability to embrace a state of unknowing, to live in the present and to open themselves with every pore of their body to feedback.

I am often asked if NLP translates into other cultures. I reply, "It is about culture – our individual and collective culture." NLP is a means of respecting and embracing difference. When asked recently how I "sell" NLP to other cultures, I replied, "I don't!" I use NLP to learn about the beauty and uniqueness of other cultures and to help those whose culture it is to learn about the structure of what they have in a way that enables them to share it fully with others.

What I want you to gain from reading this new edition is a sense of wonder and mystery – there is always more to learn. If you finish the book with more questions than answers, if something touches you and you feel emotions well up, if the hairs on the back of your neck stand unexpectedly on end or your face starts to flush, if you are inspired to know and experience more, then my writing will have been a success.

Let me now get out of the way and allow you to get on with your reading. You will find lots more on my website, www.sueknight.com, where you have the opportunity to let me know what you think. I value your opinions.

Sue Knight
September 2009

What is NLP?

What we see and hear is what we think about. What we think about is what we feel. What we feel influences our reactions. Reactions become habits and it is our habits that determine our destiny. –Bob Gass

Neuro linguistic programming (NLP) is the study of excellence. It is an attitude of learning, curiosity and respect for unique ways of being in the world. Over the years NLP has uncovered an increasing number of tools and techniques for discovering what constitutes excellence. In particular, it is a means of finding the *essence* of that excellence – the difference that makes the difference – and doing so in such a way that it can be coded and reproduced. We can have excellence at our fingertips, available whenever we choose. As a result, we can coach ourselves and others to consistently achieve the results that we want for ourselves, our business and our life.

NLP is a means of finding the essence of excellence

WHAT IS NEURO LINGUISTIC PROGRAMMING?

Neuro linguistic programming (NLP) is a process of modeling the conscious and unconscious patterns that are unique to each of us in such a way that we are continuously moving toward a higher potential. NLP is not a thing – it is the study of what works, especially of what works well. What is there not to like about that?

NLP is the study of what works

• **Neuro** refers to our brain and our physiology. We learn habits, some of which we need to get by in life: how to walk and talk, how to breathe, how to drive, how to ride a bike, how to eat, how to laugh and cry, and how to feel the way that we do.

We learn habits – some good, some bad

Most of our habits are stored in our unconscious mind. Some will be for the better and some will be for the worse. By increasing our awareness of the patterns in our thinking, we can learn how we are influencing the results we are getting in work and in life more generally. The key to finding personal and business success comes from within ourselves; learning about how we think enables us to find the answers we need.

* **Linguistic** is the verbal and nonverbal language that we use to communicate with ourselves and others. Our language is our life. What we can say is what we can think and what we can do. Learning to understand and master the structure of our language is essential in a world where communication in all its various forms is the lifeblood of our personal and business welfare.

* **Programming** is the way in which we put these patterns of thinking, language and behavior together to get the results that we do – good and bad. We run our lives by strategies, in a similar way that a computer uses a program to achieve a specific result. By understanding those strategies we give ourselves choice: choice to do more of the same or choice to enhance our potential and our individual excellence. In essence, NLP is the study of our thinking, behavior and language patterns to help us build sets of strategies for everything we do – for making decisions, building relationships, starting up a business, coaching a team of people, inspiring and motivating others, creating balance in our lives, negotiating our way through the day and, above all, learning how to learn. The good news is that we can learn how to refine our existing strategies as well as discovering new ones and even discarding those that are redundant. The bad news is that for the most part the critical pieces of these strategies are outside our conscious awareness. We do not know what we do or how we do it.

We run our lives by strategies

With NLP, we can unpack not only the conscious elements but especially the unconscious ones, so that we *can* learn how we do what we do. This allows us to do what we really want and achieve what we deserve.

The best thing for being sad," replied Merlin… "is to learn something. That is the only thing that never fails. You may grow old and trembling in your anatomies, you may lie awake at night listening to the disorder of your veins… you may see the world around you devastated by evil lunatics, or know your honour trampled in the sewers of baser minds. There is only one thing for it then–to learn. Learn why the world wags and what wags it. That is the only thing which the mind can never exhaust, never alienate, never be tortured by, never fear or distrust, and never dream of regretting. Learning is the thing for you.

T.H. White, The Once and Future King

THE RELEVANCE OF NLP

NLP will continue to increase in relevance as we embrace new cultures, break new ground, challenge traditional ways of doing things and embrace those traditions too where appropriate.

NLP has increased in relevance over time

We need to learn how to use new technology in ways that are creative and different. If you do what you always did, you get what you always got. And it is the combination of "thinking about thinking" and technology that will set the new breed of leaders and independent business owners apart from the rest. There is nothing else in the world of human development and learning as powerful as NLP. Emotional intelligence, spiritual intelligence, visualization and various other concepts are derivatives of the NLP process.

The only route to understanding would have to come through creating a practical working model in your mind that could be used to rise above the detail… Every successful entrepreneur I've ever known has worked this way… From this high level view of the world, they create simple, rule of thumb formulae that can be used as the basis for decision making.

Peter Small, The Entrepreneurial Web

We live in a world of unprecedented change. We are immersed in unpredictability and complexity. The more we discover, the more there is to discover. Every question reveals yet more questions. We need skills and attitudes to help us learn how to make sense of this chaos. When everything around us may seem to challenge who we are, we need to know how to find certainty within ourselves about what we want and what we believe. We need to take care of ourselves and stand alone in our self-assurance and empathy for others, yet we sometimes need to be able to show others our vulnerability and ask for help. We need to know how to pick ourselves up when we are down, to learn from uncertainty and disappointment, to shape our direction and even to be prepared to lose everything.

We need the capacity to move more quickly than ever before and at the same time to stand still and drink in the richness of the moment. We need to know how to communicate with people of vastly different cultures and, more than anything, how to communicate with ourselves. We need to understand others' perceptions even if they are poles apart from ours; and we need to listen to the wisdom of our own bodies.

We need to know how to laugh, to let go, to learn, to grow, to mourn, and to move on. We need humility and graciousness and the strength to absorb our own and others' inconsistencies. We need the resilience to remain in situations that cause us pain and to be able to find the joy in everything and everyone. We need to know how to find the excellence that is within us all and to celebrate it with every part of our heart and soul. We need to forgive others, but first we must forgive ourselves. We need to know how to forget, and we need to allow ourselves and others to be who they truly are. We need to learn as we have never learnt before. And above all, we need to love.

Above all, we need to love

How can we achieve all this? In some ways the answer is a paradox. Far from embarking on courses of accelerated learning and speed reading to be able to learn faster, we need to look within ourselves and find our unique resources. In this way we can develop our own formulae for success. We need to know how to learn from every situation, every person and every intuition.

There is so much to learn in both technology and personal development that it is impossible for anyone to learn everything. It is our ability to manage our thinking, our conflicts and our experience that will ultimately make the difference between those who will lead the way into an exciting, creative and cooperative future, and those who will rapidly fall by the wayside as they attempt to follow. This is what we can learn with NLP.

WHAT CAN YOU GAIN FROM THIS BOOK?

Success comes from within. Our success depends on our ability to be excellent in everything we think, say and do. NLP provides us with a way to achieve this excellence.

By mastering the concepts in this book and making them your own, you will discover the essence of your own and others' excellence. You will achieve more of what you really want and become more of who you truly are.

Excellence is context specific. Many business models fail because they assume that what works in one environment will work in another, yet what makes a leading entrepreneur in one environment may be quite different to what constitutes success in another. NLP is a means of coding excellence and enhancing it so that you can establish what really works for you in your environment and with your skills.

More specifically, NLP can support you in learning how to do the following:

Excellence is context specific

- Discover the essence of your excellence so that you can tap into that in whatever context you choose.
- Learn how to bring out that excellence in others.
- Accelerate your ability to learn so that you can not only manage change but initiate and embrace it, enabling you to excel in your particular specialism and field of work.
- Learn how to laugh at situations with others in ways that create healing and learning.
- Discover how you relate to and use time and make choices that will enable you to experience time as you want.
- Learn how to listen with respect and naivety in a way that allows you to truly learn about others and their needs and wants.
- Continually develop new ways of thinking that support you whatever the changes in the external world.
- Let go of old, traditional patterns and habits that constrict your growth and release hidden talents that are appropriate today.
- Embrace feedback in a way that enables you to develop new ideas and products with the involvement of all your customers, colleagues and friends.
- Set compelling outcomes for yourself, ones that by their very nature take on a momentum of their own and maximize the

chances that you will achieve what you want, both personally and for your business.

• Develop formulae for yourself to enable you to respond to, and more importantly take a lead in, the world of high technology so that you combine the best of high-tech thinking with awareness of yourself and others.

• Build high-quality relationships with significant people in all contexts of your life, in whatever medium is appropriate.

• Heighten your awareness of yourself and others, so that you are sensitive to the subtle shifts in behaviour and attitude that provide feedback on the effects of the way you communicate.

• Develop your flexibility so that you have more choices and consequently more influence over the situations in your life.

• Improve your ability to generate commitment, cooperation and enthusiasm in the people around you.

• Manage your thoughts and feelings so that you are in control of your emotions and your destiny.

• Develop your ability to tap into your unconscious mind and draw on its superior power and potential.

• Accept and love whatever you have and in so doing love yourself and others in a way that transforms your business and your life.

You will find your own applications and your own formulae for success – that is the real joy and power of NLP. In business especially, NLP is the difference that makes the difference in personal and business coherence, communication, strategic thinking, e-business, motivation, influence, negotiation, leadership, entrepreneurship, self-development... the list is endless.

Overall, the purpose of learning NLP is to generate further learning and to be the best you can be. If you want readymade answers, NLP is not for you.

HOW DOES NLP WORK?

NLP pays very little attention to what people say they do, as that usually bears very little or no resemblance to what they actually do. You might think that by asking top achievers how they succeed you would get precise answers. You would be wrong! The key to success is often unknown at the conscious level. Being able to access the previously unknown pieces is sometimes referred to as the magic of NLP. It is not magic, merely an awareness of what really makes the difference that is so often missing in more traditional models and techniques. Using the tools of NLP you can elicit these unknown pieces so that you can "code" talent.

There will be things you do that you do not (yet) understand. Do you know, for example:

+ How it is that in some situations you have moments of brilliance yet you can't reproduce them whenever you want?
+ How it is that sometimes you bring out the best in others yet at others seem only to trigger the worst?
+ What you do that is different in those relationships where you have exquisite rapport, where you know what the other person is going to say before they say it?
+ How you control your feelings in some situations when in others you lose control?
+ In those situations where you feel especially confident, how you generate that inner feeling of calm and certainty even when everything is stacked against you?
+ How you attract people who want to be around you in work and life?
+ How it is that some of your remote communications achieve as much if not more than face-to-face conversations?
+ What it is about the way you use technology at those times that influences people to want to do business with you?
+ How it is that sometimes everything you do seems just right, you feel at one with yourself and you achieve new personal bests?
+ What happens at those times when you are able to shift gear to a more successful way of being so that you achieve more than you previously dreamt was possible?

When you know the answers to these questions and others like them, you begin to have more choice over the way you think, feel and behave. You have more influence over the way you respond to your unique calling in the world.

REFERENCES

Bob Gass (1999) *Word for Today*, UCB Broadcasters.

John Grinder & Judith DeLozier (1996) *Turtles All the Way Down: Prerequisites to Personal Genius*, Metamorphous Press.

T.H. White (2001) *The Once and Future King* (new edn), Voyager.

William James is usually considered the father of American psychology. He was once invited to deliver a series of lectures at Harvard on a topic of his choosing. These lectures were presented on the green and were special in that they were open to the public. After some deliberation, he chose boldly and the title for his first presentation was "Can One Prove The Existence of God," a topic sure to raise eyebrows in the early part of [the twentieth] century in New England.

Thus, it was with some trepidation that he watched the audience file into the lecture hall and, sure enough, at the very last moment, a little old lady rushed down the center aisle and deposited herself front row center. Professor James presented his topic with his usual wit and charm. He noted as he worked his way through his lecture that the little old lady was very attentive and seemed to be enjoying herself–he did mark the fact that she seemed to laugh when no one else did. Nevertheless, all seemed quite in order.

At the end of the presentation, which was very well received, the inevitable queue formed. And, of course, at the end of the queue was the little old lady. When her turn came, she looked up brightly at James and said: "Dr. James, I very much enjoyed your lecture. But I do still have one question."

"Please, Madam, ask your question!" returned William James courteously.

"Well, Dr. James," she replied with a glint in her eye. "If there's no God, what keeps the earth from falling down?"

James quickly reviewed his options… he considered such explanatory notions as centripetal force, gravitational systems… but wisely chose to respond in such a way as to learn something from this woman. Turning his attention back to her, he said, "Madam, I would be happy to answer your question, but tell me what it is that you believe that keeps the earth from falling down?"

"Why that's very simple, Dr. James, the earth is resting on the back of a gigantic turtle!"

James mused to himself over her extraordinary response for a moment and then with a hint of triumph in his voice asked the obvious question. "Then pray tell me, Madam, what keeps this gigantic turtle from falling down?"

"No, no, no Dr. James!" replied the little old lady. "You can't get me there… it's turtles all the way down!"

Taken with permission from the preface to *Turtles All the Way Down* by John Grinder and Judith DeLozier.

Part I
The Elements of NLP

NLP continues to grow

NLP produces the elements that in turn feed the modeling process

NLP brings together many techniques that have been around for years and combines them with discoveries that are new. It is both the study of masters of change, some of whom are no longer alive, and a recognition of the talents that exist within each person today. NLP is a journey of discovery.

NLP didn't evolve in a neat chronological sequence; it exploded into the world of therapy and then did the same in the world of business. And it continues to grow in part because it is an evolving subject. The form that is common to all living systems is that they make themselves. They are produced by particular elements and in turn produce other elements. Take a compost heap, the beauty of which is that it exists to support the production of the very things that make it work. We put biodegradable material on the compost and that in turn is used to fertilize the production of more of that very same material – plants. This is how a living system works and this is how NLP works. It is used to "produce" more of the elements that in turn feed the whole process of modeling.

Rapport is a good example of this. When John Grinder and Richard Bandler first studied great exemplars in the world of hypnotherapy, they discovered that one of things that made the difference was the quality of the rapport these therapists created with their clients. The knowledge they gained about building rapport was then used to enhance the process of modeling itself by enabling the modelers to build a trusting and respectful relationship with their clients, thereby increasing the speed and effectiveness of the whole modeling process.

When I wrote the first edition of this book, my publisher and I discussed in detail how I could structure the subject in a way that enables you quickly to grasp the elements and begin to appreciate and experience the power of the whole. I experimented with many approaches before we decided to use the name Neuro Linguistic Programming as the basis for the structure. But that's easier said than done!

The elements of NLP don't fit perfectly into the categories of **Neuro**, **Linguistic** and **Programming**. Nevertheless, these headings act as useful umbrellas under which to introduce the subject. I ask for the tolerance of the purists among you who could argue about the exact categorization of each of the elements. The feedback I have received since the first edition is that readers have found this structure helpful and so I have continued with it and expanded the content of each section.

I have chosen those pieces of the subject that I believe serve as a useful introduction and are most relevant to work and our rapidly evolving world. I have written both an easy introduction to NLP and source documents for those who want support for their coaching and training; indeed, this book contains the material that forms the basis of my own NLP Practitioner training. In the last few years many NLP trainers have told me that they use the book as their reference material for courses and with this in mind, I have included some more steps for utilizing the skills in several of the chapters.

The first "technique umbrella" is **Neuro**. Neuro is to do with the way we use our minds, our bodies and our senses to think and make sense of our experience. The more awareness we have of our thinking patterns, the more flexibility and therefore the more influence we have over our destiny.

Neuro

I start this section with **Chapter 2, Thinking patterns**. The discovery of the unique ways in which we think opened the doors to many of the models for change covered in the subsequent parts of the book. Many books encourage you to "think positively," to "stay calm," to "keep control." NLP is much more than this, offering "how" to achieve these results.

NLP gives us the "how"

NLP is "thinking about thinking," and this chapter in particular will help you expand your thinking power. NLP does this not by prescribing fixed techniques that work for some, but by enabling you to explore what it is that *you* do when you "think positively," "stay calm," and "keep control." You have your own unique ways of accessing and using these kinds of resources, no matter how infrequently or how briefly you may have used them in the past. Once you understand the elements of your personal "program," you can distill it down into the essence of its excellence and run that program when you choose. This chapter will raise your awareness of how you do what you do, a stepping stone to personal mastery. Increasingly, you will find that leadership models and models for change talk about mental maps. With NLP you can discover the nature of your own mental map and how it influences everything you do.

You can distill the essence of your excellence

Also in the Neuro section is **Chapter 3, Filters on your world**. The filters through which we experience the world govern our perception of situations and of people. By recognizing these filters, we can capture what it is that we and others are doing and thinking in achieving the results we do. And we can understand more about our ability to relate to the unique styles of others. For example, have you ever noticed how in meetings some people talk about what is different about ideas and proposals, whereas others search for what they like and how these ideas compare to other similar ones? And have you ever experienced people who are inspired by a vision of the future trying to get through to others who want to dwell on the problems? We need to learn how to accept all the differences and similarities that exist between us if we are ever to exist as a unified world.

We need to learn how to accept differences and similarities to live in a unified world

Chapter 4, Thinking with your body, is a central part of NLP and still draws the greatest interest in those embarking on this study of human behavior. This is an important chapter, as so many people have come across more traditional theories of body language where, as examples, scratching your nose means that you are lying and folding your arms means that you are defensive. NLP offers a very different kind of understanding, one that is unique to the individual and respectful of the person. It does not put gestures into predetermined boxes, but enables us to develop the subtlety of calibrating our own body language and that of each person we meet, no matter what the context of the communication. In this chapter you will learn how to recognize different patterns in behavior and consequently different patterns in thinking. In this way you can improve how you communicate with anyone in any situation.

Linguistic

Under the **Linguistic** heading are chapters on **Enriched communication**, **Metaphor**, **Precision questions** and **Hypnotic language**, all of which contain new material, and a completely new chapter on **Clean questions**. This addition is significant. Clean language is a discovery that was the product of modeling a remarkable therapist, David Grove. Clean questions are designed to work only with the client's way of experiencing the world and the symbols they use to code their experience. It is one of those elements that became integral to the whole process of modeling, a vital part of that fertile compost heap I mentioned earlier. If you were to only read one chapter, read this one. You will go a long way with the learning that we have the fortune to benefit from here.

Clean questions are a vital part of the compost heap!

The ways of using language to facilitate change formed a large part of the early work of John Grinder and Richard Bandler, the founders of NLP. In business, language is one of the most readily available forms of influence. When you are aware of your language patterns you can use each of your senses to enrich your language and bring it alive. With precision questions you can learn how to generate quality information, the lifeblood of business. Precision questions are also undoubtedly one of the most powerful tools for challenging the constraints that we create for ourselves. Precision questions exist to reconnect us with our sensory experience.

The section of this book on language now covers the remarkable range of questions and premises on which we can work both with ourselves and others to discover the excellence that exists and to facilitate change. The questions are not reserved for the world of coaching and change. Learning language patterns and ways of responding to them will support you in achieving excellence in the way you communicate, build relationships, lead, present, negotiate, manage conflict, show respect, learn and of course model… and much, much more.

In my quest to promote NLP in the world of business, I initially played down the role of hypnotic language. I wanted to concentrate on how we could make the unconscious conscious, rather than promoting the use of working with trance. I have since moved on. Business has also moved on and I think that there is now a much greater understanding that hypnotism is more than a stage performance. My aim in including this chapter is to help you realize just how much we are influenced by the hypnotic language that is around us every day, and through this awareness how we can learn to use this language to good effect. Many of the techniques that are essential to business and our personal development rely on our willingness to draw on our unconscious mind, and hypnotic language is a way to work with that.

To make room for the new material, I took out one of the original chapters on Metamessages. This is still available from my website, www.sueknight.com.

Programming

I have once more expanded the **Programming** section of the book to reflect the increasing importance and interest in this, the heart of NLP. The knowledge and skill that exist in NLP in business have grown significantly since the last edition of this book. I have more delegates for advanced levels of training than ever before. Most major companies have a significant population of NLP Practitioners and Master Practitioners. The level at which I start my training is well beyond what I would have done some years ago. So the realization that modeling is really what NLP is all about is reflected in my developed chapters on **Modeling** and **Strategies for successful living**.

Our knowledge of NLP in business has grown significantly

I had feedback that many readers did not really get the significance of the TOTE model, included here in Chapter 11, so I have rewritten this. It is too important for it not to be understood.

All of the elements of NLP can be used in different ways. As independent techniques they will enable you to improve the quality of your relationships and gain greater control and choice over the way you live your life and the results you achieve. Additionally, even though many of these elements were discovered through the process of coding excellence, they are now also used to enhance the quality of the coding process itself. For example, your awareness and understanding of the finer distinctions in language and behavior will enable you to elicit and refine the essence of excellence in the models of excellence you choose to study.

There are many ways of teaching NLP. There was a time when I knew most of the NLP trainers running certification courses. There are now thousands, with a multitude of styles and emphases. What I have aimed to do in this book is accurately to reflect my own style, my passion for the integrity and accessibility of NLP. I have been described as an NLP junkie, in that I don't just write about NLP and teach it, I aim to live it. I believe that we were born to aspire to our excellence and that NLP is part of the route to achieving that.

What I offer is my truth. If that inspires you find yours, then all will have been worthwhile.

Neuro

The spiritual life is a life beyond moods. It is a life in which we choose joy and do not allow ourselves to become victims of passing feelings of happiness or depression.

Henri J.M. Nouwen, The Road to Daybreak

W e cannot change other people, we can only change ourselves. Our environment is tempered by our mental models. There are some people who only see good in others. They have no representation for bad. In their world bad doesn't exist.

Our thoughts leak out in everything we do, often in ways that are outside our conscious awareness. These thoughts send out signals to the world about what we want, what we believe and who we are. And the world responds to those signals. Consequently, the key to influencing the responses is to change the inner signals.

Learn to manage your mind

NLP offers us the opportunity to manage these inner representations and signals. In doing so we begin to tap into the potential of the world's most powerful computer – our mind. By learning how to manage our thoughts we can:

- Change our experience of situations and people.
- Influence the reactions we get.
- Hold memories in a way that supports the person we want to be.
- Create the future we want.
- Build the relationships we would really like.
- Discover the thinking that releases our unique excellence.

That list is only for starters. We can learn to manage our mind in ways that work for us and help us lead the life we are meant to lead.

At the tip of Argentina is a region named Tierra del Fuego (land of fire) by Magellan's explorers, who noticed fires burning on the shore. The natives tending the fires, however, paid no attention to the great ships as they sailed through the straits. Later, they explained that they had considered the ships an apparition, so different were they from anything seen before. They lacked the experience, even the imagination to decode evidence passing right before their eyes.

Philip Yancey, Rumours of Another World

2
Thinking patterns

Our achievements of today are but the sum total of our thoughts of yesterday. We are today where the thoughts of yesterday have brought us and we will be tomorrow where the thoughts of today take us. -Blaise Pascal

The structure of excellence exists to a large degree in how we think. What we think influences how we act. So learning to identify how our thinking is shaping our actions enables us to capture and reproduce moments of excellence.

Learning to recognize how we think gives us the ability to reproduce not only others' talents but our own. With the awareness that we can develop with NLP, we turn what might have seemed like "luck" into choreographed success.

Learning how we think enables us to understand and relate to the many different cultures with which we come into contact. Most of the teams with whom I consult are multicultural, and even when team members originate from the same country and speak the same language, each person still has their own unique language and personal culture. We can learn to recognize, respect, accept and relate to these unique styles and in so doing navigate our way successfully through the diversities of the global network of which we are a part.

By exploring the structure of how we think and how others think and act, we can begin to understand the subtleties of these different cultures. We can do this as we encounter them; we do not need to research for months in advance. The value of learning NLP is that we use it in real time.

The connections we make and the way we represent memories, ideas and information are unique to each one of us. Everyone has their own way of thinking. When we understand the nature of our representations, we begin to influence our

We can learn to relate to all cultures

What we think is what we are

thinking, our emotions and consequently our experience. What we think is what we are.

We take in information through all the senses of sight, hearing, touch, taste and smell. We represent this information in our mind as a combination of sensory systems and inner feelings. These thinking patterns are a part of how we "code" our experience. By learning to manage our thoughts, we learn how to create the life and career we want for ourselves. Life is literally what we make it.

Life is what we make it

PREFERENCES IN THINKING PATTERNS

Let's explore some differences in thinking patterns. Think of "coffee." What comes to mind?

A picture? Maybe you imagined coffee cups and a coffee maker?

Or maybe you heard the hiss of the coffee machine? Or the noise of the coffee being poured into the cup?

Then again, maybe it was more of a feeling? The feel of the coffee cup, perhaps? Or the feeling of relief you associate with your morning coffee break? Or the taste or aroma of the coffee?

Possibly it was a combination of some or all of these.

These different ways of thinking are:

- ◆ **Visual** We think in pictures. We represent ideas, memory and imagination as mental images, e.g. a picture of a cup of coffee.
- ◆ **Auditory** We think in sounds. These sounds could be voices or noises, e.g. the sound of a coffee machine.
- ◆ **Feelings** We represent thoughts as feelings, either internal emotions or the thought of a physical touch. We can include taste and smell in this category of feelings, the taste of the coffee, for example, or the aroma.

You will find that you have a preference for some systems over others, both in the way you think and in the way you communicate.

When we are relating to the world at large it helps if we appeal to all the senses. In this way we connect with all the preferences of our readers, our listeners, our viewers and our potential clients. At the time of writing there is a backlash against some e-business propositions, and yet there is also a boom in interest in "clicks and mortar" businesses. These are established high street businesses (the mortar) that have developed ways of attracting people to their premises through the web (mouse clicks). Given what we know about our need to appeal to all senses, this is not surprising. The combination of the technology with a physical outlet appeals to both our intellectual and our physical needs. So people are currently more likely to search for what they want on the web but follow through with a visit to a store where they can see, hold, touch and talk through the items they want to buy.

Is it any surprise that communication is one of the most widely spoken about problems in business? Consider the level of frustration so many people express with the meetings they attend. Even when an objective is agreed, it is likely that each person at the meeting will represent a successful conclusion in a different way. For example, outcomes could include:

- **Visual** An image of all the agreed proposals written up on a whiteboard with names against each one.
- **Auditory** People talking to each other at the close of the meeting, making comments such as: "That's been really useful. I know exactly what my department has to do next."
- **Feelings** Thoughts about shaking hands with other people at the meeting and a satisfied, warm feeling.

My husband got a new car with a satellite navigation system. We can choose the style of the display. My husband selects the smallest-scale map that can be displayed with the symbolic indicators for which way to turn in preference to a pictorial map. I choose the pictorial map with the largest scale possible. When traveling through France I like to see where we are in the context of the whole country, whereas my husband likes to see the details and names of the immediate vicinity.

The ability to offer choice has become a key differentiator in business

What is significant is that the makers had the wisdom to offer this choice. The ability to offer choice has become a key differentiator in business. We can choose the layout of our home page on the web, the colour of the displays. We can choose how we want our orders sent to us in the post. We can choose what extras we want to pay for when we book travel tickets. To do so we need to understand the way our customers think, even if they themselves do not consciously know (and they often don't). This awareness of unconscious need is becoming much more important than the information that we gain from standard customer surveys. We don't know what we don't know! We need to be able to offer choices that our customers only realize are important to them as they experience the difference.

A clue to the way we think is in how we move our eyes. For example, is there someone near you now who considers themselves a good speller? Ask them to spell "phenomenon" without writing it down. Watch their eyes as they do so. If they are really skilled, ask them to spell "phenomenon" backwards. Good spellers will typically look up, eyes right or eyes left, to see the word in their mind's eye. (Some may look straight ahead but in a defocused way.) Because they can "see" the word written out they have no difficulty in spelling it backwards. It is as if it is there on the page in front of them.

Our eye movements contain clues to how we think

Did your schoolteacher ever say to you, "You won't find the answer on the ceiling"? The truth is that you probably would!

Your eyes are an indication of how you are thinking. I have come across managers who when interviewing candidates for a job, have been suspicious of people who break eye contact. The implication for them is that they may very likely have recruited people who do not think!

The details of all the eye movements and their meaning are in Chapter 4, Thinking with your body.

FINER DISTINCTIONS IN THINKING

Within each of the main thinking patterns of visual, auditory and feelings there are finer distinctions, for example the color and clarity of an image, the tone and volume of a sound, the strength and location of a feeling. People who can influence their emotions and their experience have the ability to choose these fine distinctions in their thinking. Learning to exercise and extend your range of thinking patterns leads to mental agility, just as physical exercise leads to bodily flexibility.

You return home and walk into the kitchen area. The working surfaces are clean and white. On one surface is a blue ceramic bowl filled with fruit, vivid green apples, purple grapes, and several bright yellow lemons. You pick up one of the lemons and feel the textured surface with your fingertips. You raise it to your nose and smell the sharp aroma.

Also on the surface is a sharp kitchen knife and a wooden chopping board. You place the lemon on the board and slice through the middle of it. A fine mist of lemon juice sprays into the air. You pick up one half of the lemon and see the defined segments and pips, some of them cut through. You raise this half to your mouth; the sharp aroma is even stronger now. You sink your teeth into the skin.

Mind and body are one

How is the saliva flow in your mouth now? This is the power of thought. The way you think affects your internal state, which in turn triggers a physical reaction, in this case the saliva flow. Your mind does not distinguish between what is imagined and what is real.

For example:

Jim often had to give presentations as part of his work. Although he felt comfortable in one-to-one meetings, whenever he had to present to groups of half a dozen or more he felt anxious, tense and nervous. It was worse if he knew about the presentation several days in advance, because he would start to imagine what could go wrong. In particular, he would imagine a dark room, and the faces of the people that he imagined there would be blurred. He would typically start telling himself in a harsh, critical internal voice the problems he might have. For example, he wouldn't be able to explain his points clearly, he would lose his place in his notes, and people would get bored. If he heard himself speaking it would be in almost a whisper. He could see people straining forward to hear, or sitting back and looking away. He would feel a heavy, sick feeling in his stomach, his heart began to beat faster, and his mouth felt dry. Beads of perspiration would break out on his forehead and hands. And all this even before he gave the presentation!

Our lives are self-fulfilling prophecies

We "dry run" our lives in our minds to such an extent that we influence the eventual result. Our lives are self-fulfilling prophecies. We are what we think.

MANAGING YOUR THINKING PROCESS

Think about something you did last week. Now think of something you could have done last week but didn't. The question is, how do you know you did one and not the other?

After all, these are only memories, one remembered, one created. How often have you had the experience of not knowing for sure whether you did something or not? "Did I lock the front door?" "Did I turn off the light?"

Think of something you did yesterday that you will do in an identical way tomorrow. It might be getting out of bed, brushing your teeth, or setting the alarm. How do you distinguish between the one you did yesterday and the one you will do tomorrow? In fact, *can you* distinguish between what you did yesterday and what you will do tomorrow?

Many people distinguish between the past and the future according to where they position the images in their mind. For example, the past might be behind you or to your left. The future for some people is in front of them or to their right. Where is your past? Where is your future? And where is the present? There is more about how we code time in Chapter 16.

Identify two people, one you like and admire and one you dislike. Now take the one you like and admire. In your thinking about this person:

- Do you see them and, if so, what is the quality of the image? For example, is it bright or hazy, color or black and white, moving or still?
- Are there any sounds associated with the thinking?
- What are the qualities of the sounds? Are they loud or faint, harsh or soft?
- What is the location of the sounds?
- And what about the feelings? What exactly do you experience and where?

Now think of the person you dislike and consider the same questions. What is similar in the quality of your thinking about the two and what is different? The content is irrelevant. It is the *nature* of your thinking that makes the difference.

This ability to distinguish between the various aspects of your own and other people's experience is a way of determining the difference that makes the difference between those who do achieve what is important to them and those who don't.

How do you distinguish events in time?

It is the nature of your thinking that makes the difference

VISUAL DISTINCTIONS

Let's consider these distinctions in thinking patterns in more detail by taking a few simple images and experimenting with them.

Think, for example, about your journey to work. You can change your experience of this journey to make it better or worse by experimenting with your thinking about it. Start by changing some of the visual distinctions. For example, if it is dim turn up the brightness. Then put it back as it was. If it is still, make it into a movie. Each time you experiment with a distinction, return it to its original form before you experiment with another. This way you will be able to establish how a change in a specific distinction affects your experience of the situation, in this case the journey. You may find that your thinking about it becomes more relaxed, more stressful, more interesting, or maybe even more exciting.

Brightness	Bright or dim? Dull or sparkly?
Clarity	Dim and hazy or sharp and in focus?
Size	Larger than life, life size, or smaller than life?
Color/black and white	Full color, shades of gray, partial color, black and white?
Location	In front of you, to one side, behind you?
Distance	Close to or distant?
Motion	Still snapshots or movies?
Speed	Fast/slow?
Framed/panoramic	Enclosed in a frame or panoramic?
Sequence	In order/random/ simultaneous images?
Associated/dissociated	Are you seeing as if out of your own eyes (associated) or can you see yourself in the picture (dissociated)?

You may find initially that you are not aware of any pictures in your thinking. This is not unusual. If this is the case, do the exercise with your eyes closed and allow yourself to become aware of what you do notice.

AUDITORY DISTINCTIONS

Take another memory, for example your last disagreement at work. Experiment again, this time with the auditory distinctions.

For example, if you can recall voices, make them soft and whispery. Now give them a different accent. Make them loud and boomy, remembering to return the memory to its original state before experimenting with the next distinction.

Volume	How loud/quiet?
Speed	Fast or slow?
Location	Where is the source of the sound? Is it in front of you, to one side, behind you?
Distance	Is the sound close or far away?
Voice/sound	Is it a voice or can you hear other sounds? If it is a voice, whose voice and what tone is it in?
Pitch	High/low/mid range?
Continuous	Is the sound continuous or intermittent?

Note how this experiment affects the quality of the memory. What starts as an unpleasant memory can become an amusing one merely by changing the nature of the voices. Give someone the voice of a cartoon character, such as Bugs Bunny. What effect does that have?

FEELINGS DISTINCTIONS

Now think of a time when you felt happy. What does "happy" feel like to you and where exactly in your body do you experience it?

What does "happy" feel like?

Experiment again, this time with the intensity of the feeling. Can you turn it up and down? Return the feeling to its original state. Change the pace of the feeling. Continue to experiment with each element of the feeling, returning it to its original state before you experiment with the next one.

Pressure	What sort of pressure can you feel? Is there a sense of being pushed, a general or specific pressure?
Location	Where in your body do you experience any sensations?
Motion	Is there movement to the feeling? Is it fluttery, steady, intermittent, tingling?
Temperature	Hot/cold/damp?
Intensity	Strong/weak?
Pace	Is it a fast feeling, a slow one?

You will find that in each case there will be one or two key distinctions for you. By changing these distinctions you can change the quality of your experience.

Jim experimented with his thinking about presentations, first thinking about one-to-one meetings in which he felt confident and relaxed. He discovered that the key distinctions for him were brightness, focus and the tone of voice with which he spoke to himself. By bringing the quality of his thinking about presentations into line with his thinking about one-to-one meetings, by making the image bright and in focus, and by softening his internal voice tone, he noticed that he felt a steady rippling feeling in his chest. This was the same feeling he experienced in one-to-one meetings. This was the feeling that he associated with confidence.

Everyday expressions indicate trends in thinking

There are some general trends in the distinctions associated with feelings of confidence, happiness and certainty. Not surprisingly, there are expressions in everyday language that reflect this. For example:

+ "The future is looking brighter" or "The future looks black."
+ "That's becoming clearer" or "That is a bit hazy."

- "We had a rough ride in that discussion" or "That went smoothly."

The richness of our internal thinking leaks through into our communication and into the way we influence ourselves and others. Enrich your thinking – enrich your life.

Enrich your thinking – enrich your life

SUMMARY

Once we have experienced something it becomes a memory. When we react to a memory we are reacting not to the direct experience but to the way we store that memory in our mind. Managing the distinctions in our thinking gives us the ability to influence and change the nature of our memories, so that we can store them in a way that results in us feeling the way we want to feel.

You can choose the state you want

Many people develop the habit of storing memories in a way that leads to depression, anger or other negative feelings. Why choose these when you could choose pleasure or peace? The same is true for the future. Why make yourself worried or frustrated about an event that hasn't occurred when you could be making yourself confident and comfortable? You might choose to keep some of the worry in the form of concern. The point is that you choose the state you want rather than its choosing you. Our ability to manage our state is more and more important in a world that defies control and seems to be increasingly chaotic. Or is that just my thinking?

Why choose to worry when you can choose to feel pleasure or peace?

You can be sure that you already use distinctions in your thinking patterns in this way. Whenever you change your experience of something you are almost certain to have reprogrammed the way you think about it, even though you may not have realized that this was what you were doing.

SHORTCUT TO MANAGING YOUR THINKING: THE SWISH

The SWISH is a technique for utilizing these distinctions in thinking to replace a problem state with a desirable state. It is fast and powerful, as well as being great for dealing with unwanted behavioral habits. Note that the SWISH will not necessarily be ideal for deeper, more significant issues; there are other techniques later in the book that can help with these.

1   First, identify the response in yourself that you want to change. What exactly is the reaction you would like to replace? For example, you might want to change a state such as anxiety or apprehension.

2   Identify precisely what it is that triggers this response. There will be something specific that immediately precedes your reaction. Identifying this trigger is a key part of the process. If, for example, it is a response to the way in which someone speaks to you, identify what it is they say or what it is about the way they say it that triggers your reaction. Recreate this in your thinking in exactly the way it happens. If it is the way in which someone speaks to you, then hear them saying the words in exactly the way they do. If it is the sight of an audience in front of you, imagine yourself in that situation looking out at the audience in the way you do. See exactly what you would see if you were there.

3   Now determine which facets of the way you think about this trigger have the greatest effect. There will be some elements that intensify your reaction. The SWISH lends itself most readily to visual triggers; often the size and brightness of the image have the greatest impact. For example, if it is the sight of a certain person who works for you that triggers a response, experiment with each distinction in turn, putting the image back the way it was before you experiment with the next one. The aim is to find the one or two that intensify the response. Although these elements are currently triggering the response that you don't want, the aim of the SWISH is to hook these elements to the response that you do want. In so doing, you are making your own resources work for you rather than against you.

4   Think about something completely different to "break your state." For example, what color was the front door of the last house in which you lived?

5   Now imagine the person you would like to be, irrespective of what you have been in the past and irrespective of any specific behavior. This is an opportunity to imagine how you would

like to be, the sort of qualities you would really like to have, the style that fits with who you truly are. Imagine this as if you are looking at yourself as an observer, dissociated. Develop this until you have an image that is compelling and desirable. Check that this "you" really fits in with the significant people in your life – it needs to be a real benefit to them too for you to be this new way. Explore how this fits with whatever sense of purpose you have, with your beliefs and values, with every aspect that is important to you. Check that this new you meets any needs that you may have been satisfying in less healthy ways in the past. If, for example, you have been getting attention for being stressed, check that you are going to get the level and quality of attention you need from this new way of being in the world.

6 Think of something completely different to break state again – for example, your telephone number backwards.

7 Make an image of the trigger, the stimulus that prompts the response that you want to change. Use the key factors that enhance the trigger. For example, if the distinctions of size and brightness intensify the trigger, make this image bright and big.

8 Take the image of the "new you" and make it small and dark. Place this small, dark image in the corner of the bigger image.

9 Very quickly, make the large image small and dark and at the same time make the small image large and bright. Do this as fast as you can; the speed is important. You can make a sound to accompany this movement, a SWISH sound, hence the name of this process. (You can choose another sound if you wish.) The sound can become the association for the feelings of becoming the new you.

10 Break state again. Clear the images so that you start afresh. Create a new image so you break the image before you start again, otherwise you may set up a loop in your thinking.

11 Repeat the process five times and check to see if it works. You will know this when you either experience or imagine the trigger for the original state and your response to it has changed to what you want it to be – you SWISH into the new you immediately. If this is not happening, go back and experiment with different parts of the process until it does.

THOUGHT PROVOKERS

1   What sort of jobs do you think would best suit people whose thinking preference is (a) visual; (b) auditory; (c) feelings?
2   Think of a successful outcome of a regular meeting that you hold/attend. How do you think about this? Is it a picture? Do you hear sounds or conversation? Do you experience certain feelings?
3   Look at a website that appeals to you. Which senses does it employ to capture your attention?
4   Think of a part of your work that you really enjoy. Now think of a part that you enjoy less well. How do the distinctions in your thinking vary?
5   Think of someone with whom you have a really good relationship. Now think of someone you find it difficult to deal with. Compare the differences in your thinking about each person. What are the main distinctions?
6   Take out a letter or email that you received recently. Which senses are you using as you read it?

REFERENCE

Steve Andreas & Connirae Andreas (1987) *Change Your Mind: And Keep the Change*, Real People Press.

One day a traveler was walking along a road on his journey from one village to another. As he walked, he noticed a monk tilling the ground in the fields beside the road. The monk said "Good day" to the traveler and the traveler nodded to the monk.

The traveler then turned to the monk and said, "Excuse me, do you mind if I ask you a question?"

"Not at all," replied the monk.

"I am traveling from the village in the mountains to the village in the valley and I was wondering if you knew what it is like in the village in the valley?"

"Tell me," said the monk. "What was your experience of the village in the mountains?"

"Dreadful," replied the traveler. "To be honest, I am glad to be away from there. I found the people most unwelcoming. When I first arrived I was greeted coldly. I was never made to feel a part of the village no

matter how hard I tried. The villagers keep very much to themselves; they don't take kindly to strangers. So tell me, what can I expect in the village in the valley?"

"I'm sorry to tell you," said the monk, "but I think your experience will be much the same there."

The traveler hung his head despondently and walked on.

A few months later, another traveler was journeying down the same road and he also came upon the monk.

"Good day," said the traveler.

"Good day," said the monk.

"How are you?" asked the traveler.

"I'm well," replied the monk. "Where are you going?"

"I'm going to the village in the valley," replied the traveler. "Do you know what it is like?"

"I do," replied the monk. "But first, tell me, where have you come from?"

"I've come from the village in the mountains."

"And how was that?"

"It was a wonderful experience. I would have stayed if I could but I am committed to traveling on. I felt as though I were a member of the family in the village. The elders gave me much advice, the children laughed and joked with me, and the people generally were kind and generous. I am sad to have left there. It will always hold special memories for me. And what of the village in the valley?" he asked again.

"I think you will find it much the same," replied the monk.

"Good day to you."

"Good day and thank you," replied the traveler, smiled, and journeyed on.

3
Filters on your world

The appliances and machines around us will soon remember us individually and anticipate our needs.

Don Peppers and Martha Rogers, Enterprise One to One

We need to be smart at knowing our clients' needs

Technology is becoming ever more intelligent at knowing and responding to, and influencing, our personal needs. In a culture so infused with technology, we had better be pretty smart at knowing our clients' needs too. If we want to build lifelong relationships, either in our personal lives or, as is becoming the expectation, in our business lives, we need to learn how to read other people's styles and requirements with ever-increasing sophistication.

The better able we are to identify needs, the better able we are to present ourselves, our products and our services in a way that is excellent. Companies talk about doing much more than keeping customers satisfied – they talk about customer delight. To delight our customers we need to be able to "model" their thinking and behavior to ensure that we appeal to what really matters to them. We not only need to "read" these styles, we need to have the flexibility to respond to them.

At one time I decided that I would learn some Danish so that I could open my next program in Denmark in the native language. I felt that this would be respectful of the time my delegates give to listening to me speak in English. I asked a Danish delegate on a program I was running in England if he would translate a passage I had prepared so that I could practice what I wanted to say. I asked if he would send the translation to me via email. He made a decision that it would be more helpful for me if he were to record the translation so that I could hear the words instead. In his heart he was being helpful, but auditory is not my preferred choice for learning a passage like this. I wanted to see the written word, having already learned some of the pronunciation.

It can be tempting to make choices about presenting material in ways that fit our own preferred ways of thinking rather than suiting the preferences of our customers. We may think we know best in terms of what our customers "should" have. And we make unconscious as well as conscious choices about the people with whom we want to do business, depending on how well they skilfully match our needs. In the instance I quote what happened led to learning for us both, but in business making the wrong choice might cost you the work.

We may think we know best!

In our choices about how to present ourselves to customers, the margin for error has become significantly smaller. The way we use the internet is a good example of this. If you haven't grabbed your potential clients' interest by relating to the way they think within six seconds of their logging on to your web pages, research shows that they will not wait to make sense of what you are saying – they will move on.

In this chapter I illustrate some fundamental needs. There are hundreds, even thousands of needs and it is your skill in detecting not only those I have explained here but the unique ones you can discover for yourself that will enable you to model what is happening. Being able to do this and having the flexibility to adapt to what you discover can determine your success in working with, dealing with, communicating with and living with other people.

So let's consider some of the patterns in thinking and communicating that enable us to recognize what is happening in our thoughts, language and behavior, and in other people's. As we understand this we can learn what affects how we present ourselves so that others can relate to what we are doing and saying, and so that we can relate to them in a language and style they understand.

We are bombarded with stimuli throughout our life. There is no way we can take in and pay attention to everything that happens to us. So what we do is *filter* for some things over others. This is what makes our perception and experience what it is. It is not the experience itself that affects us but how we process it. When we understand what we and others are doing, we can begin to understand how we get the results that we do.

It is what we do with experience that makes the difference

LEARNING TO RELATE SUCCESSFULLY

Have you ever bought a car and suddenly become aware of all the other cars of the same type on the road? Or have you ever had an experience, maybe an insight about yourself, only to discover that many of your friends have had the same or a similar experience, even though you weren't aware of that before? Do you see the glass as half full as opposed to half empty by looking for what is there as opposed to what is not?

These are examples of ways in which we have subconsciously chosen to pay attention to some things and to delete others from our awareness. What we think about is what we get.

Here is a conversation that highlights the need to be able to understand and relate to different filters.

When Janet and Bill had a conversation, each found the other frustrating. Janet liked to discuss the details of what was needed, whereas Bill preferred to discuss the broader strategic concepts. For example, Janet would say, "I'd like Peter to go to the next meeting," and Bill would reply, "We haven't decided on the main areas of the plan that didn't work." Janet's conversation centered on future actions, whereas Bill concentrated more on the past. Janet would pay attention to the similarities between one situation and another: "This is like another idea I have about what we might do to improve the office layout." Bill would concentrate on the exception by saying things like "No, this is different" or "We didn't include an overall plan." It was as though they were talking different languages. They had different filters on their experience. They didn't find meetings with one another easy!

When two people are using the same filters there is a greater chance that they will be communicating with each other in a way that both understand. They are likely to experience rapport. If the filters you use are different to those used by your partner then, as with Janet and Bill, you may experience discord and frustration. By using similar language patterns to your partner, you are increasing the level of mutual trust and influence.

Learning to recognize the filters that we and others use is the first step. Developing our flexibility in the way we use the filters then gives us a greater chance of finding a way of communicating with each person we meet. We make hundreds, thousands, even

---

Do you see the glass half full or half empty?

What we think about is what we get

By using similar language patterns you increase the level of trust millions of unconscious choices every day about what we pay attention to and what we don't. And that is fine, provided those choices work for us. However, if we are not getting the results we want, we can learn to make new choices until we find what does work.

In our example, Bill could have replied in the following way

Janet *"I'd like Peter to go to the next meeting."*
Bill   *"Yes, Peter would make some useful contributions. Let's note that, so when we have decided what areas of the plan didn't work we can also decide who else we might want to include" (matching Janet's preference for agreement and future thinking yet still registering his concerns).*
Janet *"This is like another idea I have about what we might do to improve the office layout."*
Bill   *"You come up with lots of ideas, Janet. Can we discuss those when we have gone through my idea about the overall plan?" (acknowledging, future referencing and then making his request).*

Overall his strategy now has a much greater chance of gaining agreement from Janet.

We don't always know what will work in advance, but by having an awareness of what is and what isn't working we give ourselves choices.

Let's explore some of the filters. What follows is a "starter set."

ASSOCIATED/DISSOCIATED

Think of a conversation you had recently with one of your colleagues. As you think about this conversation, pay attention to *how* you are thinking about it. For example, are you seeing, hearing and feeling the situation as if you are in your own body – seeing it out of your own eyes, hearing it with your own ears and experiencing the feelings of being there? Or are you experiencing the situation as if you are outside of your own body – seeing yourself in the situation, hearing yourself as if you were an observer? The experience of being in your own body is referred to as *associated* and the experience of being outside of your body is known as *dissociated*.

We can make new choices until we find what does work

Pay attention for a moment to your surroundings. You may begin to notice what you see around you, the quality of the light, the colors and shapes, the shadows, and the clarity of the scene. As you notice the scene you may begin to hear sounds close to you and farther away. As you become aware of even more sounds, turn your conscious mind toward them. Be aware of the location of the sounds, their loudness or softness, their tone and speed. You can become aware of what you feel, of the textures and pressures on your body. Sense those parts of you that are touching the ground or a chair. Allow yourself to notice any smells or tastes that you experience. As you do this, pay attention to the feelings within you, to any tensions or internal emotions, their precise location and intensity.

The above is an associated state.

Now step back or stand behind the chair in which you were sitting and see yourself sitting or standing, as you were a moment ago. Look at yourself so that you can see the whole of you. Notice how the "you" there interacts with the environment. Be aware of how the "you" there in front of you looks and sounds.

In this dissociated state you will be detached from the feelings. You have the ability to consider situations with a detached objectivity without getting involved in the emotions. Both are valuable. There are times when associating is the best option, for example if we want to engage our emotions, create a state of motivation or show vulnerability. However, people who are able to "keep their heads" in the midst of a crisis can usually dissociate.

One of the people responsible for coaching and supporting the people in the London Fire Brigade discovered that the members of the crew who experienced the highest levels of stress were those who relived their memories in an associated way. As they recalled what had happened, they re-experienced the emotions they had felt at the time. So as well as experiencing the trauma of each situation, they were experiencing it over and over again and subsequently intensifying the stress they felt. The coach also established that those who had the lowest levels of stress were those who were able to dissociate from what they experienced.

Game designers have discovered that software that encourages us to "associate" into the role of one of the players gives us an intense emotional experience. It is as if we are there. Considering that we make many decisions in an emotional state, these game manufacturers are also potentially influencing our addiction to the experience. It is important to be aware of how these tactics are used *on* us and how they can potentially work *for* us.

These tactics can be used on us or for us

When I first worked in IT, we would send off programs to a nearby computer center and wait for the results to come back, ideally later that day or more often later that week. Not so today. We are accustomed to getting a response from our computer in a split second. It is important that we too can work in this real-time way, and we can only do this successfully if we are willing to immerse ourselves in a climate of feedback. One of the elements we need is the ability to dissociate from feedback that we might otherwise take personally and reject, and then associate once we have the resources we need in order to let the feedback in and act on it. Chapter 20, Giving and receiving feedback, explores ways of doing this.

The skill lies in choosing an associated or a dissociated state for a purpose. The appropriate choice depends on your desired outcome. You might choose to dissociate to protect yourself from painful emotions, or you might choose to associate in order fully to experience all the feelings of a situation. Most people's decision-making strategy results in a feeling, no matter how much logical analysis might have preceded that. If your preferred style is to keep yourself and others dissociated, don't be surprised if you and they struggle to make decisions!

Most decision-making strategies rely ultimately on what we feel

If your business depends on supporting others in making decisions, you need to know how to associate and how to help others do the same.

One of the directors of a marketing company found that she was struggling to get potential clients to make a decision about the work her company was proposing. She ran through what she had presented and how she had done that. What we noticed was that she came across very objectively and factually. Everything she said was logical, but she gave no space to feelings. Her voice communicated a consistently auditory way of thinking; the tone was even and slightly hard. There were few pauses in her presentation.

Once she'd been given feedback about her style and the likelihood of her client's needing to make decisions through a feeling, she associated

into the presentation and changed her tone of voice to make it softer and lower (communicating and inviting feelings). She spoke with greater certainty, whereas before she had raised her voice at the end of most sentences. The next time she presented to this customer, they stopped her part way through the presentation and told her that she need not continue – they liked what she was saying and she had got the business. This presentation and subsequent ones broke the record for the time needed for the client to make a decision.

TOWARDS/AWAY FROM (Desired state/Problem state)

Think of a goal you have for yourself right now. It can be a personal goal or a work goal. It can be short or long term. Be aware of how you are thinking about this goal. Are you imagining what it is like to achieve the goal, what you are seeing, hearing and feeling? Or are you aware of what stops you and what you *don't* want? For example, if you are thinking of being healthy, do you imagine yourself slim and fit or do you think of the food you want to avoid and the weight you want to lose? What is in your mind? Your ability to think about what you really want is known as *towards* thinking. Your ability to think about what you don't want is known as *away from* thinking.

I have just received a request for some training with the senior management team of one of my clients. Their request is framed as follows:

"How to avoid letting strength of personal view get in the way of management."

Do NOT think about kangaroos right now

This is a classic "away from" statement. Before I commit to the work I will want to know what it is they really want. And I've drawn some conclusions already!

The concept of towards/away from is explained further in Chapter 4. In the context of goal setting, the principle is that what we think is what we get. Our mind does not recognize the "not" part of a problem-centered statement. For example, if you tell yourself not to worry you are effectively programming yourself to worry. If you think about being confident, then the likelihood is that this is what you will begin to experience.

What we think is what we get

MATCH/MISMATCH

Look at the shapes below and describe their relationship to each other.

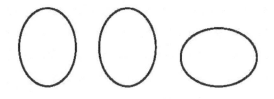

Describe what you see. Do you notice in what ways they are similar – that is, they are all oval – or do you notice that two are upright and one is on its side? In effect, do you look for what is the same – *match* – or do you look for what is different – *mismatch*?

When meeting a person for the first time, someone who sorts for a match might think of similar people, similar situations, or how the other is like them. Someone who sorts for a mismatch will identify what is different about this person and this situation compared with others they know.

Certain professions train people to think in a particular way. For example, I have come across more mismatching patterns of thinking in professions associated with information technology and finance than I have in many other fields of business. There is no right or wrong. Certain jobs depend on a person's ability to match, just as some depend on an ability to mismatch. A software engineer trained to uncover system "bugs" may be skilled at mismatching, looking for what doesn't fit, as indeed will someone in accounting whose job it is to find the imbalance. What matters is to what extent our choice takes us closer to the outcome that we want. If they do then the choice is presumably a "good" one, and if not then it is time to find a new choice.

The "yes, but" pattern in conversation is an example of mismatching.

Yes, but...

"I'm really pleased with the way this project has gone."

"Yes, but there's a danger we're going to get overconfident."

"You're right. Let's review objectively what we've achieved so that we build some of the good practices into future projects."

"That's all very well, but we don't have the time right now."

"Well, how about putting a date in the diary in a few weeks' time?"

"That's easy to say but not so easy in practice. Things change so rapidly around here."

Everything before the "but" is bull!

As someone once said to me, everything before the "but" is bull****!

Dealing with this in conversation can be hard work unless you are another mismatcher who enjoys a good argument.

BIG CHUNK/SMALL CHUNK

Look around you at the room you are in. How would you describe the room to someone who has not seen it before? To what do you pay attention: spaciousness, feel and style? Or do you pay attention to number of windows, color of furnishings, the details? Is it a mix of both? The spaciousness, feel and style are examples of *big chunk* thinking, whereas the details are *small chunk*.

This pattern of thinking can apply to anything. For example, if you have set a specific goal for yourself you could *chunk up* to more global goals or *chunk down* to milestones, which you could set along the way.

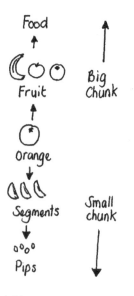

Let's suppose you are in a cookery class. You need an orange for the dish you are preparing. Another member of the class also needs an orange, but there is only one. Without flexibility in thinking the usual solution would be to accept the facts as they appear and cut the orange in two, taking half each.

If, however, you chunk up in relation to your needs in the situation by asking "What do you need the orange for?" you will discover broader needs. For example, you might want the orange for a cake and your colleague may want it for a soufflé.

If you chunk down on the request for the orange by asking "What specifically do you need for your soufflé?" you might discover that the other person needs just the pulp. You know that you only need the skin, the zest, for your cake. It is possible for you both to have exactly what you want.

This is a demonstration of skilled negotiation. The ability to chunk up and down is an ability of excellent negotiators. This is most likely to uncover the possibility of a win/win outcome in which all parties achieve not just what they want but, more significantly, what they need.

You can increase the likelihood of a win/win

PAST/PRESENT/FUTURE

Where in time do you put your attention? Some people live their lives in the past, thinking about what has gone before. Some people live for the moment and their attention is on the present. Some are continually planning and thinking about the future.

Some people live for the moment

You may have experienced these kinds of questions that look to the future:

+ What's for dinner?
+ How long until we get home?
+ Where are we going on holiday?
+ What's next on the agenda?
+ What I want to achieve by the end of the project is…

Or you may know someone who concentrates on the past:

+ What did you say earlier?
+ Did you see what that person was wearing?
+ Do you remember when we were on holiday?
+ The last meeting we had was important.

The ability to be present is an important skill in many contexts, including coaching, listening, presenting …

+ What is happening now?
+ What is that like for you?
+ What you mean is…?
+ What I am experiencing is…
+ What else is true right now?
+ The way that I understand what you are saying is…

There is no right or wrong, no good or bad, but this does have implications for how people communicate with each other.

A friend called to invite me to a school reunion to talk over old times. As someone whose attention is more on the present and the future, the thought of reminiscing about the past didn't strike me as an attractive proposition! (However, since first writing this I have been to a 50-year anniversary reunion of my old school and loved it, which demonstrates how we change over time.)

ACTIVITY/PERSON/OBJECT/PLACE/TIME

Think of the best meal you had in the last few weeks or months. The filter you use will determine your memory of this. For example, if you sort by:

Activity You recall what you and others did at this meal. Maybe you had a memorable conversation or there was a band playing.

Person It was your companion who made it special.

Object Your memories are associated with the food, a present you were given, the pictures in the restaurant, the type of furniture.

Place Your memories are of the location: the restaurant, the town, the country, or possibly the location of the table at which you sat.

Time You remember the time and date, an anniversary or another special occasion. You might remember that it was the first day of your new job or a farewell dinner at the end of term.

INTERNAL/EXTERNAL

How do you know when you've done a good job? Which of the following responses would be most likely to be true for you?

I know I've done a good job when:

- I see people using the results of what I have produced.
- I feel good inside.

- I know I've met the standards I set myself.
- We get more orders.
- I can say to myself, "That was a job well done."

These are examples of external references. *Externally* referenced people rely on external sources for their evidence of fulfillment. For example, they rely on what other people say and do. They may also rely on external factors such as "more orders," or "people use the results of what has been produced." *Internally* referenced people use their own internal feelings, images and voices as their evidence of fulfillment.

Your preference here will make a big difference to the way you work. If you are externally referenced you are more likely to depend on having others around you. If you are internally referenced, you tend to be independent of external people and events.

People who are independent in style are usually internally referenced. This is a characteristic pattern of senior managers. They can be concerned about what happens outside themselves; they need to be! However, they do not depend on external circumstances to feel satisfied. Can you imagine a managing director who depended on having his staff tell him that he was doing OK?

SELF AND OTHER

Have you ever had one of these conversations:

"We are thinking of moving home."
"I decided to that last year, but have changed my mind now in the light of the economy."
"Well, we have the offer of work in Spain."
"I got offered work in the Danish branch of our business – I'm still thinking about it."
"It is an opportunity for us to introduce a new training program into our new offices there."
"We have developed a wonderful new training program for our staff."

Compare that to this:

"We've been thinking of moving home."

"Oh really, what has prompted that?"

"Well, we've been traveling a lot lately and we feel we would prefer a more stable permanent base now."

"Have you thought where that might be?"

We have very different conversations depending on whether our attention is on self or other. Neither is universally right or wrong. Both can be good and bad, depending on the outcome. In my experience I come across more of the former example than the latter, though. One of the biggest elements of NLP training is learning to put one's own agenda to one side and give full, undivided attention to the other.

In some cultures it is the norm to put other people first. That would be the experience of many Indian women, for example, whereas in Denmark the expectations for women are somewhat different. These are generalizations, but nevertheless there are cultural trends. With an awareness of all of these filters, we can unpack what is happening and when it is appropriate to make a particular choice or not.

"Have you ever noticed? Anybody going slower than you is an idiot, and anyone going faster than you is a maniac."

George Carlin

CONVINCER PATTERN

I was explaining to a client how he might restructure his management team. He seemed unsure, although he accepted the principle of what I was saying. We discussed the plans in a number of different ways. I eventually reflected his uncertainty back to him.

He replied, "I just don't see it, Sue."

I explained again and he replied, "I just don't get the picture."

At that point I drew it on the whiteboard.

"Now I see what you are saying," he said.

Everyone has a specific means by which they become convinced. In this client's case the principal factor was that he needed to see the ideas visually before he was convinced they would work. So part of what makes someone convinced is the channel through which they receive the information.

Other people might equally well have been convinced by:

+ Hearing what I had to say.
+ Trying it to find out if it worked in practice.
+ Reading the plan in more detail.

There are differences in the way people need to receive information within these broader categories. Some people need to be told a number of times or have a number of examples before they are convinced. Others need to be convinced over a period of time; time is the deciding factor for them. Some people make decisions on the bare outlines of the facts – they don't need the detail in order to be convinced– yet others need to have something proved to them over and over again. They will be convinced, but only for one situation and one context at a time.

If your job involves you in having to convince others to achieve the result you want, you need to know the pattern by which they operate. You can then match this pattern in the way you present your information.

"Bring in someone who can take the pulse of your customers online."
David Siegel, Futurize Your Enterprise

With NLP, and especially by learning to recognize the ways in which your customers take in information through filters, you can provide a level of sophistication in your support that few have yet achieved. Most people know what they need to know, but few know how to gain that knowledge. Learn to recognize the filters in yourself and others and you will master the "how."

SUMMARY

The filters on our experience determine how we make sense of the world. When we can differentiate between the various choices we make about how we choose to experience life, we can begin to understand how our experience is the way that it is.

When we can determine what choices are affecting our lives, we can begin to replicate those times of excellence, choose to relate to people in the way that makes sense to them, and debug those moments when we are taking ourselves down a rabbit hole of emotions. The choice is ours. Never has it been more important to choose how we make sense of this world. Our choice will influence the way it is for us and for future generations.

"It is not the place, nor the condition, but the mind alone that can make anyone happy or miserable."

Roger Lestrange

THOUGHT PROVOKERS

1   Read the following passages and determine which filters each author is using.

a   I'm someone who enjoys life to the full. I play squash, I write, I work full time as a salesperson, and I have a young family who keep me busy in any spare time I have! I get a lot of satisfaction from what I do. I set myself goals and I know by my own standards when I have achieved them. I enjoy travel, and I love eating out.

b   I can be a difficult person, or so others tell me. I can usually see the alternative point of view. I enjoy a good discussion, some would say argument. I like perfection. If something isn't quite right it irritates me. I spend a lot of time working and I am meticulous in the way I go about that. I am a programmer and the work I do requires attention to detail and the ability to see immediately if something is wrong.

c   I am a good listener. People come to me with their problems. I have always had this sort of role, not only in my work life but also with my friends. I have spent most of my life in the same part of the country. I have always liked the people here. I can recall some very special occasions that I have spent with friends in the past. I have always been a bit indecisive about what I might do next. I have always let others push me into new situations or jobs, and have tended only to change if I have been dissatisfied with what I was doing at the time.

2   Take a letter or email that you have received recently. What filters do you detect in the language the writer has used?

3   Take a letter or email that you have written recently. What filters do you detect in the language you have used?

4 Compare the filters you are using in response to a communication from someone else. To what extent have you matched/mismatched the filters the other person is using?

5 Select one of your key customers. Take examples of their behavior and writing and identify some of their key filters.

6 Take a context in which you want to appeal to a wide audience, one in which people will have a wide range of filters. Identify how many filters you are using in the way you are presenting yourself, your products and your services.

REFERENCES

Fiona Beddoes-Jones (1999) *Thinking Styles: Relationship Strategies that Work!* BJA Associates.

Shelle Rose Charvet (1997) *Words that Change Minds: Mastering the Language of Influence,* Kendall Hunt.

Don Peppers & Martha Rogers (1998) *Enterprise One-to-One,* Piatkus.

David Siegel (1999) *Futurize Your Enterprise: Business Strategy in the Age of the E-Customer,* John Wiley.

One of our course delegates was recounting an incident with his 3-year-old daughter.

"How many times do I have to tell you to put your toys away?" he asked her.

"Four times," she replied categorically.

4
Thinking with your body

It is impossible to not communicate. –Paul Watzlawick

Our eye movements contain clues to our thinking

NLP is a process of identifying the essence of excellence. And the essence is very often the elusive part of what we do.

Suppose I am skilled in the way I can build rapport in business meetings with potential new clients and you want to know how exactly I do that. I could tell you that when I prepare for a meeting with a new client, I think about the outcomes for the meeting. I can also tell you that I review what I know about the company and pay attention to how I build rapport throughout the process, especially in the first few moments of our meeting. That is all very sound, but the question is: Can you reproduce the procedure I have explained well enough to get the same result?

The clues lie not so much in the content of what I say as in my nonverbal behavior and my actions. As you watch me speak, you might notice that as I talk about a new client I look fleetingly up and to my right. What I am doing in this moment is imagining visually what this company would be like if it were to implement my thoughts for the future. I do this each time I approach a new client, but I take this thought so much for granted and it is so unconscious that I did not for a long time think to mention it in my explanations of my client-facing strategies. However, this eye movement of looking up and to the right is a very strong clue that what I am doing at that moment is creating a visual image I have never seen before. By being sensitive to my eye movements, you know that I am creating something visually, even though you may not know the content of what I am doing. This clue can give you the prompt to ask me something like: "What do you think about just after you have considered the outcomes?" You could be more specific and say: "At that moment, what are you picturing?" That could be the prompt for me to realize that I am creating this visual image. This is one small clue that opens the door to one of the most significant pieces of my thinking when I meet a new client.

By learning to be sensitive to body language, you can begin to detect the pieces of the strategies that really make the difference. And these are the pieces that otherwise lie undetected. It is the ability to detect body language patterns in this way that is unique to NLP and makes the process of modeling so special and important in the way we learn.

THE EYES HAVE IT

Our eyes give powerful clues to the way we are thinking. Ask someone who claims to be a good speller to spell Mississippi. What are their eye movements? Watch carefully, because some of the movements are fleeting. Most good spellers visualize the word they are spelling by picturing the word as if it were on a screen in front and slightly above them. They typically look up and to their left, but some may look up and to their right or straight ahead with a defocused stare. These eye movements usually characterize visual thinking, a key part of a successful spelling strategy.

The way we use our eyes indicates the kind of thinking that is going on. Bear in mind, however, that these are not facts, just tendencies – everyone is unique. It is vital to calibrate to the individual rather than to apply these universally. For example:

Eyes up and left (your left) – Visual remembered
This is where we look when we are remembering images we have seen before: the face of our partner, the last place we went on holiday, our workplace, what we did yesterday.

Eyes up and right (your right) – Visual constructed
This is where we look when we are constructing images we have not seen before: ourselves in a location we have always dreamt of but never been to, a colleague with an expression on their face we have never seen, our home redesigned, the vision for our business.

Eyes straight ahead defocused – Visual
The clue as to whether this is remembered or constructed can be determined by how the weight is distributed in the rest of the body: to the left and it is remembered, to the right and it is constructed.

Eyes to the side and left (your left) – Auditory remembered
This is where we look when we are remembering sounds that we have heard before: a favorite piece of music, the sound of a friend's voice.

Eyes to the side and right (your right) – Auditory constructed
This is where we look when we are creating a sound that we have never heard before: someone we know speaking in a completely different tone of voice, for example.

Eyes down and left (your left) – Auditory digital, inner dialogue
This is where we look when we are having a conversation with ourselves or asking questions in our heads.

Eyes down and right (your right) – External feelings and emotions
When we experience feelings, this is where we look.

The direction may vary, in that left and right may be reversed, but visual is always up or straight ahead defocused, and auditory is always looking toward the ears, which can be a good way of remembering it. There is a theory that left-handed children of left-handed parents are more likely to have the sides reversed.

HOW ELSE DO WE THINK THROUGH OUR BODY?

Our thoughts leak out through our body language, which is one of the reasons it is important to be aware of what thoughts are being communicated through this medium. Body language is everything in our behavior with which we communicate other than words. However, the way we say those words – the tone, the volume, the pitch of our voice – is our body language.

So in detecting whether we are thinking in a visual, auditory or feelings way, not only can we use eye movements as clues, we can also detect clues in body language.

For example, someone thinking in a **visual** way will typically:

+ Speak quickly in a high voice (they are trying to use words to get across the images they can see, so they need to speak quickly to do this).
+ Breathe high in the chest – rapid, shallow breathing.
+ Gesture high in the air, often trying to depict the images they can see internally.
+ Often show tension in their body.

Someone thinking in an **auditory** way will typically:

+ Speak in a rhythmic way, almost tunefully.
+ Talk mid tone.
+ Breathe mid chest.
+ Gesture lower than someone who is thinking in a visual way.
+ Often have their head tilted to one side as if to accentuate the amount they take in through their ears.
+ Frequently touch their ears and mouth and often have their hand against their face as if on the telephone

And someone thinking in a **feelings** way will typically:

+ Speak in a resonant way, slowly and with frequent silences.
+ Breathe low in the chest – deep, slow breaths, as if sighing.
+ Gesture down and to their right (you'll have heard the expression downright angry – down and right is usually where people go when accessing feelings).
+ Have a "laid back" body posture, relaxed and free moving.

So body language is:

Voice	Head and face
Body	Intonation
Tone	Accent
Rhythm	Pauses
Facial expressions	Eye movements

Muscle movements	Muscle tension
Skin color	Body movement
Posture	Arm and hand gestures
Frequency and nature of touch, both self and others	Body rhythm – the kind of movement or stillness that
Stresses	is characteristic
Speed	Hesitations
Emphasis	Frequency of response to others
Head movements	Facial lines
Eye contact	Head position
Mouth expressions	Proximity to others
Timing of movements	Breathing rate
Breathing position: high, mid or low in chest	Position and direction of legs and feet

All of these elements and more are communicating our innermost thoughts every moment of every day. It is not that people don't recognize these signals – they do. The staff in one company I worked in knew very well that when the managing director's lip became taut and whitened slightly, it was time to stop asking questions!

We do all read one another's body language, but many of us have become used to ignoring signals we detect unconsciously. We have learnt to delete or distort what we pick up intuitively. By developing our conscious awareness of what these signals might be telling us, we start to draw on an immense untapped potential in our communication.

THE IMPORTANCE OF READING BODY LANGUAGE

Learning to be aware of body language and the differences between one person and the next and one culture and the next creates a marked improvement in how well we understand and influence other people and they us. Some people seem to have a natural ability to influence, creating a climate of instant rapport in which all parties feel at ease with each other. Others may find these people eminently approachable, easy to talk to on any issue, with an obvious advantage in any negotiating, communicating or influencing situation.

The outstanding conclusion reached by researchers in this field is that typically more than 90 percent of our ability to influence lies outside of the content of what we say.

If we don't understand and respect difference, we are liable to judge what we don't know as negative. For example, in the UK there is a very much higher expectation of feedback to what we say (even if it is just a grunt) than is the norm in many other cultures. Consequently, we can find lower levels of response to what we say (especially when we are talking on the phone) very disconcerting. We might, for example, be tempted to misread it as disinterest.

We not only limit ourselves by what we can say, the choices we make about how we use words make communication even more risky. When we don't understand what we hear, in a meeting for example, most of us are unlikely to say so. If we don't entirely agree with what someone is saying, most of us are likely to say that they do agree or say nothing. However, whatever choices we make with the words we do and do not use, our nonverbal behavior signals what we truly feel.

By learning to pay attention to body language signals we can:

There is a higher expectancy of feedback than in many other cultures

* Know when to end a conversation.
* Tell to what extent the person we are speaking to has understood what we are saying.
* Determine the level of agreement we have achieved.
* Recognize the degree to which we have touched the core motivation of the person we are talking to.
* Establish how we represent time and the impact of that on the way we use our time.
* Recognize when we have created a connection.
* Determine when we have established a deep level of rapport.
* Recognize what kind of emphasis in a presentation will work best in getting our message across.
* Ascertain whether we have read and respected the culture of the person with whom we are dealing.

In the NLP process of modeling particularly, it is by watching and listening to body language that we can:

* Find out how someone structures their thinking to achieve what they do.

- Elicit the unconscious (and therefore taken-for-granted) ways of thinking that make the difference in the results we achieve.
- Do an inner benchmarking of excellence rather than relying only on external behavior.
- Deduce the values and beliefs behind someone's behavior.
- Recognize other people's different emotional states.

By developing our sensitivity to body language signals, we can tell when someone has changed the way they are thinking. We can begin to determine what strategies they are using when they are achieving what they want and when they are not.

I was talking with a client about her goals for her work and her life. She talked about two goals. The first was a goal she had been given in her work. As she talked about this her face was pale, her lips were taut, and she sat forward with her shoulders hunched. Then she talked about a goal she had to travel and work in Canada. The moment she began to think about this her face flushed slightly, her shoulders dropped, the muscles of her face relaxed, and she began to move her arms in a fluid, easy way as she gestured while she spoke.

What we established (with not too much difficulty) was that when she was thinking about her work goals she was very much into problem thinking, concentrating on what she had to do and what she ought to do. She was dissociated in her thinking as she did this. When she thought about her goals for working in Canada, she immediately imagined herself there doing the kind of work she really wanted. She was thinking about this in an associated way: she could see it as if she were looking through her own eyes and hearing it through her own ears. Most important of all, she was feeling what it was like to be there. The body signals she was evidencing for the second goal were characteristic of what was, for her, compelling motivation.

We have two characteristic states

Most people have two key characteristic states: one when they are aligned and in touch with their unique skills and attitudes, and one when they are out of touch with who they are and their true capabilities. Each state has its own characteristic thinking patterns, beliefs and body language. By learning to recognize the characteristics of each and the distinctions between the two, we can learn how to choose the most effective one for the outcomes we want to achieve.

TRADITIONAL WAYS OF READING BODY LANGUAGE

You may have read books on body language saying that, for example, if someone is crossing their arms it means that they are defensive. Or maybe you have heard that if someone touches their nose with the back of their finger this means they are lying. In my experience it is foolish and disrespectful to make such judgments.

The way body language is used in NLP is very different. In NLP we respect that each person has their own unique patterns of body language. The challenge is to be sensitive to that and not make assumptions – positive or negative – about what those signals mean.

One of my friends was commenting on someone they had just met.
"She is very intelligent," he said.
"How do you know this?" I asked.
"She speaks very quickly," he replied!

We might find, for example, that crossed arms for one person mean something completely different to what they mean for someone else. One of the aims of NLP is to heighten our awareness of patterns in body language for everyone we meet, so that we can learn how to flex our behavior to connect with them if we so choose and in a way that is respectful of who they are.

MIND AND BODY ARE ONE

What we think is how we are. Through our body language we show our skills, our values, our beliefs, what kind of person we are, our cultural preferences, and even our purpose in life. By a handshake we reveal everything that anyone can ever know about us if they are sensitive to us in this way. We show what we are feeling every moment of every day. If we are expecting disagreement in a meeting we are about to attend, we show that in our body language.

We reveal all in a handshake

When Peter expected disagreement in a meeting he ran a negative inner dialogue, imagining the worst that each person might say to each other. Consequently, his eyes went down and to his left. At the same time, the muscles in his face became taut and he lowered his head. You wouldn't have to have too many meetings with Peter in this state to begin to know what was going to happen next!

As we remember happy memories, we show that in our body language too.

When Julia thought about the success she had achieved in her involvement with the board of directors, she looked up and to her left initially (remembering what one of the most successful meetings looked like). She then started to smile slightly and looked down and to her right (as she associated into her feelings when the board had achieved a major agreement about the way forward in the business and had done so in a very creative way). She looked sideways and to her right as she imagined some of the conversations she expected to have in the next meeting. All the time she was rhythmically swinging her foot from side to side.

Our body language reveals the truth of our inner thoughts and feelings. There is little we can do about the subtlest of signals that we communicate to the world at large.

SPOTTING THE FILTERS

Body language reveals the truth of our inner thoughts and feelings

In Chapter 3 I explained some of the different filters we use to think and communicate. We can detect these filters through our language. And we can deduce someone's type of thinking by the patterns in their body language.

Remember that the patterns are only clues, not absolute proof. It is our awareness of patterns in body language, verbal language and our knowledge of a person *over time* that enable us to get closer to what is really going on in their thinking. Nevertheless, the more we read the signals, the more we are likely to choose the way of communicating with each person we encounter that will enable us to relate to them effectively.

Let's explore some of these body language patterns in more depth.

ASSOCIATED/DISSOCIATED

In Chapter 3 I described how we might be associated, engaged in what we are saying and thinking, by experiencing situations standing our own shoes. In this state we are connected with our feelings. Or we can be dissociated, observing and listening to events as if we are a fly on the wall. In this latter state we are disconnected from our emotions.

Our body language changes dramatically according to which of these states we are in. In meetings it is easy to detect those people who are in an associated state. They usually lean forward and gesture animatedly to show their feelings. They often interrupt as their emotions rule their actions. When talking about their feelings, they hold their hands to their chest, close to their heart. In contrast, someone who is dissociated is usually sitting or leaning back. By putting some distance between themselves and the situation they keep themselves objective. They do this mentally as they do it physically. When dissociated, they often talk about themselves and point to themselves as if to an imaginary self in the air in front of them (which in their thinking is often how it is).

Try selling to someone who stays in a dissociated state and you will probably find that it is hard if not impossible. For most people the decision to buy is associated with a feeling. The skill in this kind of influencing situation lies in knowing how to achieve that and recognizing when you have it.

PROBLEM STATE/DESIRED STATE (Away from/Towards)

The ease or tension we hold in our body is a result of how we think. Think for a moment about something you must or should do today. Notice what happens in your body as you do this. Now think about something you would really like to do. Imagine yourself doing this. Notice what has happened to your body. How are your shoulders, your neck and your back? Can you tell what expression you have on your face?

When we think in terms of problems or what we don't want in our lives, we concentrate on what we want to move away from. This kind of motivation is often based on moving away from pain or discomfort. Consequently, the body language we demonstrate when thinking this way is tension. In this problem state we are likely to frown, hold our shoulders tense and hunched, and show tension in other parts of our body. Not surprisingly, one of the most common reasons for absence from work is back problems. What do you think that says about how a large proportion of the population feels about the work they do?

On the other hand, when we imagine what we *do* want we have corresponding body language. This is how people who think this way influence the achievement of their goals: They are acting as if they already have achieved them and the world responds accordingly. Their behavior is likely to "hang loose," they are relaxed, have loose facial muscles, easy-moving limbs, flowing movements. If we watch and listen to the way we are using our bodies, we can get clues about what we are doing that is either helping or hindering us to achieve what we really want.

What is your face telling you?

Our posture, our gestures and our facial expressions and lines communicate the habits we have developed in our lives. Take a look in the mirror: What is your face telling you?

MATCH/MISMATCH

Some of us like to be liked and to please other people and some of us would rather have confrontation and argument. Sometimes we prefer one approach in one context and another in a different context. Whichever approach we like better shows in the way we behave. Someone who searches for similarity (matching) will seek to be like the person or people they are with in every way they can. They will move like them, dress like them, look like them.

You may have noticed how couples who are close to each other seem to grow to look alike. This is not surprising when you think that people who are fond of each other or in love will match each other's behavior and expressions. Over time, the lines that form on their faces will be similar. Even if their basic face structure is different, the habits they form together will show in the way their bodies develop over time. Take a look at your partner: Do you like what you see? You may be looking at a mirror image of yourself!

So someone who creates a climate of rapport naturally – someone who is very approachable and is easy company – is usually someone who matches others around them. This doesn't mean that they agree with everything other people say. However, they will be searching for the opportunity to support other people in some way, building them up rather than knocking them down. Their behavior, including their movements, their posture, their facial expressions, their gestures, even the rate at which they blink and breathe, will be similar if not the same as the person to whom they are relating at that moment.

This matching of nonverbal behavior is influential in situations of discord. We can communicate at a nonverbal level that although we do not agree, we do support the other person. You may have noticed how some people with critical feedback to give will simultaneously touch the other person on the arm or on the shoulder. In effect, what this is saying is that I am still connected to you even though I am giving critical feedback.

Notice what happens when someone whose preferred style is to match in this way is faced with someone who mismatches. As the other person changes to be different, the matcher will look confused, and will often be shocked into silence. Mismatching behavior is alien to them. Alternatively, they will skillfully follow the other person, not allowing them to be out of synchronization.

Similarly, someone who searches for difference, preferring to mismatch, will show that in the way they behave. They will use body language that is contrary to the person they are with. If their partner in conversation is leaning forward in an associated manner, the mismatcher will lean back, dissociated. It is a pattern for them to be different and they will show it in the way they dress, behave and speak.

You can easily notice someone who prefers to mismatch: they stand out from a group as the one whose behavior is different to the rest. Mismatching externally with others often stems from conflict going on inside the person, and they may indicate this conflict by talking about or experiencing parts of themselves at odds with each other. They show this by spatially indicating the parts as being in separate hands, hence the expression "on the one hand… on the other hand…" Trying to match someone whose preference is to mismatch can feel somewhat like nailing jelly to the ceiling! This kind of behavior is characteristic of someone who may have difficulty in relationships, who may not be easy to converse with, and who seems to put obstacles in the path of any connectedness to anyone else.

PAST - PRESENT - FUTURE

Consider your office or your home for a moment. Do you know where everything is? Do key items have their place in your environment? If you have an office and use a computer, you very likely file different sorts of information in their allocated places. Even if you are not orderly about this, it is likely that there is some method in your world.

We do the same with the space around us. You will have a place in that space where you represent the past, the present and the future. Think about it now. Where are your past memories: behind you, to one side, above you? Ask someone close to you – you might be surprised to find that they have their time zones allocated to very different parts of their personal space.

It is as if we have a spatial filing cabinet that goes with us wherever we go. We typically have a place for parts of ourselves that we like and identify with and quite another space for the parts of ourselves that we would prefer to dissociate from.

When I am coaching, I note where these parts are stored. I can gradually make the person I am coaching aware of this storage system so they can make more choices in how they use it. It is often the case that we keep the parts of ourselves that we like close to our chest and the parts that we don't like at arm's reach, in front or to one side of us. Watch people's hands and where they gesture as they speak to you and you will learn where they store their memories, parts of themselves, visions for the future, and much more.

We have a spatial filing cabinet

PROCEDURE/CHOICE

We give clues about how we make decisions by where we gesture. Think for a moment about how you make decisions. How, for example, did you decide to read this book? Did you have a choice of books or was its purchase part of a planned approach and this was one step in a sequence? Whichever it was indicates your preference for choices or procedures.

And if I had asked you to explain that choice to me, I wonder how you would have indicated your preference in your body language. Someone who prefers choice tends to wave their hands in an arc in front of them, indicating the array of choice. Someone whose preference is procedural is much more likely to make a chopping action, moving their hand away from them, indicating the steps stretching before them in sequence.

INTERNALLY OR EXTERNALLY REFERENCED

Have you ever noticed a person who, when making a suggestion in a meeting, glances in the direction of someone from whom they are seeking approval? It may not be the person to whom they are making the suggestion, but it is the person whose feedback and acknowledgment they rely on for feedback on how they are doing. This is characteristic of someone who is externally referenced, in that they need feedback from an external source to know how they are doing.

Someone who is internally referenced has an internal yardstick that they use to know how they are doing. Someone with this preference is much more likely to look straight at the person to whom they are making a suggestion, or even not to look at anyone but perhaps to be reading the next item on the agenda.

Someone who is externally referenced is much more likely to seek feedback than someone who is internally referenced.

Externally referenced people glance, seeking approval, from key members of a meeting

USING BODY LANGUAGE TO INFLUENCE OUR STATE

It works the other way round: How we behave influences how we think and feel. If we hunch our shoulders and tense our neck, we are likely to think about the problems in our lives. If at the same time we look down and (usually) right, we will also feel the emotions attached to those problems.

Saying "keep your chin up" to someone who is feeling down is very sound advice. By lifting our head up we disconnect from our feelings, which are experienced in a head down position for

"Keep your chin up" is sound advice

most people. And when we say "distance yourself from it," we are inviting our listener to imagine themselves outside of themselves in their thinking and to dissociate from their feelings.

By changing one or two factors in the way we are thinking about a situation, we can significantly change how we feel about it.

SHORTCUT TO USING BODY LANGUAGE TO ACHIEVE AN ALIGNED STATE

1 Work with a partner to do this.
2 Ask your partner to think of a time when they didn't feel at ease with themselves, when they felt out of balance, possibly stressed in some way. Ask them (but only briefly) to step back into this time so that they are seeing, hearing and feeling it again.
3 Note their body language. See how many characteristic elements of this state you can detect.
4 Ask your partner to break state (think about something completely different).
5 Ask your partner to think of a time when they felt completely at one with themselves. Ask them to associate into this time by seeing, hearing and feeling it from their own shoes.
6 Note their body language. How many characteristic elements of this state do you detect?
7 Feedback to your partner what you noticed to be the differences between the body language of each state.
8 Ask them to do the same for you.

SUMMARY

Our body can know much more than our mind alone. If we limit our learning to what we can know intellectually, we significantly compromise what we can learn.

We live in an age when learning is key. We not only need to learn how to learn, we need to use every resource to do so. Whole body learning comes from using our body to tell us what our mind doesn't consciously know. And the quickest and most effective way to learn how to respond to the different cultures we come into contact with each day is to listen to and look at their body language.

Making people aware of their body language can often have the effect of lifting them out of the issue, so that they can take a more dissociated view of what is happening. This can be valuable if they are so emotionally caught up in an issue that they cannot break out of it. Awareness of body language creates a meta state from which we can watch and listen to the patterns of what is happening and how it is happening.

In the context of modeling excellence, it is the body language that contains most of the clues about how we and others are achieving the results that we want to be able to reproduce.

Treat the spoken word as unsubstantiated rumor unless supported by nonverbal behavior

THOUGHT PROVOKERS

1 Watch someone talking in regular conversation on a TV program. Notice where they put their hands. Notice also where they look when they speak. You don't need to know what their gestures mean, just be aware of them.

2 Ask someone you know to compare the holiday they had last year with the one they plan to have this year or next year. Notice where they look or indicate with their hands when they are talking about the past compared to when they are talking about the future.

3 Listen carefully to someone on the phone. Determine when they are associated and when they are dissociated, by the emotion (or absence of it) in their voice.

4 Pay attention to one person in the next meeting you attend. (Choose a meeting where you do not have a key role so that you can give time to observing someone else.) Determine how much of the time they are in the present with the other people in the meeting and how much time they spend elsewhere. Do this by noticing their eye movements.

5 When you are next with someone from a different culture (and that might still be from the same country as yourself), adopt as much of their nonverbal behavior as you can. When you do this, what do you learn about their underlying values (what has to be true for them to behave in this way)?

According to my mother's elder sister, our favourite aunt (who could count up to ten in Bushman and utter his formal greeting for our delight although invariably she went dangerously purple in the process), it was fatal to remark on the Bushman's smallness in his presence. More, it was often perilous to show in one's bearing that one was aware of dealing with a person smaller than oneself.

Our old 'Suto hands strongly supported my aunt with their own colourful illustrations. They said they had always been warned never to show any surprise if they unexpectedly came upon a Bushman in the veld in case he took it to imply they could have seen him sooner had he not been so small. When, unexpectedly, one ran into a Bushman the only wise thing to do was promptly to blame oneself for the surprise and say, "Please do not look so offended. Do you really imagine a big person like you could hide without being seen? Why, we saw you from a long way off and came straight here!" Immediately the fire in those shining eyes would die down, the golden chest expand enormously and gracefully he would make one welcome. In fact the oldest of the old Basutos once told me one could not do better than use the Bushman's own greeting, raising one's open right hand high above the head, and calling out in a loud voice: "Tshjamm! Good day! I saw you looming up afar and I am dying of hunger."

Laurens Van Der Post, The Lost World of the Kalahari

Linguistic

Language and word choice form a manager's primary tool. Used wisely, sound guidance can grow from the seeds of aligned words. Used poorly and all you get are weeds.
Michael Lissack and Johan Roos, The Next Common Sense

In the beginning was the word. Your words are your life. Your language is an embroidery of patterns of words that tell your story. Your language is either your gateway to learning and choice, or your jailer.

In business especially, language is a powerful tool. It is the currency of business transactions. By learning to develop mastery of your language you can:

- Improve the quality of the information you exchange with others in whatever medium you choose.
- Increase the level of understanding you create with your communication.
- Influence the outcomes of situations.
- Empower yourself and others by challenging the constraints that show themselves in language.
- Bypass conscious resistance by engaging the unconscious mind.
- Communicate in a way that is captivating and compelling.
- Enrich your language and consequently your life.
- Learn what messages you are communicating to others' unconscious minds and discover if they are those you want to be communicating.
- Learn how to recognize the signals that you and others are sending through your body language.

Your words are your life

The opportunity to practice your skill with language is available to you not only when you interact with others, but more so when you interact with you.

5
Enriched communication

Words as I speak or write them, make a path on which I walk.
Diane Glancy

Personal success relies largely on our ability to communicate. What we say matters little compared to how we say it, no matter what medium we use to convey the words.

The quality of language is one of the significant factors that make the difference between outstanding communicators and influencers and those who would aspire to achieve their standing but who do not ignite the hearts and minds of their listeners in the same way. When Barack Obama was campaigning for election as President of the United States, his name was linked to that of John F Kennedy, Martin Luther King and other great leaders as people with the ability to engage and inspire, to create an enticing vision for the future and to move people to action.

Great communicators and leaders ignite the hearts and minds of their listeners

One of the early discoveries in NLP was that skilled communicators use language in a way that creates a climate of trust and understanding. A study of powerful communicators also revealed that they naturally use language that is rich in its use of all the senses. The richer our language, the richer our internal experience and the richer the experience of those with whom we engage. Read these lines from *Love's Labours Lost*:

A lover's eyes will gaze an eagle blind;
A lover's ears will hear the lowest sound,
When the suspicious head of theft is stopp'd:
Love's feeling is more soft and sensible
Than are the tender Horns of cockled snails:
Love's tongue proves dainty Bacchus gross in taste.

What has Shakespeare's writing got to do with writing in business today? Everything! What constitutes excellence transcends time. He has embraced virtually every sense in this short passage. This is enriched communication. You may not use his words, but be aware that the reason his writing has reached so many people over so much time is because of the way he influences us with his style of writing. There's nothing bland in the words he uses, and in using our senses he engages our unconscious mind, the part of us that finds this kind of communication irresistible. It fires our imagination.

Compare that example to part of an article I received today:

"I had the opportunity of developing alongside a group of people who came from all aspects of life and from various parts of the country. During my time I recognized the confluence of the different parts of this experience in which I was involved and the connections it made for me. I also had the opportunity to have interactions with teachers who were undertaking a new approach to teaching, in terms of their technique, approach and attitude."

I know the person who wrote this and I had expected to find their writing exciting and inspiring; it wasn't. I was surprised and my reaction prompted me to take a closer look to find out what it was about the style that had left me untouched in this way. Given that the writer was hoping to "touch" many more people with this article, this was important. The language is not enriched. The writer uses neutral language with very little appeal to the senses. Neutral language is likely to keep the intellectual, critical, unimaginative side of the brain engaged rather than the imagination.

Contrast that example with selections from speeches by Barack Obama.

"Our task is to continue the long march of those who came before us, a march for a more just, more equal, more free, more caring and more prosperous country. I chose to run for the presidency at this moment in history because I believe we cannot solve the challenges of our time unless we solve them together – unless we perfect our union by understanding that we may have different stories, but we hold common hopes; that we may not look the same and we may not have come from

*the same place, but we all want to move in the same direction – towards
a better future for all of our children and our grandchildren."*

*"A good compromise, a good piece of legislation, is like a good sentence;
or a good piece of music. Everybody can recognize it. They say 'Hey, it
works. It makes sense.'"*

It is reassuring to know that we can learn the enriched style of
great leaders, authors, poets, communicators and influencers.

MY INTRODUCTION TO NLP

Ironically, it was over 20 years ago on a creative writing course
that I first came across NLP. I wanted to be able to write with
interest and style. The course I attended was run by two people:
one an author, the other a consultant who had "coded" the
writing skills of this author in order that we might reproduce
some of his writing style in our own work. I became curious about
this process of coding talent, which is how I came to be interested
in NLP.

NLP is a process of
encoding talent

Since then I have modeled many writers. I had the privilege of
listening to Brian Keenan talking about the process he went
through to write *An Evil Cradling*, about his harrowing
experiences as a hostage in Beirut for four and half years. His
discussion of the writing was as compelling as the writing itself.
Both his spoken and his written communication are rich in the use
of all senses. When he spoke to our course you could have heard
a pin drop, such was the quality of his communication.

You can code the writing or speaking style of any great
communicator. It sometimes seems that the qualities of
compelling communication have been stripped away, to leave
the cold, neutral language that fills so many hours of business
presentations and pages of reports. By studying the difference
between the people to whom you are more likely to give your
attention and those whose reports you shove to the bottom of
the pile, you will uncover the secret of enriched
communication.

SENSORY-SPECIFIC LANGUAGE

The Shakespearean passage contains language appealing to the eyes, the ears and the feelings: "gaze an eagle blind," "hear the lowest sound," "soft," "tender," "gross in taste." Shakespeare engages our every sense so that we can see, hear and feel what he is saying. Feelings language is what encourages the reader to associate and connect with what is being said and this is at the heart of this passage. And finally, he leads to us a less usual form of language – leaving a sweet taste in our mouths?

You may not want to communicate exactly like Shakespeare in one of your project review meetings, but you probably do want to capture and hold your audience's attention. And you want to speak or write in a way that increases the likelihood of your listener or your reader understanding what you say.

ADAPTING TO OTHERS' PREFERENCES

It is important to be able to use all the senses as you speak or write

It is important to be able to have the choice of using all the senses in the way you speak or write. You will discover that your listeners and your readers have preferences, as in the following example.

Pete and Joe rarely agreed. They both complained that they found the other frustrating. As senior managers in a rapidly growing organization, it was vital that they understood each other's point of view.

Whenever they got together to make decisions, Pete wanted to gain a grasp of the situation and make decisions based on his gut feeling. He'd had a lot of success working this way. Joe, on the other hand, liked to talk his ideas through in full. Typically he would have a list of points that he wanted to discuss. Pete quickly got frustrated with this and usually cut the meeting short. Their inability to reach a satisfactory conclusion had resulted in Pete moving Joe to a new position where they had less direct contact.

It seemed as though Pete and Joe were speaking a different language; in a way they were. Pete thought and talked mainly in terms of feelings. He made decisions based on "gut feel." Joe had a very auditory way of communicating: he would "talk his ideas through" and have "points to

discuss." They were using different senses to communicate, or rather to try to communicate.

If your means of communicating is the same as the person to whom you are speaking, then you are literally talking the same language. If, like Pete and Joe, you use different systems to communicate, then you will have difficulty understanding and accepting what the other has to say.

Once you get to know someone's preferences, you can adapt the way in which you communicate to match their style so that you increase the likelihood of them understanding what you are saying. And that in turn increases the chances that they will relate to what you say and potentially agree with it. If, however, you do not know the person or perhaps you are talking to an audience greater than one, whose thinking and communication styles are going to be varied, enriched language is the style to use. In this way everyone will be able to relate to some of the style that you are using.

EXAMPLES OF LANGUAGE IN VARIOUS SENSES

Your speech is an expression of the way you think. For example, when you think visually you are likely to say:

- I get the picture.
- It's clear now.
- I see what you mean.

However, when you think in an auditory way you are more likely to say:

- That sounds good.
- It rings bells for me.
- I hear what you are saying.

When your experience is more feelings based, you tend to say:

- That feels right.
- It made an impact on me.
- I was moved by what you said.

Then we have the language of taste and smell (often grouped under the category of feelings):

* It left a bad taste in my mouth.
* There was something fishy about that suggestion.

Some of the key words for each of the three systems are:

Visual	Auditory	Feelings
see	sound	impact
focus	hear	taste
clear	tell	feel
bright	say	touch
picture	click	smell
hazy	bang	tense
color	talk	rough
view	volume	bitter
dim	loud	relaxed
look	snap	whiff

Some of the key expressions for each of the three systems are:

Visual
Things are a bit hazy
I take a dim view of that
The future looks bright
The outlook is bleak
Seeing things through rose-tinted glasses
He is in a black mood today
We're in the pink
I look forward to seeing you
Things are looking up
We've a clear way forward
A colorful expression

Auditory
I tell myself to take care
I'm glad to hear it
Tell me how it is
My teeth are chattering

Things clicked into place
Let me explain
We're in harmony
Listen to yourself
We're in tune with each other
It was music to my ears
I'm pleased you said that

Feelings
Racked with pain
The sweet smell of success
Get in touch with reality
A taste of fear
I've got a grasp of what you mean
Warm regards
I've got a handle on it
I was moved
It was a blow to my pride
Let's firm up on this
I savored the moment
Hold on

Excellent communicators naturally use the system preferred by the person to whom they are speaking, at least initially. This ensures that they are talking the same language and are more easily understood than if they were to use a representational system that was less favored by their audience.

USE OF ENRICHED LANGUAGE IN BUSINESS

Ships that pass in the night, and speak each other in passing;
Only a signal shown and a distant voice in the darkness;
So on the ocean of life we pass and speak one another,
Only a look and a voice, then darkness again and a silence.
    Henry Wadsworth Longfellow, "The Theologian's Tale: Elizabeth"

You'd scarce expect one of my age
To speak in public on the stage;
And if I chance to fall below

Demosthenes or Cicero,
Don't view me with a critic's eye
But pass my imperfections by.
Large streams from little fountains flow.
Tall oaks from little acorns grow.
                    David Everett, "Lines Written for a School Declamation"

These are examples of compelling, inspiring language. By developing your ability to use all sensory systems in your language, you will be developing your ability to communicate in a way that is interesting and compelling.

Contrast the following:

"As you walk down the corridor to the main office you will see a pink notice on the wall to the side of the EXIT door. Read this – it will remind you of the emergency procedures we have demonstrated this morning."

This has a very different effect to saying:

"Be sure to take account of the emergency procedures on the way out."

The first example is more likely to engage the listeners' attention. It uses sensory-specific language, and it encourages association into the experience of reading the procedures. It is therefore likely to be more memorable than dissociated, neutral language.

Compare this:

"Things have been difficult for some time now. As a result of this our objective for the next period is to introduce a quality program. It will be crucial to the future success of the company. By giving attention to quality we will be understanding and meeting the requirements of our customers, both internal and external. I cannot stress the importance of this enough. For the last year our sales and it seems our spirit in this team have fallen."

With this:

"Because of what I feel to be the problem and because you tell me that our focus of attention now needs to be different, I have written out my thoughts on our outcomes for the year to come. I would like to explain

these to you; I'd like you to listen and ask yourself, 'How can I make this work for me?' I want to hear the answers to this question. My vision of the future is one where each of the people – staff and clients alike – with whom we come into contact will see a new image emerging, one that communicates attention and care and concern that we really meet their needs. I believe we can do this by ensuring that we see each and every one of them to ask them all, 'What do you really need from us in order for you to feel that you are being served well?' and 'What would have to be true for you to want to continue to keep us as your main supplier for the next three years?' We will know when we have achieved our goal when our customers invite us to meet with them to discuss their needs and when they say, 'You understand us and demonstrate that you will act to ensure our needs are met.'"

Each style of communication has its place. Unfortunately, neutral, abstract language is often used in business through habit rather than choice. If you want to increase understanding, motivate and inspire, then enriched communication is the way to do it.

Language that encourages association is memorable

SHORTCUT TO USING ENRICHED LANGUAGE

1 Choose something that you want to communicate to someone. It could be via an email, a letter, a report or a presentation.
2 Decide on the outcome that you want to achieve. (See Chapter 15 on well-formed outcomes.) Work out how you will know when you have achieved this, for example what you expect to see, hear and feel that indicates your success.
3 Think of the person you are going to communicate with. What do you think is their preferred way of communicating: what is their most preferred sense, next preferred, least preferred? If you aren't sure, take a look at any communication you have had from them. If you are communicating to a group of people, use all the senses unless you know there is a cultural norm for the group that you can match.
4 Imagine yourself associated into the situation that you want to communicate so that you can see, hear and feel it. (This could be a past, present or future situation.)
5 Choosing the preferred style of your audience, write down what you are seeing/hearing/feeling (matching the way they

would use these). Aim to convey with language what it is that you see, hear and feel. If you are not sure of some of the vocabulary, check back to the lists on page 72.

6 After you have communicated what you wanted to say, check out how far you achieved your outcome. To what extent have you achieved the indicators of success that you set yourself at the outset?

7 What have you learnt about how to use enriched communication in the process of doing this?

SUMMARY

Enriched communication is the essence of motivation and commitment. Appeal to the eyes, ears and feelings of your listeners and you will have their understanding and their attention. Inspirational leaders throughout history have instinctively had the ability to capture the hearts and minds of their audience. By understanding the components of enriched language, you too can inspire and delight your listeners. Bring your business meetings and presentations alive with your skilled use of language.

THOUGHT PROVOKERS

1 For someone you haven't met before, how could you prepare to present your ideas so that you take account of each of the visual/auditory/feelings systems?

2 Rewrite these sentences using enriched language:
   a   It is important to me that I progress within this organization.
   b   I want to know what we aim to achieve with this meeting.

3 Select someone you work with. Listen to the language they use. Identify any preferences for visual/auditory/feelings systems.

4 How can you ensure that you address each of the senses when giving a presentation?
   a   Visual.
   b   Auditory.
   c   Feelings.

5 Pick one of your favorite books. Read the first page and note examples of each of the sensory systems that you detect being used.

6   Watch the adverts on television. For each one, note which senses it appeals to predominantly.

7   Log on to the internet and select a website. Which senses does the home page appeal to? How attracted are you to continuing to explore this site?

REFERENCES

Brian Keenan (1993) *An Evil Cradling*, Vintage.

Gregory Bateson was one of the influences on John Grinder and Richard Bandler, the founders of NLP. Much of his thinking about change and learning has been incorporated and developed in the concepts of NLP. Some of his discoveries about learning came from the time he spent studying porpoises, which involved watching porpoises in performances for the general public

In particular, audiences were shown how a porpoise learnt to do a trick. As the porpoise circled in the pool, the trainer would wait and watch for the porpoise to do something different: flipping its tail or spinning around. As soon as it did this different behavior – it didn't really matter what it was as long as it was different – the trainer would blow a whistle and give the porpoise a fish. As soon as the porpoise repeated the behavior, the trainer would once again blow a whistle and give the porpoise another fish. In this way the porpoise learnt what it had to do to get its reward and would demonstrate the new behavior in order to obtain the fish.

There were usually several shows each day, so at the next show naturally the porpoise would swim out into the pool and begin to demonstrate the new behavior that had previously earned the fish. Of course, this time the trainer wanted to demonstrate to the audience how the porpoise learnt new tricks and consequently didn't give it the fish. The porpoise would become increasingly frustrated and toward the end of the show would do something else: jump out of the water, for example. As soon as it demonstrated this new behavior, the trainer would blow the whistle and give it a fish. The porpoise quickly realized that this was what it needed to do and would continue to jump out of the water, and each time it did so the trainer blew the whistle and gave it a fish.

At each subsequent show the same pattern was repeated, the porpoise getting increasingly frustrated each time until in desperation it performed a new behavior by chance, at which point the trainer immediately blew the whistle and gave it a fish. The frustration in the porpoise increased to such a point that occasionally the trainer would break the procedure and give the porpoise a fish without its demonstrating a new behavior.

Eventually, after many shows. the porpoise seemed to change dramatically and became very excited as it was waiting to be let into the show pool. When it was released into the pool the porpoise put on an amazing performance that included eight completely new behaviors, some of which had never been witnessed before.

When asked about the unearned fish, the trainer replied, "Those fish were to maintain my relationship with the porpoise. Only by maintaining our relationship can we communicate in this way and achieve the kind of results you have just seen."

6

Clean questions

There is ecstasy in paying attention. You can get into a kind of Wordsworthian openness to the world, where you see in everything the essence of holiness, a sign that God is implicit in all of creation. –Anne Lamott

Pause where you are right now. Where is your attention? Where has it been over the last ten minutes? Have you been concentrating on the pages of this book or has your attention wandered onto other things? Are you paying attention to what I have written here? Has your attention been at any time on the way I am saying it? Are you noticing any patterns in the way I am communicating with you? If not, let's begin!

I was watching the Commonwealth Games. The coverage had been of the cycling, but it now cut to the shot put. I suggested we switch off as I found this boring. My friend looked surprised and asked how I could find this boring.

"Look at the different techniques!" he exclaimed. "This guy is spinning around before he throws the shot. And look at the speed with which he does that. Do you realize that he is turning in such a way that the shot is coming away from him at maximum possible speed? And notice how he is using his neck as a spring. No wonder they have such huge necks."

I began to pay attention in a way I had not done previously. This sport, which had been so alien to me, started to come alive. Gradually I began to notice the differences between the different athletes. And bit by bit I became intrigued.

In contrast, I was doing an exercise with a group of delegates on one of my courses. The challenge was for one of the group members to explore the goals of one of the other people on the course using open questions. The person doing the questioning looked disinterested through most of this process. When we explored this subsequently he said, "I was waiting for them to talk about something I am interested in!"

My experience of watching the Games, which has been repeated many times in other ways and with other people, is that there is a richness in many things that I often overlook. Yet when I become sincerely and openly curious about another person's area of interest, I begin to take on their passion for the subject.

"All of us are watchers – of television, of time clocks, of traffic on the freeway – but few are observers. Everyone is looking, not many are seeing."
Peter M Leschak

AN ATTITUDE OF CURIOSITY

Richard Bandler, one of the founders of NLP, said:

"NLP is an attitude characterized by the sense of curiosity and adventure and a desire to learn the skill to be able to find out what kinds of communication influence somebody and the kinds of things worth knowing… to look at life as a rare and unprecedented opportunity to learn."

Consider this conversation. We were explaining the plans for the development of our house to one of our friends and were comparing the design on paper to how the house was at that time.

Me   *"This is the artist's impression of how the house will be."*
Sam   *"So you are going to lower the roof?"*
Me   *(a bit surprised) "No, the roof will stay the same."*
Sam   *"So that door is where that opening is now?"*
Me   *"No, no, the door will be over there and that opening will be a window."*
Sam   *"So you are going to have another window to the side there?"*
Me   *(now beginning to feel frustration) "No, that will be the same as it is now."*
Sam   *"So you are going to add another room in the roof space?"*

Me   "Well yes, at least one."
Sam   "So you are going to lower the roof to do that?"
Me   (now having given up communicating with any accuracy what
       was planned) "Yes, that's right!"

I had not found a way to explain what was true about the plans and my friend in turn seemed intent on working out the answers for himself without really listening. This is not unusual. The ability to question and listen in an open and "clean" way is rare, in my experience. And yet without this ability we go through the world confirming our already established ideas and learning little that is new. A tendency to impose our "map of the world" on others is sadly the norm. That is true at many levels and I believe is the root of many of the problems we experience in the world today.

> The ability to question and listen in a "clean" way is rare

Many of the participants in my programs in India are tempted to recreate their world as they know it in their country of origin. They are likely to want the food to which they are accustomed, to dress the way that is their habit, to speak with their own familiar language patterns. I avoid returning to some of the Greek islands that I first visited over 40 years ago for fear that the loss of their natural beauty and absence of tourism might shake the memories I have of their unspoilt charm. I class this tendency to impose our way without permission as a form of bullying. With this attitude we are unlikely to discover the unique excellence that exists in the world around us.

So what is the alternative?

CLEAN

David Grove, on whose work the concept of clean questions was founded, unfortunately died in 2008. His work as a therapist was remarkable in the profound change and learning that he was able to facilitate with extreme efficiency and elegance. There are a few people who have influenced the subject of NLP and, in particular, the way we use it, and he, ironically, is one. I say ironically, as he would never have classed himself as an NLP coach or trainer. He was nevertheless without doubt an exceptional therapist, linguist and coach.

I was spellbound when I first saw him working with a group. His skill with language and awareness of patterns of behavior was captivating and profound. When I consider the similarity in the people who have had this effect on me, I realize that one of the factors that makes this remarkable difference is the quality of their attention.

It was no surprise that NLP modelers and trainers Penny Tompkins and James Lawley decided to model his attitude and his skills, despite his initial resistance to the whole idea of NLP. And thank God they did. We have some of his thinking and qualities available to us now through the results of their work. And his greatest legacy must surely be clean questions – simple, common sense, yet elusive to all but the naturally curious and the experienced and trained coach.

WHAT IS CLEAN?

To be "clean" is to be naïve, present, open, not knowing, alert, aware, fascinated, eager to learn and selfless

To be clean in the context of modeling excellence is to be naïve, present, open, not knowing, alert, aware, fascinated, eager to learn and selfless. If that were not enough, it is the ability to know the effect of every word and sound and nuance of language you use, to employ your language and silence completely in the service of discovering what lies beneath the surface, and to do so in such a way that, together with the client, you are able to elicit the essence, the truth of their experience, so that you have either a description of their excellence or the key to change. Yet even though they can achieve so much, the structure of clean questions is remarkably and astonishingly simple.

An example of a clean question is:

And… (mirror their words) **in what way…?**

The attitude that is the backdrop to the words needs to be dedicated, sincere, nonjudgmental and curious.

Let us consider this question in context.

Jim   *"I felt I made a really good connection with the customer."*
Me   *"And a really good connection in what way?"*
Jim   *"Hmm, good question, we just sort of gelled. I guess I was*

expecting this to be the case."

Me   *"Expecting, how do you mean?"*

Jim   *"Well, I did a lot of thinking about this meeting beforehand and I had imagined how it might be."*

Me   *"When you say imagined how it might be, in what way?"*

Jim   *"Thinking about it now I realize that I pictured me and the customer and I even imagined us talking together in the way that I wanted the meeting to develop."*

Me   *"And when you imagined yourselves talking together in the way that you wanted the meeting to develop, what is that like?"*

Jim   *"Oh, it is a dream – a good dream where everything is happening the way that I want it to happen and I feel really confident."*

We'll push the pause button on this conversation for a moment to explore what is happening here.

Jim initially said what had happened. And he did so in the way that most of us would initially explain our experience, in an abstract way: "a really good connection." This conversation was part of a coaching session, so it was appropriate for me to explore with him what he meant. "And" indicated that I was listening and going with his comment.

"And" is a small yet powerful word. This magic word is often used in hypnotherapy, as it communicates that as a listener you are with the client and they can relax. "And" says "I want to build on what you say." It's a friendly word.

Then I repeated the abstract words that Jim had used: "a really good connection." He had deleted the details of what he meant, although not deliberately; it would be impossible to have everyday conversations if we were to include all the details, so we usually rely on others making correct assumptions about what we mean most of the time. Repeating the words exactly as they were said seeks to assure the listener that they have been accurately and truly heard. This mirroring back of the language also encourages the recipient to reflect: to go inside themselves and find out what they meant by what they said, as up to this point they might not consciously know.

And finally, I asked: "In what way?" This is the essence of clean. Note that I did not ask: "What does that feel like or look like or sound like?" Nor did I ask: "So what did you do?" I used a question that was without any of the filters described in Chapter

> "And" is a small yet powerful word

> Repeating words exactly assures the listener that they have been accurately heard

3. It is a neutral question, allowing the other person to answer in the way they choose. If I were to ask "What did you say?" and they had not actually said anything, the question would jar and interrupt their state of reflection.

You can see how much is going on in this one sentence. Of course, the measure of whether the question worked is the result. If Jim had looked confused or startled at the question, then that would tell me that I had not asked the best question or had not asked it in a way that obtained an open and fuller response. Many of the essentials of clean questioning are encapsulated in this sentence.

I introduced a slight variation on this question later on:

"And when you imagined yourselves talking together in the way that you wanted the meeting to develop, what is that like?"

This is a classic clean question. It has the same "and" opening, the mirroring of the words that Jim used, and then the question: "what is that like?" Note that most clean questions are asked in the present tense. This has the effect of encouraging the client to remember their experience as if it were now (to associate into the experience). And this question does more than that. It invites the client to access the metaphor by which they hold these experiences; see Chapter 7. Metaphors bypass our unconscious mind and hold so much more than we can encompass in our conscious thinking. Once we access a metaphor it is a bit like striking oil (to use another metaphor). They are a rich source of detail for our experience – exactly what we want when we are modeling excellence.

When Jim compared his experience to a dream, I might have asked him what kind of dream, but he has already answered this one (an indication he has started to internalize the questions):

"A good dream where everything is happening the way that I want it to happen and I feel really confident."

We begin to get the structure of Jim's experience. There is much more, but we now have a framework for how he builds good connections with his customers. This is not a one-off occurrence – it is something he does intuitively and now we and he can begin to understand the structure of how he does this. Once we have the detailed structure (the program), that structure is available to Jim whenever he wants it so that he can access this ability with consistency. And we or he can teach this program to others (maybe colleagues in the same business), so that they can achieve his level of success in the way he works with customers.

Some of the rest of this modeling/coaching session follows:

Me   *"And this confidence, whereabouts is that?"*

Jim   *"I feel it in my chest." (pointing to the center of his chest)*

Me   *(pointing toward his chest where he indicated he had this feeling) "What is this feeling of confidence like?"*

Jim   *"It's a very steady feeling running right through me. I feel really good when I feel like this. I feel as though I can achieve anything."*

Me   *"And when you have this feeling, what happens just before?"*

Jim   *"Hmmm." (pauses and thinks) "I remind myself of some of the recent times when I have had good connections with customers."*

Me   *"You remind yourself, in what way do you remind yourself?"*

Jim   *"I run a sort of video of some of the highlights of recent times that have been good and I can hear the sort of things that I and others were saying and I feel the confidence that I felt then. Hmmm, that is interesting. I hadn't realized I did that."*

Me   *(I wait to let him really appreciate this. Pausing at times like this allows a person to integrate their learning. I can see that he is reflecting within himself. I wait until he looks up and back to me. He smiles. Silence.)*

Me   *"And so you run a sort of video of the highlights and you hear what you and others were saying, and you feel confidence." (I point to that same area in his chest where he had indicated that he felt this) "This is like a good dream where everything is happening the way that you really want it to happen and you feel confidence... and then what happens?"*

Jim   *"Then I feel in this very good state" (he lifts his shoulders, smiles and gives a small laugh as he moves his hands and arms freely in a wide sweep) "and I trust that we will have a really good and interesting discussion no matter what the issues are."*

We have the key elements of Jim's structure for building good connections here, the depth and some of the sequence. I have come across similar structures in successful leaders, salespeople, husbands, wives.

> Pausing allows the person to integrate their learning

WHAT ARE THE CLEAN QUESTIONS?

Some of the questions encourage the client to expand and go deeper into the perception that they are describing in the moment. These are the "developing questions."

And what kind of (their words) is that?
This invites the client to expand on what they are saying. It is likely that as they do so they become more associated into the sensory-rich descriptions that are characteristic of the way we hold experiences in our unconscious minds.

And (their words/a summary of the key words so far) anything else?
This is a very useful question to test for how to know when to stop. Sometimes it prompts much more at a deeper level and sometimes it highlights that you have emptied the cache of information and thoughts available in this area. By asking this question you are allowing the person to determine the stopping or moving-on point.

You allow the person to determine the moving-on point

And whereabouts is (their words)?
This can help the person become precise about the locality of a feeling, for example, or the way they are using this space in their thinking. Some examples of how this question can be used are in Chapter 15, Well-formed outcomes.

And that's like what?
This is a classic clean question and invites a metaphor.

And is there a relationship between (their words) and (their words)?
This question encourages the person to explore how the elements of their thinking are connected.

And when (their words) what happens to (their words)?
This question also explores the connection between elements and how a change in one affects another. The presupposition that is enforced here is that all elements in our experience have an impact on everything else.

Then there are questions that invite the client to put their attention outside their current perception and locate their experience in time.

And (their words), what happens just before?
This can help to identify the trigger for a key state. If, for example, we feel confident and we know what that is like and the whereabouts of the feeling, then to know what happens just before is to know what step we can take to switch this feeling on. We begin to have access to our emotions, which enables us to get at more of the sequence in the strategy.

We can learn how to switch on feelings

And (their words), then what happens/what happens next?
This question helps to elicit the sequence of actions that form part of the strategy. We begin to get the order of the steps to achieve the result.

And (their words), where does that come from?
When this is asked in relation to a feeling we can begin to identify the cause or the source of our emotions. We challenge the belief that things or emotions "just happen."

Jim now has the conscious awareness of the specifics of a key state that is essential to the way in which he builds good relationships. And we do too. Only when we ask the right kind of questions and listen with a totally open mind do we have the possibility of truly learning and respecting the talents of other people.

THE VALUE OF CLEAN QUESTIONS IN EVERYDAY CONVERSATION

Clean questions are not only the property of coaches and therapists, they can enrich the way in which we relate to others on a daily basis. Consider this example of someone who was not using clean questions:

Clean questions enrich the way we relate to each other

Just recently my accountant invited me to a meeting with a financial adviser, someone he thought might act on my behalf. After a few pleasantries, this adviser proceeded to question me.

"You probably know about some of the changes to pension schemes?"

"No, actually I don't," I replied.

"Well, you will probably be wondering how you can secure your future in the light of the downturns in investments."

"Not necessarily," I replied.

"I can see that your business has done very well over the time that you have been independent and I guess you will be wanting to wind down in the not too distant future."

"Not at all," I replied, not sure whether to feel irritated or amused at the wild mindreading in which he was engaging.

He gave me no time to elaborate on my answers before he fired another loaded and assumptive question at me. This continued for quite a while, at which point he pushed a piece of paper across the desk for me to sign to give him permission to explore the state of my current pension scheme. I refused. He looked puzzled!

How often do you jump in and make unhelpful assumptions about another person's experience? I most certainly do, for all the training I have had. However, now I am much more likely to wait and react after some thought and questioning than I would have done in my youth!

It is now always appropriate to jump straight in with the questions. Nevertheless, you can create a clean foundation and follow up with the questions. Can you imagine how the above conversation might have gone?

"Hello, pleased to meet you. Harry has invited me to meet with you and I was wondering what goals you might have for this meeting?"

"Well, I value Harry's advice and I am curious as to why he thought us meeting might be important."

"Well, I can fill you on what I believe and we can check that out with Harry too. He did suggest to me that it might be useful for me to explore with you the changes in pension schemes and investments, as they might have an impact on your future."

"OK – well, I have not taken any interest in these things so I am curious what changes he and you think might have an impact on me."

"Great, so let's proceed on that basis. Can I ask you what are your thoughts about the future in terms of your work and possible security?"

"Well, I'm keen to continue the work I do no matter what age."

"When you say 'continue', in what way continue?"

And so the clean basis and then the more specific clean questions would have led to a very different outcome.

OTHER APPLICATIONS OF CLEAN QUESTIONS

In some ways it would be easier to list the times when clean questions are not appropriate! The times when they are valuable include:

- When collecting information about the style and needs of a new or existing client, so that not only do you understand their needs precisely, you also understand the style with which they would like you to deal with them.
- When someone has an issue that they want to talk through with you. Clean questions may be all they need to work out this issue for themselves. By asking the questions, you raise their awareness of how they are making their experience what it is.
- When you are not sure what someone means. Rather than assuming a meaning, check using a question.
- When you want to encourage someone to know that they have all the resources they need within themselves. By not providing the answers or suggestions, you encourage them to take ownership of their issues and find their own resources to deal with them.
- When you want to delegate and encourage independent thinking and working.
- When you want to show respect for another person's experience and knowledge.
- When modeling excellence.
- When coaching.

There are thousands of everyday specific contexts when clean questions are called for. Enjoy finding out more!

THOUGHT PROVOKERS

1. Think for a moment: When did you last have a conversation when the only agenda present was that of the other person? When did you last listen with your whole being, with the sole purpose of understanding and

appreciating what the other person had to say? If you say "today," then I applaud you. That is not the norm.

2. Decide on a time or a conversation when you will choose to listen in an entirely open and clean way. Choose a time when practicing new skills will not be critical to the outcome of the discussion. Take some time beforehand to make sure that you are in a relaxed state of sincere curiosity. Evaluate how you think you did and with what results. If you have the opportunity and it is appropriate, ask the person with whom you had this conversation how it was for them.

REFERENCES

Penny Tompkins and James Lawley (2000) *Metaphors in Mind*, Developing Company Press.

You can download two summary cards of clean questions from my website, www.sueknight.com.

The Thunder-beings were busy giving birth to new clouds, sending them to dance in the blue playground of sky. Grandfather Sun provided the glittering sunbeams, which acted like jump ropes for today's newborn white, puffy Cloud People.

One of the most curious little clouds wandered off on the winds. She decided she was going to have a talk with Sacred Mountain. "Grandmother Mountain, I've come to ask you if your forests need rain today," she said. "I want to be of service, and so I thought I had better find out what is needed most."

Sacred Mountain told the little cloud that there was plenty of moisture today, but the little one could help in another way. Sacred Mountain taught the little cloud how to understand the thoughts and questions that the human beings were having. It was fun for the little cloud to capture the waves of human thoughts rising from the Earth and to answer the humans' unspoken questions by becoming shapes that formed a series of ideas. The answers needed were found through linking ideas.

The little cloud approached Sacred Mountain at the end of the day with another question that caused Cloud to have a heavy heart. "Grandmother Mountain, I've worked all day to reflect helpful answers to the Human Tribe, but now I have one very important question. How can we get them to look up and pay attention?"

7

Metaphor: The key to the unconscious mind

*Engaging the book as a listener forced me to consider the awesome power of metaphor, and
how thoroughly it defeats our attempts to contain it.*
Kathleen Norris, The Cloister Walk

When preparing for each race in the Olympic Games and subsequently receiving the gold medals for both the 100 metres and the 200 metres sprint, Jamaican runner Usain Bolt adopted the pose of an archer. And he did so in a playful way. This is a powerful metaphor: he was reinforcing his beliefs about his speed and the ease with which he was approaching the race, and at the same time communicating that to his competitors and the watching world. There was a lot of influence packed into that one posture.

WHAT IS METAPHOR?

A metaphor is a way of understanding, expressing and experiencing one kind of thing in terms of another. For example, we may think of life as "a bed of roses," work as "a battleground." Whatever the metaphor, it emerges in the words, expressions and physiology we use and it influences our own and others' experience.

Metaphors correspond to the original experience they are describing; the symbols are different, but the structure and the organization of it are the same. Usain Bolt, for example, was representing his running ability as an arrow (or a bolt, perhaps!). The arrow corresponded to him being released from the bow, the starting blocks, and aiming for the target, the finish line. The symbols were different, but in both cases the runner gets released just as the arrow gets fired. Both have a target.

Metaphors represent the essence of who we are

A metaphor captures the essence of the structure of our experience. Much is reconstructed from what is presupposed. If we experience home as a prison, then this presupposes that there is someone or something that keeps us in that prison, that there are boundaries beyond which we cannot go, that there are rules we must obey, that we have done something that has got us in there and that we have no control. If, however, we talk of realizing our vision for the future, this implies that we have had it all along and we are just discovering it, that it is a moving process, that we can see it and that realizing what is important happens over time.

Metaphors say a lot in a little package

Metaphors communicate a lot of complex information in a very compact package. We can say more with a metaphor than we can ever say with a literal description.

WHERE DO WE FIND METAPHORS?

Metaphors permeate our lives

Metaphors permeate our lives. They exist in our language, in our stories, in fairytales, in parables, in our dreams, our gestures, our movement, the way we use space, our choice of environment and the way we position ourselves in that environment. The photo that a training colleague of mine was using to promote herself was slightly off center, for example; she spoke of feeling incongruent in her expertise.

We are subject to metaphor in our everyday lives: the advertising we see and hear incorporates metaphors, as do the films we watch and the books and magazines and newspapers we read. If an advertisement shows someone dining and drinking in a centuries-old building, there is an implication that this has been true for centuries and will continue to be true for centuries into the future – that there is a security over time about this product.

Metaphors can be enchanting, enticing and mesmerizing. Their effects may be enlightening and empowering when they are developed and recounted constructively. Used carelessly, however, they can be damaging and disturbing. The more we can learn to notice and listen to the metaphors in our life, the more we can choose the way we influence ourselves and the way we allow ourselves to be influenced.

In all aspects of life we define our reality in terms of metaphors, which subsequently shape our everyday behavior. The structures of the metaphors are the structure by which we live our life. These might be productive and contribute to our unique excellence, or they might be patterns of destruction. Once we become aware of our metaphors, we can recognize how they limit or empower us. They can therefore be explored as a means of modeling excellence or as a means of healing, transforming and enriching lives.

Ken often described his experience in life as being between a rock and a hard place. He went from one seemingly irresolvable conflict to another, and that is the pattern that repeated itself throughout his life. He reeled from one law suit to the next, always feeling "badly done by."

Discovering the metaphors by which we live our life helps us elicit the essence of excellence as we model someone we admire, or even as we model ourselves. We might also do this in order to coach someone to become aware of their limiting patterns and let their excellence develop and emerge.

METAPHOR IN THE CONTEXT OF MODELING EXCELLENCE

It is certain that at some point of the process of modeling excellence we will uncover a metaphor that captures the essence of a person's way of being in the world. That metaphor is unique to this person; only they have the representation of its meaning. If we want to discover how they are, then it is vital that we respect their symbols, their meaning, their way of expressing their world. If I introduce my terms and my meaning, I have trampled on their map – I will have learnt very little about them and only imposed my way of doing things.

Clean questions (see Chapter 6) are the means by which we can discover the unique meaning of another person's way of coding their experience. In particular, the metaphor symbolizes what it is like to be that person. *Like* is a significant word in the world of metaphor. A metaphor is expression of something in different symbols but in a *like* way.

Listen to the language that colleagues and friends use. Have you heard these sorts of statements? Consider too what they

> The metaphors by which we live our lives shape our everyday behavior

> Metaphors capture the essence of a person's way of being

might presuppose that is not explicitly said.

I need to combat his response	*Interaction is a battle*
We can overcome objections	*They need to be overcome*
We need to keep our heads down	*We are at the mercy of others*
On track to achieve what we want	*A track exists*
Steaming ahead	*An old form of moving!*
We will carry no passengers	*We are capable of carrying them*
Everything in the garden is rosy	*Life is something that can grow*
They are blooming	*They grow and do well*
Business has died down	*Business has a life cycle*
Life is a ball	*Life is play/a game*

A metaphor is unique to the person holding it. If we wish to explore the metaphor as the basis for modeling their excellence, then it is vital that we give that person choice about how they explore it and even if they do want to explore it. As they do so, they will not only talk about what this metaphor means to them, they will show it with their gestures and the way they move and use the space around them. And it will be not only their words but their exclamations, their erms and coughs, laughs and pauses that communicate meaning. We need to pay attention not to what the person is saying but to what they are doing as they say it.

Pay attention to how rather than what

When we are aware of the metaphor by which we, friends and colleagues live, we are aware of the way we and they are thinking. It is a way of making sense of life. Understanding the metaphor both in and behind the communication can help us make sense of an individual's experience. A metaphor gives form to what it is like to be that person.

If you know someone who thinks in terms of overcoming objections, you may begin to understand any resistance they experience from their colleagues, staff and customers. Imagine how you would feel if someone were attempting to overcome your objections!

Metaphors are rich in their ability to enhance communication. Opposite are some examples of visual metaphors drawn by course delegates to depict either the way they saw themselves then or the way they wanted to see themselves in the future.

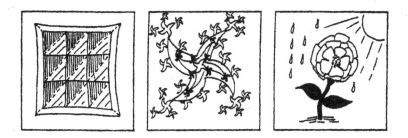

These pictures provide a wealth of information, not only for the observers but also for the owners. Questions can reveal many implications of the metaphor that have sometimes been outside the awareness of the owner.

"Metaphor and symbolism enable us to give form to those aspects of life which are the most mystifying; namely, our relationships, our problems and their solutions, our fears and desires, our illness and health, our poverty and wealth, and the love we give and the love we receive."
                    James Lawley and Penny Tompkins, Metaphors in Mind

When thinking about what metaphors are true for you, you may find that your unconscious mind pops an image or a thought into your head. Your unconscious mind is the source of your real hopes and fears. The more you learn to acknowledge what your unconscious tells you, the more you will have access to this powerful resource. Major breakthroughs in thinking are believed to have come about through the power of metaphor. It is held that Einstein discovered the theory of relativity as he lay daydreaming, imagining himself riding a sunbeam.

Your unconscious mind is the source of your real hopes and fears

EXCELLENT COMMUNICATORS

Excellent communicators and influencers use metaphor to capture and hold attention.

"The present life of men on earth, O King, as compared with the whole length of time which is unknowable to us, seems to me to be like this: as if, when you are sitting at dinner with your chiefs and ministers in wintertime... one of the sparrows from outside flew very quickly through

the hall; as if it came in one door and soon went out through another. In that actual time it is indoors it is not touched by the winter's storm; but the tiny period of calm is over in a moment, and having come out of the winter it soon returns to the winter and slips out of your sight. Man's life appears to be more or less like this; and of what may follow it, or what preceded it, we are absolutely ignorant."

The Venerable Bede

USING METAPHORICAL STORIES AS A FORM OF INFLUENCE

Metaphors may be single words, expressions or stories. To understand how to construct and tell a story metaphor is to know how to influence with elegance and respect.

Milton Erickson, a therapist of world-class stature who was studied by John Grinder and Richard Bandler as part of their early research into what made a difference between outstanding performers and the rest, was a master of the metaphor. He was also a master of change. Although the context in which he worked was therapy, his methods apply equally to business. The following is an example of one of his stories, told to explain the way he worked with his clients:

One day an unknown horse strayed into the yard of the farm where I lived as a child. No one knew where this horse had come from as it had no markings by which it could have been identified. There was no question of keeping the horse–it must belong to someone. My father decided to lead it home. He mounted the horse and led it to the road and simply trusted the instinct of the horse to lead itself towards its home. He only intervened when the horse left the road to eat grass or to walk into a field. On these occasions my father would firmly guide it back to the road. In this way the horse was soon returned to its owner.

The owner was very surprised to see his horse once more and asked my father, "How did you know the horse came from here and belonged to us?"

My father replied, "I didn't know, the horse knew! All I did was to keep him on the road."

This story illustrates not only the way Milton Erickson worked with his clients, but also the way most NLP is conducted today.

By providing guidance only where it is needed, NLP respects the fact that everyone has all the resources they need to solve their problems. Given the space and encouragement to use these resources, you are more likely to find solutions that are congruent with who you are. These solutions are therefore much more likely to be ones to which you are committed and will therefore work to produce the outcome you want.

When presented with a metaphor, we make our own unique interpretation of it in a way that makes sense to us. Most significantly, it is our unconscious mind that makes sense of it, and so metaphors bypass conscious resistance and embrace our unconscious. If you are faced with someone who will not intellectually consider what you are saying, try telling them a story, a parable for what you want them to learn.

A client of mine was unhappy with what she experienced as the dominance of her business partner. She thought of working independently, although she did not have experience of marketing, nor did she have financial expertise to manage her own business. She was not listening to the advice others were giving her about having someone with her who could support her in some aspects of her business. I told her a story:

Once upon a time there was a trapeze act. They were famous, although in any promotions the elder acrobat always got first billing. The younger acrobat was increasingly doing all the new stunts and had managed a triple somersault swinging from the trapeze on one side of the tent to the other, where her partner would wait with arms outstretched to balance her as she landed on the waiting platform. She decided to practice some new acts on her own and was increasingly confident with her mastery of a quadruple somersault with a twisting turn at the end. She did not tell her partner about this, although he could tell how much more skillful she was becoming and had congratulated her on that.

One night in the circus tent during a live performance, she decided that she would attempt her new act. She whispered to her partner that she was going to do something solo and for him to trust her. He looked surprised, but stood back on the platform. She prepared herself and swung out high and far. As she gained momentum, she launched herself into this mid-air somersault, but as she did so realized that she might not have given herself quite enough momentum. She turned in the air and looked toward the waiting platform. With fear she pushed herself toward

> People have all the resources they need within themselves already

> Metaphors bypass the conscious mind (and its resistance) and embrace our unconscious

it and at that moment her partner, sensing the danger, reached out, catching his hands in hers...

You will know if the person is making a connection with the metaphor by their state as they listen. The stronger their reaction, the more likely it is that the metaphor has triggered something for them. The beauty of metaphor is that people make sense of it in their own way. What it does is allow them to hear what you perceive to be the structure of their experience in another form. It gives them the opportunity to discover the wisdom that an observer might have and yet at another level to recognize the structure of the story in such a way that at an unconscious level, they know it is for them. My client in this case went into a very deep, thoughtful state and much later came back and asked me questions about the story. Neither her unconscious nor her conscious mind could forget it.

Another client had difficulty detaching from her emotions. Most circumstances in life were a drama. She would be very unlikely to stand back and use the wisdom of a third-party observer. She reeled from one dramatic situation in her life to the next. She could make a cup of tea at breakfast a drama!

Traveling in the car one day, she asked for my feedback. I had often given her feedback before, but had not seen much evidence of her taking this feedback on board. So this time I said:

I have a story for you. I have a friend and this friend was fascinated by mazes, the sort of maze you might find in the expansive green gardens of a grand English country house. She had heard about this one very famous maze, famous because so few people had found their way to the center – where there is said to be a tower. So this tower had rarely been reached by the visitors to the grounds.

The friend decided to visit the maze and was determined to find the center. And so she paid her admission price and as she was entering the maze, she overheard someone on the way out saying that they had made it to the center and the strategy worked. She stopped them and asked what the strategy was. They explained that if you kept your left hand always in touch with the side, you would find your way to the center. She was a-maze-d (!) and decided to try it out.

So she entered the maze between the dark, deep foliage of the hedges that lined the pathway. It was such an old maze that she had to strain

People make sense of metaphor in their own way

her neck to look up to see the sky. *Keeping her left hand always in contact with the leaves, she continued. Sometimes she was tempted to take her hand off the hedge, as she could see that the path was obviously a dead end, but following it round she came out the other side and continued closer and closer to the center. She could tell that she must be close, since the path was less worn as fewer people had trodden the ground here.*

Eventually the bushes opened up and there was a clearing. In the center of the clearing was a wooden tower with a winding staircase to the top. "Success!" she said to herself in a congratulatory voice as she climbed the steps. At the top was a view not only of all the winding maze but of the countryside beyond. It was view that astonished her and she stayed there for some time just appreciating this novel perspective of the path and how she was going to get out of the maze to enjoy the rest of her day.

WRITING YOUR OWN METAPHOR

Maybe in your role as a coach, facilitator, trainer or leader you want to use a metaphor that will communicate a particular message to others. How do you go about constructing one? Here are the principles.

+ Identify the message that you want to give.
+ List the elements of the current situation, e.g. confusion, lack of overview, no strategy, little ability to detach from emotions.
+ Choose a parallel context, and in that context choose symbols that you will use in the metaphor to correspond to each of the key elements. Select symbols that have the qualities of the original elements, e.g. for confusion, a maze; for lack of overview, a viewing platform in the maze, a strategy for getting through the maze.
+ When you write or tell the metaphor, tell it as a story: "Once upon a time..." (though you may not use those actual words).
+ Keep it simple, one story thread that builds anticipation and curiosity.
+ Decide how you will use the metaphor to communicate the message so that you leave the listener with the space to work it out in a way that fits for them – you don't have to spell out an answer!

Communicate the metaphor in a way that gives the listener space to interpret in their own way

- Now write or tell the metaphor as a story. Use enriched language with all the senses – visual, auditory, feelings. This keeps people's attention. Done well it is mesmerizing. That is what you are aiming for.
- Leave the moral of the story untold. An open ending is compelling. The unconscious mind will hold on to to the story until it has a meaning and an answer. It may take days, weeks or months for someone to get a meaning. Be patient!
- Give the listener(s) space and time to digest it. Stay silent. Your listeners may well be in a trance at this point. Use it.

USING METAPHORS IN BUSINESS

A director of a company was confronted with the unenviable task of announcing to one of the divisions that they had to lose half of their workforce in the following two years. This meant making 2,000 people redundant. Everyone was tense. Rumors of the cutbacks had already spread throughout the site and it seemed unlikely that the employees would be willing to listen to what the director had to say, let alone participate in the implementation of the cutbacks.

The director cared about his employees and believed that there was a possible future if they all cooperated and thought together about how they could reconsider the future. He called his staff to a meeting. This director was a much admired man; everyone trusted him and knew him to be a man of great integrity. Nevertheless, they were all apprehensive and resistant, sensing that he was going to announce some very bad news.

He explained the facts. Then he said, "This business is like a snowball rolling downhill. It is gathering snow and momentum as it gains speed. There are two possible routes that this snowball can take. One is that as it continues to roll it gets heavier and larger as it gains speed and it speeds down the hill, only to roll onto the plain where in the heat of the sun it gradually melts and disappears. The other possibility is that the snowball rolls on down the mountain beyond the plain. It has gathered such speed that nothing can stop it and, although it slows momentarily as it crosses the plain, its momentum keeps it going and it rolls on and on until eventually it reaches the fertile plain at the bottom of the valley. We can influence the path that snowball takes," he explained.

They did.

As another example, I was involved with a company whose directors talked in the following terms:

* Being in the firing line.
* Attacking the competition.
* Aiming at the target.

They described the workforce as the "troops." Employees in this company did not "step out of line," nor did those with any entrepreneurial style stay very long. I even saw a slide in one of their presentations headed, "We will fight them on the beaches." Fight whom, I wonder?

It is important to question whether and how these metaphors fit with the network culture that is absorbing the business world, in which we need to learn how to help our customers to thrive, how to support our employees to grow, and how to flourish in conditions that are right for us personally. Individuals and companies have metaphors that express their unique culture. The question is whether or not these are metaphors that support the culture and style they really want. The clue is in the language and behavior of individuals, as in the military example above. Not surprisingly, many of the older managers in this company had spent time in the forces. Now the company was searching for a way of developing a new style of leader who encouraged autonomy and cooperation. It was time to change the metaphor that underpinned the culture.

Metaphors communicate company culture

SUMMARY

Metaphors have been with us in many forms for as long as we can remember. Stories in the forms of fairytales, proverbs and parables are passed down from generation to generation. Metaphors are so rooted in our upbringing that for many people they act as an anchor for relaxation and involvement.

As such, metaphors bypass any conscious blocks or resistance and slip into the unconscious mind. The unconscious mind responds to the challenge of the metaphor by finding a unique solution that fits the listener's experience and needs.

Metaphors are powerful and memorable. Many of the best speakers and leaders use metaphor as a way of communicating what they want to say. A skilled storyteller is a skilled communicator.

Metaphors are also used in our everyday lives. The metaphors in an individual's or company's language provide many clues to the patterns by which that individual lives and the culture of the company of which they are a part. By learning how to construct and recount metaphors, we are learning how to open our listener's or reader's mind to new possibilities and choices. And by learning how to listen to the metaphors that our unconscious mind gives us, we learn to use our internal wisdom and to develop our coherence so that we become more of who we are truly meant to be.

By learning to listen to metaphor we learn to use our internal wisdom

THOUGHT PROVOKERS

1   If you were to draw a metaphor for yourself, what would you draw? As you read that question you may have noticed that a picture popped into your mind. What is it?
    ◆   What does this represent for you?
    ◆   What are the characteristics of this metaphor?
    ◆   What are its strengths?
    ◆   What are its weaknesses?
    ◆   How are the elements of the image related?
    ◆   What does this signify?
    ◆   What is missing and what does that signify?
    Show the drawing to someone else and encourage them to ask you questions about it. Their questions may give you insight into the deeper significance of the metaphor for you.

2   What metaphors would you use to describe:
    ◆   Your career?
    ◆   Your relationships?
    ◆   Your social life?
    ◆   Your past?
    ◆   Your future?
    How do the characteristics of the metaphor manifest themselves in these areas of your life? For example, if you say "Life is like a dream," what does that mean? Is it unreal? Dreams can be intangible. Dreams have many meanings and the purpose of them can be unclear. There are pleasant dreams and nightmares. Explore the possibilities of the metaphor for you.

3 Think of a situation that you would like to influence. It could be a presentation, a meeting, or a discussion with one of your colleagues. Develop a metaphor that you can use the next time you are in this situation.

4 Think of someone you admire, whose abilities you would like to model. What metaphor underpins their excellence? What is your evidence for this?

5 Think now of the company that you manage or work for. Is there a metaphor that expresses itself through the language and actions of the employees? Set yourself the task of identifying any metaphors that you hear being used in your company or in the companies of any of your customers during a particular day.

REFERENCES

James Lawley & Penny Tompkins (2000) *Metaphors in Mind: Transformation through Symbolic Modelling,* The Developing Company Press.

Michael Lissack & Johan Roos (2000) *The Next Common Sense: An E-Manager's Guide to Complexity,* Nicholas Brealey Publishing.

I hired a carpenter to help me restore an old farmhouse. After he had finished a rough first day on the job, a flat tire made him lose an hour of work, his electric saw quit, and now his ancient pickup truck refused to start. While I drove him home, he sat in stony silence. On arriving, he invited me in to meet his family. As we walked toward the front door, he paused briefly at a small tree, touching the tips of the branches with both hands. When opening the door, he underwent an amazing transformation. His tanned face was wreathed in smiles and he hugged his two small children and gave his wife a kiss. Afterwards, he walked me to the car. We passed the tree and my curiosity got the better of me. I asked him about what I had seen him do earlier. "Oh, that's my trouble tree," he replied. "I know I can't help having troubles on the job, but one thing's for sure, troubles don't belong in the house with my wife and the children. So I just hang them up on the tree every night when I come home. Then in the morning I pick them up again. Funny thing is," he smiled, "when I come out in the morning to pick 'em up, there aren't nearly as many as I remember hanging up the night before."

8
Precision questions

Language is the only homeland. -Czeslaw Milosz

T he only person who is accountable for how you experience what happens to you in life is you. If you spend time apportioning blame, being frustrated and feeling hard done by, then you are avoiding the truth. Without doubt, you are compromising yourself and clouding if not completely obscuring your talents and true potential.

One day when my sons were very young, on holiday in Dorset, we were joined by another little boy. He and my son decided to build a sandcastle. When they were doing this I overheard them talking. My son asked him what he liked doing best at school. "I don't know," he replied. "I'm not very clever." He was six years old and his words reflected a choice he had made or had learnt already that would undoubtedly limit his future success.

The only person who can look after you is you

Ultimately, the only person who can look after you is you.

Responsible organizations, families and communities encourage their people to take ownership for themselves. To do so is an expression of love. To encourage dependency is to communicate a belief that others do not have all the resources that they need. Children pick up this message and may either accept or rebel against it.

LEVELS OF LANGUAGE

Linguist Noam Chomsky distinguished two levels of language:

- *Surface structure* – everything we say, either to ourselves or to other people.
- *Deep structure* – the underlying meaning of what we say, containing information that is neither expressed nor consciously known.

A number of things can happen between the deep structure and the surface structure of the language. The intention of the communication may be lost or changed in the process of converting one to the other. The more aligned we are between what we say and what we truly mean, the more coherent our message and the more likely we are to reveal our true excellence.

Our language is rich in clues about our willingness and skill to take on this kind of responsibility. We can learn habits to support this way of being. And we can learn to recognize the habits we have that hinder this way of being. Language is a good place to start to begin to make this kind of difference.

Our language is rich in clues

LAZY LANGUAGE

Look at the expressions below. Read them quickly. What do they say?

Now read the following passage. How many *f*s are there?

FEATURE FILMS ARE THE RESULT OF YEARS OF SCIENTIFIC STUDY COMBINED WITH THE EXPERIENCE OF YEARS

The expressions actually read "Once in *a a* lifetime," "Paris in *the the* spring," "A bird in *the the* hand." In part, the way the words are written in the triangle encourages misreading. Even so, we frequently delete and distort what we read, hear and see to fit in with our expectations. In the passage there are six *f*s. (There really are! Many people write to me saying that there must be a mistake in the number we have printed here!) How many did you count?

These simple exercises illustrate the sort of processes that occur in our thinking every day. We delete, distort and generalize information so that we become disconnected from its deeper meaning. We typically use an imprecise form of language in speech, a lazy language. This is at the heart of many business problems often paraphrased as communication issues.

We sat next to someone we had not met before at a local fête and before long he was expounding his suspicions about the "they" who were deliberately filling the skies with toxins and triggering earthquakes, among many other things. When challenged, he could not explain who "they" were. I have come across this mysterious "they" in many settings:

- "They" don't communicate effectively.
- "They" introduce changes without consultation.
- "They" don't listen.
- "They" expect you to know what's going on.
- "They" keep you in the dark.
- "They" are responsible for the problems in the world.

Do you have a "they" in your company?

"They" are very elusive. They are never in the same room as the people who are talking about them (or if they are, they keep quiet!). They are very often one or two levels higher in the management structure, even when the people referring to them in one case were the board of directors themselves! Alternatively, they are an unknown quantity outside the organization, a group of people who represent existing and future clients, suppliers, members of a holding company and so on. The "they" syndrome illustrates our tendency to put the source of problems (and therefore the possibility of change) outside ourselves. "They" are elusive and impossible to pin down, which leads to the loss of ownership of our own circumstances. Effectively, when we blame others we give away any influence we might have had.

LANGUAGE PATTERNS

Below are a few language patterns that we can learn to recognize and challenge in ourselves. Doing so will not guarantee excellence, but it will certainly clear the path toward it.

John Grinder and Richard Bandler made a study of these language patterns. They developed and refined a set of questions designed to challenge and influence the constraints that people put on themselves. These questions are designed to do so in a way that challenges the perceptions we form about ourselves in the way we delete, distort and generalize our experience. The questions challenge the way we express these patterns in our language, both internally to ourselves and in conversation to others. The questions aim to reconnect the speaker with their original experience and the truth of their potential.

By learning to challenge our language, we create greater coherence in who we are and we increase the influence we have in all aspects of life.

Precision questions challenge the constraints we put on ourselves

THE MAIN CATEGORIES

There are three main ways in which we shape our perception of the world. These are by deleting some of our experience, by distorting and by generalizing.

When we delete, we filter out some aspects of our experience and pay attention to others. For example, when a mother is apart from her baby she can typically filter out everything except the sound of her baby's cry. When we delete, we reduce our experience to something we believe we can manage.

Deletion

When we distort, we change the way we experience sensory data, for example when we assume that silence means we have offended someone or that a harsh tone of voice means someone is angry with us. Alternatively, we can, if we choose, distort our experience in a way that works for us. We can choose to believe that if someone is giving us a hard time they must care about us a great deal. None of these are hard facts – they are inventions of our creative minds – and some will work for us and some won't.

Distortion

Generalization

Generalization is the process by which an experience is attributed to the whole category of which the experience is an example. For instance, when someone is let down by one person and subsequently says "You can't trust anyone," this is a generalization. Generalizations are the basis of what we choose to believe about the world, good and bad.

In some instances all of these processes can be useful. We could not cope with everyday life if we didn't use them all in some way. The aim of learning these patterns in language is so that we can identify patterns that are limiting us in our way of being in the world and replace them with patterns that support us to be the best we can be.

Note which patterns "speak" to you in some way

If you are committed to facilitating your own and others' excellence, then I encourage you to learn these patterns. Start with you. Read the next sections through and note which patterns "speak" to you in some way. Pay attention to these first and begin to note any instances in which you might be using them. Just be aware – that is often the most useful starting point. Let the change emerge and maybe later consciously explore what options you have in what you might be saying to yourself instead.

So here are the more detailed patterns with some ways of challenging them. When we challenge we are influencing significant change, not just in the use of words but in our way of experiencing the world.

DELETIONS

Abstractions

An abstraction is the result of taking a verb (an active word) and turning it into an abstract noun. (If you can put "ongoing" in front of it, it's probably an abstraction.)

e.g. Jack and Jill went for some exercise.
What kind of exercise was that?

More examples	The challenges
It was a difficult conversation	Who was talking to whom?
	Difficult in what way?
It is a special relationship	Special how?

These are nonspecific actions or subjects where the detail of what is happening or who is being referred to has been omitted.

Vague actions and subjects

> e.g. They went up the hill
> Who went up the hill?

More examples

Fred needs to improve his presentation skills

People don't let you make decisions here

The challenges

In what way does he need to improve?

Which people?

An "opinion as fact" statement is when the speaker expresses an opinion as if it were a truth by deleting the fact that it is an opinion.

Opinions expressed as fact

> e.g. It is advisable to have regular exercise
> According to whom?

More examples

This is the right way

It is bad to be lazy

The challenges

According to whom?

According to whom?

A comparison uses better, worse, happier, more... but without a specific yardstick or measure.

Comparisons

> e.g. Jack and Jill should have been more careful
> In what way should they have been more careful?

More examples

We need more sales

A better world

We will be the best company

The challenges

More than what or how many?

Better than what?

Compared to whom or best in what way?

DISTORTIONS

When mindreading, the speaker presumes to know what another person is thinking or needing without any hard evidence in support.

Mindreading

e.g. I know why Jack and Jill fell down the hill
How do you know?

More examples

I know why you did that

You're upset

The challenges

How do you know that?

How do you know?

Value judgments

A value judgment is made when no evidence is presented to support it.

e.g. Jack and Jill were careless
On what do you base that?

More examples

I am a slow learner

Your work is substandard

The challenges

On what do you base that?

What is your evidence for that statement?

Cause–effect

A cause–effect statement attributes one thing to another.

e.g. Carrying a heavy pail made them fall down the hill
How did carrying a heavy pail make them fall down the hill?

More examples

You made me angry

How does it make you feel?

The challenges

How did *I make* you angry?

How can *it make* me feel anything?

Interpretation

In interpretation, two statements are linked in such a way that they are taken to mean the same thing: "This means that."

e.g. Jack and Jill are obviously irresponsible to fall down the hill like that
How does falling down the hill mean that they were irresponsible?

More examples

I haven't heard from him,
he is obviously angry

You're quiet, you must
be bored

The challenges

How do you know it means that?

How does me being silent mean I am
bored?

GENERALIZATIONS

Sometimes we take specific experiences and make them universally true outside their specific context.

> e.g. If you carry heavy pails of water down a hill you are always going to have an accident
> Was there ever a time when they carried a pail and they didn't fall down the hill?

More examples	**The challenges**
I always catch colds in wintertime	Always?
No one makes decisions round here	No one at all?
I have never been able to do that	Was there ever a time when you could?

Drivers are statements of need. The person making the statement is denying themselves a free choice.

> e.g. Jack to Jill: "We have to go up the hill to get a pail of water"
> Jill to Jack: "What would happen if we didn't?"

More examples	**The challenges**
I *have* to finish this	What do you *want* to do?
I *must* tidy my desk	Who says so?
I *should* visit my parents	According to whom?

These expressions imply that there is no possibility.

> e.g. Jill to Jack: "I can't carry a heavy pail of water down that hill" (She was right!)
> Jack to Jill: "What will happen if you do?"

More examples	**The challenges**
I can't do that	What stops you?
	What would happen if you did?
I won't be able to speak	What stops you?
	What would happen if you did?

A word of warning: It is vital that you have rapport as you ask these questions of others. They can otherwise be experienced as intimidating and aggressive. We don't always have permission to use these techniques on other people, so the place to practice first is with yourself. I want to emphasize this point. Far from building rapport, NLP techniques used enthusiastically but without permission will do more harm than good. It is by developing ourselves that we influence others. A goal to aim for is to be such an attractive example to others that they want some of what you have. I believe that then and only then do you begin to have permission to facilitate others' awareness and learning.

Be an attractive example

MANAGE YOUR INTERNAL DIALOGUE

The language you use may be what you say openly to others. Equally, it can be what you say to yourself internally. You can use the precision questions described above to challenge your internal dialogue and in so doing change your feelings and your experience.

We are influenced by what we hear, not only what others say to us but especially what we say to ourselves. The questions we ask ourselves are especially significant, as our unconscious mind loves questions and will work on our behalf until it has found answers. Remember those occasions when you forgot a person's name and asked yourself who they were, only for the name to pop into your head several hours later? Your unconscious was working on your behalf.

Your unconscious mind works on your behalf

However, the unconscious mind only does as it is asked. If we ask our unconscious "Why did that job go so badly?" that is what it will search for and that is what we will get. And what we will very likely get as well is depressed! Whereas if we ask ourselves "What could I have done differently and how can I learn from this for the future?" then that is also what we will get. With this answers we are more likely to move forward by learning how to be more successful in the future.

When we have awareness of the questions we are asking ourselves, we can significantly influence our emotional state. Our state influences our reactions, reactions become habits – and habits determine our destiny.

I was asked by the technical director of a software development company to help him build his confidence for the international presentations that he was often asked to give. When he explained what he wanted, I discovered that it wasn't help with the design of the presentation, but help to manage his feelings before and after. Typically, he could not sleep well for at least three weeks prior to the presentation and he often felt physically sick on the morning itself. We began to explore the conversations he had with others and himself related to these presentations. What emerged was this:

"These presentations never go well. They expect me to manage the material and all the technical demonstrations. Giving these talks makes me stressed. I know what people in the audience will think, they'll think this is all obvious. They'll want to leave. I can't relax. It will be the same experience all over again."

We discovered a series of deletions, generalizations and distortions in his thinking. Over time, we took each of these statements and challenged them in the following way; bit by bit we unraveled the complex web he had spun for himself. He gradually sorted out what he did want to achieve and how he could manage himself to do that.

His thinking	The challenges
"These presentations never go well."	Never? Have they ever gone well?
"They expect me to manage the material and all the technical demonstrations."	Who expects you to do this? How do you want to be able to do them?
"Giving these talks makes me feel stressed."	How do they do that? How do you want to feel?
"I know what people in the audience will think, they'll think this is all obvious; they'll want to leave."	How do you know that? How do you want them to react?
"I can't relax. It will be the same experience all over again."	What stops you? How do you want to be? What would happen if you did relax?

Three months later I received this letter from him:

Dear Sue,
I have just returned from giving a presentation in Paris. It was a joy to do. I enjoyed the demonstrations and I particularly enjoyed the questions I got from the audience. The hardware didn't all work perfectly but I

used this as an opportunity to show how quickly we could recover problems when they occur. You'll be pleased to know nobody left the presentation – at least not until the end! Most of all in the weeks prior to the presentation I slept well, in fact I think I can safely say my family were pleased to have me around. This was not the case in the past. I actually enjoyed the run-up to the presentation and I'm looking forward to the next one. Thank you.

Yours peacefully
John

MANAGE YOUR EXTERNAL DIALOGUE

We have choice: choice about who to use as our suppliers, choice of who we remain with in a relationship, choice of whose method of presentation appeals to us most, choice of who we want to do business with. For the fortunate, the choice is endless. So it helps to be aware of whether we are offering a choice to others that they find appealing.

Maybe you think that people choose you for how you look, for the products you offer, for the information you provide them with. You may be wrong. More than anything else, people choose you because of the effect you have on their state.

Stephen Covey, in his book *Seven Habits of Highly Effective People*, talks about the legacy we leave. It is our legacy, not our arguments or correctness, that determines whether others will choose us. And our legacy is the effect we have on others with our actions and our words.

Just as we influence ourselves with our inner dialogue, so we influence others with the words we use. And because of the unconscious mind's love of challenge, our questions have a greater influence than our statements. Questions stay with us until we have the answers, and questions that we ask of others will do the same. So awareness of the questions we ask is important in realizing what state we are inducing in the receiver of the question.

Ask yourself who you would rather do business with: someone who leaves you feeling invigorated and inspired, or someone who leaves you feeling that the world is dark and hopeless and full of woe? Would you choose someone who

Our legacy is the effect we have

Questions are irresistible

leaves you feeling confident in yourself or someone who reminds you continually of what you are doing wrong?

Consider the following scenarios and imagine the effects of each of the behaviors, some of which are in line and some out of line with a desirable outcome. Consider what overall effect each question might have and how desirable that effect might be.

You want to boost the confidence of a member of your team. They frequently come to you with questions:

a   Give them the answer.
b   Encourage them to find an answer.
c   Ask them how someone else in the department (who is good at this aspect of the work) would do it.

You want to encourage someone to do business with you in the future. You are talking about their situation, in which there are several problems:

a   Tell them specifically about all the problems you have noticed.
b   Tell them what the key issues are.
c   Ask them to imagine what it would be like if the situation were just as they wanted it to be.
d   Tell them what you believe the solution to be.
e   Ask them how they will recognize that any work you do for them has been successful.

You want to create a culture of learning in the organization by supporting a process of giving and receiving feedback. You are being given feedback:

a   Explain why you acted in the way that prompted the feedback.
b   Ask the giver of the feedback to expand on it.
c   Ask the giver of the feedback to explain what you could do for them to know that you have learnt from the feedback they are giving you.
d   Give immediate feedback to them.

There are no prizes for the correct answers. This is common sense, after all – but are you aware of how often you use your common sense? And more important than that, can you imagine what it would be like if you always acted on the common sense you know you have?

SHORTCUT TO CHALLENGING PERSONAL LIMITATIONS

Consider for a moment something you would like to do in the future but haven't done yet. It could be something simple and short term, for example:

*   Clearing your desk.
*   Writing a letter to a friend.
*   Reading a book you have bought.
*   Giving a colleague some information you promised.

Or it might be on a bigger scale, such as:

*   Learning a language.
*   Taking the holiday you have always wanted.
*   Changing jobs.
*   Starting a family.

1   Which ones would you put into the category of "must" or "should" do? Which ones feel more appropriate when you precede them with words like "want to" and "can do"?
2   Take one of the "must dos" and one of the "can dos." In your mind, step into the "must do." For example, "I must clean my desk." What sort of feeling do you get when you say this to yourself?
3   Now try on "can do." For example, "I can learn French." Or try on "I would really like to..." Choose your own "I can" and repeat it to yourself. Say it in a matter-of-fact, encouraging tone of voice. Or use "I would really like to..." How do you feel? Usually "I can" said to yourself in a positive way generates feelings of confidence and enthusiasm. It is a way of giving yourself permission, reminding yourself of what you can indeed do.

SUMMARY

Recognizing and challenging deletions, generalizations and distortions in your own and others' speech patterns will not only improve the quality of the way you communicate, it will improve your ability to experience what you really want from life. Skilled communicators have mastery over their language. The more flexibility you have over your language, the more potential influence you have over your experience.

Given that we have less and less control over the pattern of external events, the one place where there is room for growth is within. In learning how to use technology we are looking to save time and effort, and yet the contexts in our lives where we waste the most time are when and where we create an effect in others through our language that subsequently needs repair. If we become skilled in choosing language in line with our own and others' needs, we will save hours, days, months and even years in some cases from the time it takes to achieve what we really want. How much new technology can offer you that?

Challenging deletions, generalizations and distortions in language with rapport and when appropriate will reconnect you and others with your experience. These challenges are a way of restoring ownership and they are an elegant way of increasing the choices you have available to you. The skill of questioning is a way of clarifying and influencing relationships with self and others.

THOUGHT PROVOKERS

1   Take a piece of paper and write down your ambitions for yourself and what, if anything, gets in the way of your achieving them. Do a brain dump: whatever comes to mind write it down. Set yourself a limit of five minutes and keep writing down whatever occurs to you in that time.

2   Reread the passage you wrote about yourself. What patterns can you detect? Use the questions set out in this chapter to challenge those patterns for yourself.

3   Test your own assumptions. Consider the following statements and note your immediate thoughts:

   a   A friend in a computer software company tells you they have a new managing director. She also says the MD is very young for the job. In your mind, how old would they be?

   b   A colleague tells you he is moving companies and getting a significant pay increase. He currently earns $80,000 per annum. How much do you imagine the pay increase to be?

   c   Your boss tells you she has an urgent job for you to do. When do you imagine this has to be completed by?

d   A friend tells you she has just bought an expensive new car. What price range would that fall into in your thinking?

e   A colleague tells you he is going to take a long holiday. How long do you imagine that to be?

f   A friend invites you for a long run. How long would that be?

Now ask a colleague, a friend, a member of your family or your boss the same questions. How do your answers compare?

4   Choose one of the end-of-chapter stories, one that resonates for you and holds a meaning that you believe is important. Read this story to a friend and ask them what meaning that give to that same story.

5   To challenge the language patterns in the following statements, what questions would you ask?

a   I can't change the way I am.

b   No one can help me.

c   I know they'll think I'm nervous.

d   He did it deliberately.

e   I'm annoyed because you are late.

f   There is only way to give feedback constructively.

g   My staff don't respond to my directions.

h   This relationship isn't what it should be.

i   I'm upset.

j   You upset me.

6   Think of a situation recently where the outcome was dependent on what you said and you didn't get the effect you wanted. What did you say? How much time did it take you to resolve the issue (assuming it has been resolved)? What could you have said instead?

7   Now think of another situation that was strongly influenced by the words you used and where the outcome surpassed your expectations. How did what you said affect the outcome? How might you surpass your expectations in other contexts of your life in a similar way?

REFERENCES

Richard Bandler & John Grinder (1975/76) *The Structure of Magic, Vols I and II,* Science and Behaviour Books.

Stephen R. Covey (1999) *The Seven Habits of Highly Effective People,* Simon & Schuster.

There existed a psychotherapist who believed that many of the problems people brought to him were characterized by the existence of fish in their dreams. One day a client came to him and was discussing the problems he had.

"Tell me," said the psychotherapist, "did you dream last night?"

"I might have done," replied the client.

"And tell me, in this dream was there a river?"

"I don't think so," replied the client.

"Well, was there any water, if not a river?"

"I guess there might have been."

"And was there a pool on the ground?"

"I couldn't be certain but it's possible," the client replied.

"And in this pool could there have been a fish?"

"I can't rule out the possibility that there might have been a fish."

"Aha!" said the psychotherapist. "I knew it!"

9
Hypnotic language

Tread softly because you tread on my dreams.

WB Yeats, "He Wishes for the Cloths of Heaven"

People sometimes express concerns about the "programming" part of the name neuro linguistic programming, which may be associated with manipulation and brainwashing. Given that NLP is a powerful tool, they are right to be concerned. My approach with business is to make the unconscious conscious, on the basis that through conscious awareness we have choice. I also feel this is in line with the business goals of empowering and developing individuals through awareness and choice.

It is interesting, then, that the truth is that we are programming other people and ourselves most of the time. We are manipulating our own and others' responses and we are brainwashing ourselves and being brainwashed just about every moment of every day. The problem is that without awareness and without training, we tend to do it clumsily and often in ways that are at odds with what we really want to achieve.

In a team meeting about the future of the business the group leader looked at everyone directly and said, "Don't be apprehensive…"

His words had an effect the exact opposite of the one that he wanted to create.

Our unconscious mind obeys commands

Our unconscious mind obeys commands – we seek out the commands in a sentence and ignore the rest. Embedded in the group leader's sentence was a very clear command: "Be apprehensive." I wasn't apprehensive until the group leader said this! If I say to you "Whatever you do, don't stop now," I have given you the instruction to "stop now."

I was out to lunch with my sons and on the next table were a mother, father, and immaculately dressed little girl, about four years old, in a beautiful pink chiffon party dress. She was remarkably well behaved throughout the meal. For dessert the father ordered her a huge chocolate milkshake, which arrived with a jumbo straw. As the waitress put the milkshake down in front of the little girl, her father said very clearly, "Whatever you do, don't blow down the straw." I'll leave it to your imagination what happened next!

We need to learn how we already use these hypnotic language patterns. By doing so we can learn how to be more respectful of ourselves and others in choosing language that supports what we want.

When John Grinder and Richard Bandler set out on their exploration of the structure of excellence, they modeled outstanding psychotherapists. One of these people was Milton Erickson. In studying him they learnt about the power of the voice and the influence of language, especially hypnotic language. The results of this work became known as the Milton Model.

To quote from John and Richard's book *Trance-Formations*, the Milton Model provides the user with ways of being "artfully vague." Being artfully vague allows a communicator to make statements that sound specific and yet are general enough to be an adequate pace for the listener's experience, no matter what that is. This is the opposite of the model for precision explained in Chapter 8, which is designed to specify experience more fully. The Milton Model provides the user with a language structure in which just about all specific content is omitted.

Hypnotic language is used for the following reasons:

- It stimulates altered states of consciousness: trance.
- It allows us to bypass conscious resistance.
- It gives space for the listener to make sense of the language in their way and therefore draw on their inner resources.
- It avoids saying anything that might mismatch the specific meaning of situations for the listener and can therefore be good for building rapport.

Hypnotic language is a way of being artfully vague

HYPNOTIC LANGUAGE IN BUSINESS

If you think hypnotic language (trance-inducing language) is the preserve of psychotherapists, go to any regular business presentation and check out the trances that have been induced in the majority of the audience!

The workplace is full of hypnotic language

I would first of all emphasize that this is not so much about introducing hypnotic language into the workplace – the workplace is full of it already, often inappropriately – it is, rather, about being aware of what language patterns we are using and choosing ones that fit our purpose and lead to a win/win situation. A business report or presentation is likely to contain more hypnotic language patterns than anything else. The use of vague language (and it is more likely to be "clumsily" vague than "artfully" vague) avoids confrontation and challenge. If it is too vague for you to be sure exactly what it means, it is more likely to be ignored than challenged, and that for many people in business has been the safer option. I quote from an article in a recent business magazine:

"Therefore, in view of the absence of any objective evidence provided by the original proponents of the hypothesis, and the failure of subsequent empirical investigations to adequately support it, it may well be appropriate now to conclude that there is not, and never has been, any substance to the conjecture that people represent their world..."

This is overwhelmingly hypnotically vague language and is taken from a report designed to highlight the ineffectiveness of NLP! Yet the author appears to be unaware of the patterns in his own language and the effect of those patterns on the reader.

What are some of the pitfalls we can avoid by learning about hypnotic language?

- We can choose when we want to induce a trance and, more significantly, when we do not want to do that.
- We can maintain and strengthen rapport by being aware of the effect of our words.

The managing director was discussing the style of coaching that he wanted the management team to adopt. He repeatedly asked the managers questions as follows: "What would I have to ask to be sure that he [the person being coached] came to the right conclusion?" or "How can I say this to her so that she realizes what I want?" The effect of these questions was to irritate the managers, who wanted a freer, more open style of coaching. Although he believed he wanted to encourage a coaching style in the business, he had not let go of the desire to find a way to "coach" people to come to his conclusions! On this occasion they did not reach any agreement.

What the MD was doing was using questions that contained powerful assumptions. The assumptions were ones that other members of the board didn't share, but they didn't know how to unpack the questions in a way that allowed them to challenge the assumptions. This is a pattern of hypnotic language that I explore later in this chapter.

Some questions contain powerful assumptions

So the reasons for using hypnotic language skillfully are to be able to:

- Choose language in line with the outcomes we want to achieve.
- Respect other people's unique interpretations of a situation, especially when we do not know the context.
- Recognize when other people are using hypnotic language on us and be able to challenge them.
- Create space in our language for others (possibly someone we are coaching) to draw on their own resources rather than relying on us for answers. In this way we can help build confidence and self-esteem.

AMBIGUITY

A delegate on one of my courses in Denmark was doing a coaching exercise. I was the subject for his questioning skills and he was exploring how I thought of my role in different contexts. He asked me "Who do you think you are" and was about to add "in your work context?" Because of the accent and the way he emphasized the words, I heard it as merely: "Who do you think you are?" The meaning I put on this was: "What right do you have to think of yourself this way?" I am quite sure this was not the way he meant it, but the fact I put this meaning to it meant it had a significance for me that was more powerful than the original. I began to appreciate the arrogance I was communicating.

Ambiguity is an important aspect of hypnotic language

Ambiguity is an important aspect of hypnotic language. It causes disorientation and creates space for the listener to create their own meaning, one that might take us much longer to discover at a conscious level. The significance of encouraging the listener to find their own meaning is that they are likely to have a higher level of commitment to any meaning they find for themselves than to any we might offer them.

EMBEDDED COMMANDS AND QUESTIONS

Earlier I referred to the father who told his daughter not to blow down the straw. His sentence contained an embedded command: "blow down the straw." Our unconscious mind is very obedient: it detects any commands in conversation and seeks to fulfill them. So the little girl was doing exactly as her unconscious mind believed it was being told to do when she blew down the straw.

Words shape our experience

Words shape our external experience. When the new manager told his team that they "must not lose the business with this client," he was offering their unconscious minds the structure of thinking that could lead to loss.

Words sculpt our inner world and subsequently shape our outer world. What we say to ourselves (our inner dialogue) has an influence on what we see, hear and feel. Similarly, our spoken words influence not only ourselves but also our listeners. It is vital that we take responsibility for the effect we create with our language if we want to maximize our influence. In other words, the meaning of our communication is indeed its effect.

We can embed positive or negative commands. Examples of positive commands might be:

* You can begin to *relax*.
* I've been wondering how you might begin to *see a way forward*.
* I don't know if you will *begin to feel motivated*.

There are some negative suggestions that, when our unconscious mind finds them, are stripped back to the command component:

* Don't *think deeply about what you might be learning*.
* On no account do you need to *be aware of what you are saying*.

You may already be starting to think about some of the inappropriate examples you have heard. For example, has anyone ever come to you and said: "Don't *worry*, everything is going to be all right," when probably what they meant to communicate was: "You can *put your mind at rest now*."

You can also embed questions as a way of gently prompting a response from your listeners:

◆ I am curious to know *what would you like to get from this meeting*.
◆ I was just wondering *what would you like to drink*.

Most people will answer the question without even realizing that they have not been asked a question directly. What they often experience is a respectful and allowing style of conversation. This style of questioning is entirely appropriate when dealing with someone who might feel very sensitive, say in an appraisal or coaching meeting or with someone who is feeling nervous in an interview where direct questions might be too unnerving.

Just this week on one of my courses I heard one delegate say to another (who wanted to develop a new relationship): "Does thinking like that make you feel more alone?" If they had been aware of the effect they really wanted they might have said: "Does thinking like that make you feel more connected?" Alternatively, they could have asked an open question: "What is it like when you think like that?"

One way to help embedded commands or questions be received as such is to mark them out in the way we present them. For example, we might pause before and after the embedded command or mark it out with a raised eyebrow or a hand movement. If our marking out is subtle it will be perceived but not consciously detected. The appropriate use of embedded commands and questions can be a graceful way of collecting information and a respectful form of influence. I know that with a little practice you can…

Embedding a quote in a sentence can be a very powerful way of getting a message across by bypassing any conscious resistance. For example, you might describe a conversation with one of your clients to another client by explaining that the first client had found it difficult to delegate responsibility. You might then explain that you said to her: "You will only realize your true

You can really get learning and insight now

Appropriate use of commands is a graceful way of collecting information potential when you learn to let go of control." You have in effect said what is in quotes to the person you are talking to now, but you have avoided taking responsibility for the message. The effect of this is that they cannot dispute the story; they are likely to take in the quote as if it applied to them without being able to challenge your right to offer it to them personally. This can be useful if you are dealing with someone whose preference is to dispute and mismatch what others say.

This kind of embedded command or question can be intentional and served to help me get rid of some frustration recently. I was with someone who I was increasingly finding frustrating. They were criticizing the kind of work I do. This is someone who does not take feedback easily, if at all. Rather than bottle up my frustration, I said, "I was working with someone recently and they would not see anyone else's point of view and I said to them, 'Just how naïve can you be? Can't you see how frustrating your attitude can be for others? Might you ever accept someone else's opinion?' I was talking about someone else, but I was really directing those embedded statements to the person I was with at the time. At one level they knew that, but at another level they could not challenge what I was saying as it was not seemingly directed at them. Do you know, they seemed to change after I said that! More importantly, it helped me get the things I wanted to say off my chest.

PRESUPPOSITIONS

You may have wondered while reading this how you can use these language patterns in your everyday work.

The previous sentence is a classic example of hypnotic language. It is a fact that you are reading this (unless someone else is reading it to you or you have found some other way of taking in the information in this sentence). And I have linked with that fact a response that I would like you to have; that is, wondering. And I am suggesting that you wonder about how you can use these language patterns in your everyday work. The question I have posed is how you can use these patterns.

Notice that I have therefore based this on the following presuppositions:

- That you can use these language patterns.
- That you can use them in your everyday work.
- That you want to use them in your everyday work.
- That there are such things as language patterns.
- That you are able to wonder about them.
- That you would want to wonder about them.

If you accept the introductory statement, you are accepting all these presuppositions simultaneously. Presuppositions are a powerful form of influence. Used effectively, they can accelerate your progress toward an outcome. Used ineffectively, they will irritate and provoke your listener, even though your listener may not always be sure what it is that is having that effect. The value of learning about these patterns is that you can become aware of what works for you and for others. By having this awareness, you also have the means to explain what is happening and the words to plan differently.

Presuppositions are very effective in training programs when you want a group to accept certain premises for their development. For example, if you want a group to learn how to give feedback to each other, rather than asking if they *want* to give feedback you ask *how* they will give feedback. You have given choice, but not over what you consider to be the nonnegotiables. This is why in coaching it is so important to be aware of the language you use. There is a big difference between asking someone "*Can* you make a commitment to a next step?" and "*What* commitment can you make to a next step?"

To find out what is presupposed in a sentence and therefore not open to question, there is a simple test. Take a simple statement, "Colin mowed the grass." If we negate it, we have "Colin did not mow the grass." What is still true is:

- Colin exists.
- The grass exists.
- Colin could have mown the grass.
- The grass can be mown.
- There was an expectation that Colin might mow the grass.

In the earlier example, when the manager asked "How can I coach people to come to the right conclusion?" he was presupposing that:

> Presuppositions are a powerful form of influence

- There is a conclusion.
- There is a right conclusion.
- He has a right to coach people.
- He can coach people.
- He has the right to coach people to come to a right conclusion.

This is powerful language when used by communicators who presuppose what they don't want questioned. Often the communicator does not realize what they are presupposing (especially when they are unaware or unskilled in the use of these patterns). Learning about presuppositions can help us to discover what control we are holding on to and of what choices we might be able to let go.

As I was writing this chapter I became aware of an outcome that I had set myself, to decide which option of two key opportunities I was going to take for my future. I realized I had presupposed that it had to be one or the other. With just this realization, I discovered that the way forward for me was to believe that it did not have to be one or the other but could be both.

Some more examples of sentences and questions that contain presuppositions are:

- You might wonder who is going to volunteer for this project.
- Do you want to sit down while we go through this report?
- You might ask yourselves which department will achieve its target first.
- How can I delegate in such a way that we devolve ownership in the business?

Some traditional sales closes include presuppositions, for example: "Do you want to place the order now or later this week?" For me this is an example of inappropriate and outdated use of presuppositions. One of the factors that determines whether a statement is appropriate or not is whether you have a right to assume the presupposition. Does a salesperson have the right to assume that you will place an order? I don't think so, which is why I would find this style of question offensive.

However, I will not presuppose what you can believe about it!

Do you realize how much of this you are taking in unconsciously?

DISTORTIONS

I am opposed to smoking and a colleague, who does not share my view, is aware of my feelings. We have had discussions about this where we both tried to convince the other that we were right. Recently I sent an email to this colleague talking about a fellow presenter, whom I admire very much and had met for the first time. My colleague knows this person and responded by saying how much she admired him too and how caring this presenter was at all times, even in casual moments like a smoking break. When I read this I felt an inner conflict and was not sure initially what that was about. Then I realized that my colleague was linking something with which I agreed (the admiration I felt for the colleague) to something of which I did not approve (smoking).

What my colleague had done is a form of unconscious anchoring (see Chapter 12), which works very effectively if we want the two things to be linked together. However, if it is unecological for us to link the two, the distortion leads us to experience the inner resistance that I felt when I read this email.

Nevertheless, as I describe in Chapter 12, anchoring is a valuable and naturally occurring tool. We can use it for ourselves and to support and coach others when we link something that is occurring or is true for them with something to which we want them to respond. For example:

• You are reading this sentence and you are wondering what other forms of hypnotic language there can be.
• You are taking in this information and you are exploring how you can practice these patterns in ways that enhance what you do.

In these two examples it is the use of the "and" that has the influence by linking two components of the sentence together. What happens is that you get the listener into a "yes" way of thinking and without a break you present another (nonfactual) idea to their mind. It's a bit like getting someone to open the door to accept a parcel they have ordered and while the door is open starting a discussion about the weather!

Other forms that this linkage can take:

+ *As* you sit here listening to what I am saying you can begin to wonder how what I say applies directly to you.
+ *While* we talk this through in this way you can start to think how we might take this forward.

And a stronger form of this kind of linkage:

+ Sitting here listening will *make you aware* of just how much there is to learn.
+ Watching this presentation *requires that you* relax and concentrate fully on what we are saying.
+ The way you are breathing *causes you* to begin to relax completely.

My experience is that if the motivation behind your statements is a genuine win/win and is perceived that way by your listener, these kinds of statements will be accepted and will accelerate your progress toward a mutual outcome. If they are not – if they are, for example, being used to manipulate someone against their wishes – then although the listener may not know what is wrong they will sense it. They may get that "something not quite right," instinctive reaction to you or what you are saying.

MINDREADING

You are probably wondering what I am going to say next. I am mindreading when I say that. However, if you *are* wondering or if it is plausible that you *could be* wondering or might choose to, then it nudges you down that route.

Mindreading occurs when you act or speak as if you know the other person's internal experience. As with all the other patterns, it can be helpful and an enriching experience, or it can be patronising and disruptive. (And rather than presuppose that these are the only two effects it can have, you can also think what other possibilities there are!)

Mindreading assumes you know what someone else is thinking

Some examples of mindreading:

- You are probably asking yourself what you can do about this.
- I expect you will have an answer.
- I know what you will say if I tell you.
- Your next step is predictable.
- You might be thinking what your outcome might be.

I remember a car journey into London with a colleague. It was as if this colleague had been waiting for the opportunity to tell me (without interruption) what they had on their mind. The conversation took the form of her telling me for most of the journey what I should do with the opportunities I had and with the business and what I must do for myself. The effect of this mindreading and the powerful language of shoulds and musts was that I felt as if I was under fire. I was mentally exhausted and very relieved when we got to our destination!

SUMMARY

It is important for us to be aware of hypnotic language patterns. With this awareness we can choose the patterns we use with others and ideally select those that most support us in achieving our mutual outcomes. With this awareness we can also be aware of what is not working and precisely select alternative ways of meeting our own and others' needs.

THOUGHT PROVOKERS

1 Take a piece of written communication that you have sent recently. It could be a letter, an email, a report. Select three or four sentences, especially ones in which you are making suggestions or recommendations. Negate the sentences and list the presuppositions on which you have based your statements. How many of those presuppositions were you aware of using and how many were used without conscious thought? What do you learn from that?

2 Identify someone with whom you experience a lack of choice in conversation. Write down some of the typical things they say to you. What (if any) hypnotic language patterns are they using?

3   Think of someone who typically resists any suggestions you make. Thinking back on the way you have put those suggestions, what options do you now have that might work more effectively to reach a win/win position?

4   Identify three situations where you believe that using hypnotic language would support you in achieving mutually desirable outcomes with another person.

REFERENCES

John Burton & Bob Bodenheimer (2000) *Hypnotic Language: Its Structure and Use*, Crown House.

John Grinder & Richard Bandler (1981) *Trance-Formations: Neuro-Linguistic Programming and the Structure of Hypnosis*, Real People Press.

Sidney Rosen (ed.) (1991) *My Voice Will Go with You: The Teaching Tales of Milton H. Erickson*, W. W. Norton.

Last night I watched a football game on television. One team wore their colored jerseys, indicating they were most likely the home team, while the other team wore white jerseys. Neither team had a good win–lose record, so the game seemed evenly matched. Most of the players were fairly new to the professional ranks except two on one team. I set this up this way to illustrate how beliefs influence outcomes. The team carries a belief about their ability to play effectively or not. Each individual on the team also carries a belief about his own competence. These may or may not be consistent.

What probably is true is that each of these players once carried very high beliefs about his competence. No player could even be on a professional team if he did not once demonstrate his ability to win. And we all know beliefs precede and are consistent with ability. Maybe when he played college ball or maybe when he played in high school. But no doubt he once felt certain of his competence, he believed he could and would win. He knew and remembered how to win. Well, in this game last night both teams demonstrated their current beliefs that differ from their past beliefs, they believed they could not use their competence. They seemed to forget what they believed about their ability and how to use it. The game illustrated very well the old adage, use it or lose it. Both teams tried to lose it.

So I began to wonder if all the players, except two, forgot their beliefs about their high ability and where might it be stored. One player had not scored a touchdown all year and this game was the 12th, amnesia at its worst. Yet sometimes when you look inside yourself it becomes very difficult to do so objectively. So much seems at stake that you lose some perceptual ability, you know?

So where is the objective, unbiased storage of beliefs containing high ability? It suddenly dawned on me, the ball! After all, who scored more touchdowns and field goals than any player? The ball! Who was present during each tackle or run and catch for a touchdown? The ball, wow! It contains such a rich storehouse of memories about how to play well, score and win. Just ask the ball because it knows how to score and win, it has done so for many individual players and teams and each scoring player carries something that knows how. Follow the ball and let it tell you how, guiding you to the score. To win you just need to have a ball.

Story reproduced with permission from *Hypnotic Language* by John Burton & Bob Bodenheimer.

Programming

We are what we repeatedly do. Excellence, then, is not an act but a habit. —Aristotle

M odeling is the process of coding talent, the means of discovering the essence of excellence. When we step into someone else's shoes and reproduce what they do and the results they achieve, we are modeling. Modeling involves reproducing the sequence of thinking, language and behavior patterns of our subject in such a way that we can reproduce the same result with consistency. To do this, we may also need to take on (albeit temporarily) their identity and beliefs. In effect, to use a computer metaphor, we are eliciting the program code needed to demonstrate the talent and we are running the program as and when we want it.

Reproducing excellence

The purpose of modeling talent in business is to reproduce excellence. If we want to reproduce the success of an outstanding salesperson, manager, or presenter, modeling enables us to do this. Equally, if we want to reproduce the way a successful, enterprising company or individual presents themselves through a remote medium such as the World Wide Web or email, we can do this too. If we want to discover how some people are able to thrive in the context of a network economy, we can learn how they do this so that we can do it for ourselves.

These top performers run mental and physical programs of which they are unaware and which will almost certainly not be in any book on standard selling techniques, management models, or presentation skills. The programs they run may be specific to the

Excellence is context specific

industry, the client, or even the place and occasion. Excellence, as such, is context specific. You may discover that parts of their program add little or no value and are redundant and that yet other parts can be developed.

By discovering and developing what we learn, we can not only reproduce the skill we are modeling, we can tweak and enhance it so that we can achieve an even higher level of skill than the original.

NLP is an active process. It is research into what works with the purpose of enabling us to reproduce and enhance success in ways that are unique. The more we model excellence, the more we discover. NLP operates at a higher level than most traditional training in the sense that it enables us not just to learn what works but *how* it works. When we learn NLP we learn how to think and be successful. The process of NLP offers ownership and discovery and enables us to learn how to learn. By embarking on the process that is NLP, we not only learn how to learn but increase our ownership and personal discovery in the whole process of personal and business growth.

NLP is about learning how to learn

10
Modeling

It is rare that one cannot learn from another or from life's experiences, if the effort is made. Perhaps that is the secret of achieving a peaceful society; searching for each other's unique and special knowledge. —Anon

If someone can do it, anyone can do it. That is the basis of modeling. We can learn to capture our moments of brilliance, study them, code them, and reproduce them at will. Consider any outstanding performer in sport, the arts, business, life. This is what they do. They don't just have one-off moments of luck; they reproduce their brilliance wherever and whenever they choose. That is what makes them top of their game. And we can learn to do the same.

"We take the very best of what people do, synthesize it down, make it learnable and share it with each other – that is NLP."

Richard Bandler

Modeling is a state of curiosity and selflessness. It is a desire to listen. It is an ability to watch, respect and learn from others as well as ourselves.

There is no longer any such thing as a job for life. We are increasingly directly accountable for everything we do. The number of people who are self-employed has risen tenfold in the last five years. We are only as good as the results we are achieving today. That's why we need to learn.

When my son sent emails from his travels around the world, I was initially interested in what he had to say, what he was doing, where he was, and where he was headed for next. My husband, however, was really interested in how my son's ability to communicate what he was doing matured as he traveled. His use of words and expressions developed a style and richness that we had never noticed before. On one occasion we got a copy of an email that went out to all his friends as well and I learnt things that no email addressed "dear Mum" was ever going to reveal. I was astonished at some of the content and said to my husband, "Just read what he is saying!" My husband replied, "Yes, but look at how he is saying it!"

There is talent behind every behavior, whether we approve of the behavior or not. And with NLP we can access the structure of that talent and reconnect it to new behaviors if we so choose. For example, if you regularly get depressed or stressed, you can learn how you do this irrespective of what is happening in your environment. The very fact that you repeat this behavior with regularity says that it is something that you have learnt how to do. And the fact that you can do this suggests that you have a strategy, although undoubtedly an unconscious one. My guess is that you would not choose to be stressed and so would do differently if you knew how you were creating this state for yourself. And you can. Suppose you have learnt how to let something external trigger this response, maybe someone says something to you in a particular way. Or perhaps you get stressed when you are asked to do something like a presentation. Whatever the trigger, the next thing you do is to visualize the situation getting worse. This is your strategy – and it's a strategy you can change.

MODELING IS A STATE OF CURIOSITY

Even though you may work for a large organization, the chances are that no matter how much support you receive, you either already are or most certainly will be expected to be self-reliant in the way you respond to the challenges you face. There are few easy options at work and the pace is such that others are busy looking after themselves.

However, the good news is that most people have barely scratched the surface when it comes to drawing on their inner resources and few really know how to do this. Modeling is the answer. It is not just a technique, it is a lifestyle. Wherever you are

Modeling is not just a technique, it's a lifestyle

and whoever you are with you can be learning and growing.

Modeling is a way of achieving lifelong learning and true personal fulfillment. It is a way of respecting the unique talents we all have.

I recently watched a TV program showing how the IQ tests that were once used for college selection in one part of the US discriminated against the young black population. These people did not score well on the qualities measured. However, a researcher discovered that when they experimented with another test that measured very different aptitudes, the same population excelled. The implication of relying on the original test was, in one of the boy's own words, "We have no option but to make a living by going on the streets and selling drugs." By introducing the new test the researchers were opening doors to education for this previously neglected group of people.

Modeling draws on the principle that we all have talents of value

There are powerful implications in the yardsticks we use to "box" people into what is acceptable and what is not. Modeling goes way beyond a new test. It respects the fact that whatever talents we have are of value and can be directed toward our own good and for the good of others. To learn to model is to explode the myths of IQ stereotypes. It is to learn to respect and allow everyone their rightful place in the world. As the quote at the beginning of the chapter suggests, maybe our ability to model is the key to a peaceful society.

In the business context, we need to be exploring previously untapped resources. We need to learn from what every individual has to offer. If we do what we always did we get what we always got – a recipe for business suicide. So modeling opens up a completely new world in how we recognize potential and, more significantly, release it for the good of everyone.

Modeling can take many forms. We learn some of our most fundamental skills by modeling others. Babies and young children are expert modelers. Only when they start learning by more traditional methods do they begin to lose this skill. Some traditional methods of schooling train out of us our most natural learning talent. "Sitting by Nellie" was the method by which many employees were taught to do their work. This only worked well if Nellie was a model of excellence or if the new employee was smart enough to know what worked and what didn't.

Unfortunately, it often resulted in the reproduction of bad practice.

We can model anything; people are excellent in many different spheres. We can, for example, have excellence in our ability to:

- Generate commitment and respect.
- Motivate ourselves and others.
- Sell and influence.
- Achieve a personal best in sport.
- Listen.
- Speak a language fluently.
- Communicate using the latest technology.
- Network.
- Lead and inspire.

Equally, we can have excellence in our ability to:

- Get depressed.
- Sulk.
- Lose our temper.
- Remain untouched by emotion.
- Procrastinate.
- Worry.
- Resist change.
- Respond aggressively to others.
- Panic.

By modeling any of these we can develop a conscious awareness of the process, and with conscious awareness we have a choice, which is to continue the same process or to do something else. Merely the process of studying what we are doing and how we are doing it lifts us to a level of detachment in which we can choose what we do and, more importantly, what we continue to do in the future.

Many companies now have a system of mentoring whereby members of staff, as part of their development, are allocated to a more senior or more experienced employee in order to learn from them ("sitting by Nellie" relabeled). All too often, the success of this system hinges on the experienced employee's ability to impart their skills. Often they don't know their most powerful skills nor how they use them. If, however, the learner is equipped with NLP modeling skills, they can elicit the skills they need to learn irrespective of the awareness and skill level of their mentor. The subject being modeled can also benefit from this process by learning from feedback on how they structure their experience. With this awareness they can achieve greater consistency in the skills they possess.

My very first full-time job was as a computer operator in the glass-manufacturing firm Pilkingtons. I had never worked on a computer before and I was allocated to Geoff to follow him around and learn what he did. Occasionally Geoff would explain what he was doing, but more often than not he would just do what he did (and at that time operating the computer sometimes meant a bit of engineering and a bit of fixing programs that crashed in the middle of the night when the programmers weren't around to sort out the problems). Geoff was very good at all of these things, but he wasn't very good at explaining to me what he did nor how he did it.

You can learn to reproduce a talent in one context of your life so that you can use it in another

You can apply the process of modeling to yourself. You might, for example, want to reproduce an ability or skill that you have in some areas of your life or work, in order to use it in other contexts. Let's suppose you are influential when dealing with colleagues but don't have the same level of influence with clients. You could model yourself in order to discover the difference between the two, so that you can use your influence in whatever context you choose.

One company that employed a telephone marketing team could not understand why there was such inconsistency in the results it was getting with some of its telemarketeers. With some clients they were very successful and were able consistently to convert a call into an appointment, but with others they struggled to get past the first few minutes of the conversation.

What the company discovered when it modeled what was happening with these calls was that the telemarketeers were building mental images based on what they had heard from others in the company about the different groups of people they had to call.

One of the biggest differences between the successful calls and the unsuccessful ones was connected with the mental image the caller had

in their mind as they made the call. Those who were most successful imagined the recipient of the call in a brightly lit room. The image was vivid and in color and they imagined the other person smiling. (This was entirely in their mind, as they never saw the people they phoned.) The unsuccessful callers typically imagined the recipient of the call in a dark room, the image was defocused and gray in tone, and the person had a serious expression on their face. All this before they had even dialed the number!

By modeling the successful mental strategies, the company was able to train the previously less successful marketeers in these thinking techniques. The average conversion rate of call to appointment increased significantly.

We achieve the results we do through the programs we run in our minds and in our actions. Just as computer programs are a sequence of codes, so personal programs are a sequence of mental and behavioral codes. When you walk, talk, drive, read or laugh, it is unlikely that you think consciously about how you do these things. The programs that make them happen are managed on your behalf by your unconscious mind. These programs are known as strategies.

If you want to model excellence either in yourself or in other people, your aim is to elicit these unconscious strategies as well as the conscious ones that enable you to do what you do. When you have the strategy for how someone manages their experience, you have the key to reproducing that experience for yourself.

The key to reproducing experience

When a chef produces a gourmet dinner, not only is he following a recipe for the ingredients, he is also following a recipe for thinking and behaving. He may, for example, have an image of what he wants the dish to look like accompanied by the aroma of the final meal. He may also be concerned with timing and the look and feel of the ingredients. He has a unique way of achieving the result.

I watched a program on BBC television in which companies were invited to put their business up for overhaul. One of these programs featured Mo's corner shop. This was a typical corner shop, packed full of thousands of different product lines, many of them beyond their shelf life and many almost impossible to find easily on the cramped shelves. Mo applied to the BBC team of experts to have them redesign his business.

He was under threat from the big supermarkets nearby, so not only did the BBC team want to increase the efficiency of the shop, they also wanted to find ways to differentiate Mo's shop from these bigger competitors.

The expert team set about reorganizing and relabeling the products on the shelves. They installed self-clean, maintenance-free ovens to supply daily fresh bread. They introduced a new stock control system and eliminated the 80 percent of products that had not sold for years. And they went into Mo's office, where they found that his method of personal organization was to use three-year-old diaries (or older), cross out the days, and overwrite them with the current year's days and dates. So the office came under the experts' scrutiny and revision as well.

After all of this and much more, Mo was left with a completely overhauled shop. The time needed to find and buy items had been cut by at least 50 percent and his customers were delighted with the changes. But what about Mo? He was delighted too, although he appeared at times to be a little bemused. This was not surprising really when you start to deduce what must have been going on in his head or, more to the point, how *it was going on in his head. Mo's shop was an expression of his internal structure. His shop and everything about him were a mirror of his internal experience.*

The methods used by the BBC team (the results of which were wonderful, in the short term) are the methods used by many businesses wanting to update and bring about a culture change. The remedy so often seized on is to change the environment.

It is the inner facelift that makes the difference

How many businesses and shops have you seen go about a facelift in just this way? Yet the facelift that would really make the difference is the inner facelift. By modeling what was going on in Mo's inner experience, we can deduce not only how he has got what he has but also, to take it one step further, what he might need to change in his inner world to really make a difference.

We have strategies for making decisions such as what to have for dinner, where to go on holiday, how to plan our day. There is a pattern to the way we do this.

For example, the way I decided to write this book was:

1   I saw others (close friends) write a book.
2   I imagined myself writing a book.

3 I asked myself repeated questions over time about what the topic would be and how I would do it.
4 I looked and listened for examples of how others did this.
5 When eventually I could clearly see myself writing a book (even down to seeing the context in which I would write it), I got a feeling that the time was right.
6 I committed myself by telling people what I planned to do.

Understanding a strategy gives me choice about how and when I use it. Equally, if someone wanted to influence my decision about writing, it would help if they understood my strategy rather than trying to impose their own.

Suppose you identify that your partner in negotiation has a strategy that involves:

1 Creating a picture of what they want (visual).
2 Asking themselves a question about the viability of that outcome (auditory).
3 Getting a feeling of certainty that this is what they want (feelings).

By matching this strategy you will be helping and influencing their decision-making process. Let's say their outcome was to ask for promotion to a new job. You could match their strategy by saying:

1 "Imagine what it would be like to approach your boss, to see yourself with her clarifying your future" (visual).
2 "Ask yourself if that is a feasible thing to do" (auditory).
3 "And you will instinctively know whether this is the right approach for you" (feelings).

It is important to remember that if you ask someone "How do you do that?" – if you ask them consciously to recall their strategy – it is unlikely that they will be able to give it to you. They may either say "I don't know," or they will tell you what they *think* they do. This is rarely the same as what they actually do. To elicit a strategy, the person you are modeling needs to be doing or reliving the experience you wish to model.

Modeling in business has led to significant breakthroughs in the way skills are taught. Traditionally, companies used standard

What people think they do is rarely the same as they actually do training programs to teach standard skills. More often than not, trainees were left to their own devices to adapt these skills to their unique environment. There are unique patterns that work in one company, one department or one market segment, and that will not work in another. Modeling enables you to elicit these context-specific patterns in order to reproduce excellence in a place of your choice. By choosing the people who excel within your organization, not only will you be able to reproduce their levels of success, you will also be able to help those same people achieve greater consistency in their own performance.

When PricewaterhouseCoopers wanted to reproduce the outstanding performance of some of its top project leader coaches, it decided to use NLP to model the strategies that worked. It selected its outstanding performers and I was invited to model them to find out how they do what they do. I watched them in action working with groups of trainees and talked with them about their beliefs, their values, and their sense of identity and purpose.

What emerged was a consistent pattern for the ones who achieved results significantly above the norm. All had a quality of selflessness, a purpose that was beyond themselves, and all had values that included love and care for others. At the level of behavior, they were all skilled in the way they used metaphor and visionary thinking. And they were so dedicated to meeting the learning needs of their trainees that if they did not do that to their satisfaction (in one case especially) this resulted in the coach's temporarily feeling physically sick. (I did not necessarily want others to have to reproduce that!) However, once we knew what some of the key pieces were in the strategies (and there was much more), I was able to present this to others who had not yet achieved the same level of excellence.

The joy of modeling is that you can refine the model by testing which elements add to excellence and which detract or make no difference. By taking away one element at a time, you can determine how this affects the overall result. This enables you to generate the most effective model, which you can use to teach others, including the person you modeled.

This process applies when modeling anything, whether it's an individual, a team, or a complete organization. The skills it takes to sell a luxury car are quite different from those it takes to sell a software package. The skill required to motivate a group of production line workers is quite different from that needed to motivate advertising account executives. The skill needed to communicate face to face may be very different from that needed to communicate via the internet. The skills you need in the Information Age are vastly different to those that might have stood you in good stead in previous times. Modeling enables you to uncover the uniqueness of the model, the quality of the inborn talent, and the natural skill.

A client of mine said, "This modeling is the secret weapon for today's business if everyone but knew it." It is easy to access the strategies you want, although it is not yet usual practice to do this in business. Any individual or organization that employs this kind of thinking is still going to be well ahead of the game for several years to come.

We can find useful strategies behind any behavior. It is the *process* of what we do that is always valuable, even if the content is not. We need to look at all the behaviors we use to uncover the strategies that lie behind them. By doing this, we can find that even behind some of our weaknesses we have strategies that are invaluable used in the right context.

Take the example of someone who sulks. I know of people who can sulk for hours, days, weeks, and in some cases years! This might not seem a valuable skill to have, but behind the sulking lies the strategy of maintaining one emotional state for a period of time. In this context it is a negative skill, but suppose this same person wanted to maintain a state of confidence or motivation and had not succeeded in doing so. Where do they look for the answer? Not to self-help books and not to other people – what they want is what they already have. They have the strategy for maintaining a state, all that they have to do is transfer that strategy to another emotional state.

Examples of business modeling projects include the following:

• A major car manufacturing company encouraged its employees to invest time in their personal development. It funded everyone to learn something new on one condition, that it was not to do with their work. Some people learnt a new language. Some learnt how to play a musical instrument. Some

Modeling – the secret weapon

took up a new sport or hobby. Whatever they did, they did because they wanted to. This was a smart move on the part of the company. What it was doing was strengthening its employees' strategies for doing for what they really wanted (outcome thinking) and for learning. One of the goals of the organization at this time was to be a learning organization, in which learning was a fundamental part of the culture, and the strategy it adopted was a powerful way of achieving this.

◆ A marketing company decided it would model the way the founders of the company brought in new business. Until this time no one else in the company had the same consistent level of success in the way they did this.

◆ An IT manufacturing business modeled the way one of its leaders successfully negotiated between the different cultures in the business after a merger.

◆ A building society modeled the way one of its directors inspired those who joined the business.

The point is that modeling is a very different way of thinking and working to what happened in the past. Giving people in a company the skills to model is giving them the means of generating ways of finding solutions to any situation they encounter.

A BENCHMARK FOR EXCELLENCE

The result of much of the modeling that has taken place has been the discovery of certain patterns of excellence. I offer this benchmark for excellence with caution. It is not fixed, it continues to develop. Who knows what will happen in the future?

The elements of excellence

I use the term excellence to mean individuals and organizations who consistently achieve the goals they set themselves. It covers especially people and organizations who are achieving goals that benefit not only themselves but also people and organizations beyond themselves; those whose goals are not just for personal wealth but for richness of life. People and organizations who achieve excellence in this way do the following.

SYSTEMS

They pay attention to the role they play in the larger system of which they are a part. They have a purpose to contribute to this bigger system in a positive way, to add value. Companies that sustain their success over time are now the ones who can network and create genuine win/win scenarios with their employees, clients and suppliers, as well as anyone with whom they have contact.

They have a commonly held and understood mission or identity. This mission is an expression of what each team or company members really wants and truly demonstrates in their moment-by-moment behavior. Just as a strong sense of self is the basis for individual confidence, so a coherent mission is the base for a solid and attractive business.

They hold and live out the beliefs of excellence explained in detail throughout the book.

People and organizations who achieve excellence are capable of:

- Sensitivity toward themselves and others.
- Flexibility in being able to change what they are doing and how they are doing it when what they are doing isn't working.
- Thinking in outcome terms and dovetailing their outcomes with those of others so that they achieve a win/win situation.
- Building lasting relationships and strengthening the networks that surround them.
- Learning continuously from everything that happens to them.
- Being interested in and curious about what is happening around them and the people they meet.
- Acting and speaking on a day-by-day basis in ways that live out their mission, their beliefs and their capabilities.

- Changing their behavior so that they continually increase their flexibility while remaining true to their values.
- Asking questions in a way that allows them to learn from themselves and others.
- Asking for feedback and giving feedback when they have permission to do so.
- Enacting the behavior they want from others so that they lead by example.
- Recognizing that their environment and their appearance are an expression of who they are and what they think.

- Taking responsibility for influencing their environment so that it supports the outcomes they want to achieve.
- Respecting their environment and always leaving it "better" than the way they found it.

SHORTCUT TO MODELING A SKILL

NLP is a process of modeling and the rest of this book explores the details of how you can do that with skill and professionalism. This shortcut is an introduction to that process.

1   Identify the skill that you want to model and reproduce. For example, you may know someone who can get and hold the audience's attention within seconds of the start of a presentation; make decisions; wake themselves up in the morning without the aid of an alarm clock; set realistic time targets that they consistently achieve; or start the day in a positive frame of mind. Be specific in defining the skill and the context in which you want to use it.

2   Select a person, or people, who you consider demonstrates excellence in the skill. Define excellence in terms of the results that your model of excellence achieves, what you see, hear and feel when this top performer is displaying this skill.

3   Observe your model in action to identify the following:
    ◆   What specifically they do and how they do it.
    ◆   Any specific behavior patterns.
    ◆   How they manage their environment.
    ◆   Their language patterns and filters.
    ◆   The beliefs and values they demonstrate and express.
    ◆   How they communicate a sense of identity.
    ◆   What purpose they say they fulfill, or seem to fulfill.

4   Question your model. First, ensure that they associate into an experience when they are using the skill you wish to model. Modeling is a process of discovering what the subject usually does not know about themselves; it is not about them telling you what they think they do. When they are imagining themselves using the skill, be sure to phrase your questions in the present tense to keep them associated, e.g. "What are you seeing?" "What are you saying to yourself?" You are interested in the "what" and the "how" of what they do, not the "why."
    Check out their thinking at each of the logical levels (see Chapter 13). For example, you can ask them:

- ◆ "What are you aware of in your environment?"
- ◆ "What are you saying and doing?" (Useful to compare this with what they actually said and did.)
- ◆ "What are you thinking?" (Watch their eye movements, which give more information than their conscious answer.)
- ◆ "What are your capabilities?"
- ◆ "What is important to you ar this time?" (This elicits values.)
- ◆ "What do you believe?" And "How do you hold that belief?"
- ◆ "How would you describe yourself?" (What is your identity?)
- ◆ "How do you connect with other systems of which you are a part?"

Get feedback throughout to ensure that your subject is comfortable and happy with the way you are going about this.

5 Have someone else model the skill and compare your findings with theirs.

6 Now reproduce the thinking and behavior patterns of your subject so that you take on their strategy.

7 Test your model by taking away one element at a time as you use it. If the element isn't key to the process it won't make any difference. In some cases taking away an element may even enhance the process.

8 Do the results you achieve match the results your model achieves? If they do you have been successful; if they don't, go back and find out what other elements make a difference.

9 Note down the strategy so that you can continue to use and, if appropriate, develop it.

SUMMARY

The result of modeling is conscious competence, a mastery of the skills you have and the skills you want to have. With practice, these skills and ways of thinking become a part of your unconscious competence; you don't have to think about them, they become a natural part of who you are. In its simplest form NLP is a process you have been using all your life. In its most sophisticated form it is a way of generating excellence in everything you do, as an individual, as a team, as a company.

The skills and techniques explained in the later chapters of this book are the result of modeling excellence.

THOUGHT PROVOKERS

1   In what unique ways do you add value to:
    - Your family?
    - Your role in your business?
    - Your friendships?
    - The community of which you are a part?
    - Life?
2   Think about the events you have planned for the rest of this week. Are there any about which you don't feel too confident or happy? Think of someone you know who could handle these events in the way you would like to. Step into their shoes and imagine yourself handling the events as if you were that other person.
3   Which people have been the main influences on the way you are today? What is it about each one that you have incorporated into the person you are?
4   Who would you most like to resemble in skill or in style? Is there a colleague or friend whose style and skill you admire? Imagine how you might come to resemble them.

One day a man was tending his garden, which bordered the desert in Arizona. Dusk was descending and he heard in the distance the sound of motorbikes. A gang of Hell's Angels rode up, attacked him, tied him to the back of one of the bikes and drove him into the desert. There they left him, barely alive, as night fell.

The man survived the night and began to regain consciousness as the sun appeared above the horizon. He knew that the sun in the desert means certain death. Without food, water or shelter he stood no chance of survival.

Then at his side he noticed a small bush. He crawled underneath and curled up using the little shade there was to protect himself from the burning rays of the sun. He felt despair – no one knew where he was.

Just at that moment he saw a falcon landing on the bush. To the man's amazement the falcon spoke and asked, "Can I help you?"

Shocked, the man replied, "I am dying of thirst, my mouth and tongue are swollen. To survive I need water."

"Look behind you," said the falcon. "There is a snake. Follow the snake, for it knows where the water seeps out of the rocks. There you will be able to drink."

The next day the falcon came back. "How are you?" it asked.

"I have drunk but I need food to survive – water alone is not enough."

"Stay quiet and wait until the antelope passes by. When it does, follow it – it can show you where the cactus plants are, whose flesh you can eat."

The next day the falcon came back. "Can I do anything for you?" it asked.

"Yes," replied the man. "Although I have drunk and eaten I still need salt to survive. How can I get the salt I need to live?"

"Have no fear," replied the falcon. "The fox also needs salt. If you follow the fox you will see where it finds the rocks to lick that will give you the salt you need."

The man did as the falcon said and returned to find that the bush under which he had sheltered was burnt and charred. "What will I do know?" he asked himself. "I have no shelter, I will burn to death."

Then the man realized that by following the animals he had learnt how to find food, water and salt. He knew how to survive. He noticed the rich colors of the sky as the sun dipped low on the horizon, the blues, the purples and the gold of the sun itself. He heard the exquisite songs of the birds in the distance and he felt an inner peace and joy.

"Shall I show you the way home?" asked the falcon.

The man thought for a moment and then said, "I think I'll stay a little longer."

11
Strategies for successful living

We have different gifts, according to the grace given us. –Romans 12:6

We create our circumstances

We are creatures of habit. Our lives follow patterns that we take with us wherever we go. I remember a phone call from someone I had met on a course. He explained, "I just wanted to tell you that I am going through a bad patch in my life. My relationship with my partner was not working out so I decided to finish it. And I have been very unhappy in my job so I have decided to resign. And I wanted to tell you that on top of all that I have decided to leave this country – I am fed up with the climate and the culture here." And he thought that he wouldn't take his patterns with him!

It is our patterns in thinking and behaving that create our response to our circumstances, not the circumstances themselves. And by becoming aware of these patterns or habits we can begin to choose the life we want. Running away from what we don't want is not the answer. We remain the constant that creates our circumstances.

STRATEGIES FOR SUCCESS

We have learnt strategies that can work for us or against us

In NLP these patterns and habits are known as strategies. A strategy is a sequence of thoughts and behaviors based on a set of beliefs and a sense of self. We all have characteristic elements in our strategies for both our resourceful and unresourceful states. We have learnt strategies that work for us just as we have learnt ones that work against us. Once we are aware of what we are doing when our lives are going well and what we are doing when our lives are not going well, we have choices.

"Those able to realize that the thinking of today is about strategy and communication rather than technology alone will be able to run rings around the pure technologists."

Peter Small, The Entrepreneurial Web

Here are some examples of strategies:

Harry was concerned with his response to some of the people in his organization. He was aware that he treated some people with respect and courtesy at all times and yet with others it was all he could do to contain his frustration and aggression. He knew that the former was the way he wanted to be with everyone, not only because of his values as a human being but also because it made good business sense.

When he talked about the people he treated with respect (who were also the people with whom he learnt the most), he looked directly at me and he talked about himself using "I." All his gestures were close to his chest (his heart). When he talked about the people with whom he had difficulty, he stopped saying "I" and said "you" or "one" instead. He indicated these people in his thinking by pointing to them in the air as if they were up and to his left, away from him. When he talked about the people he respected his whole face softened, he spoke in a relaxed manner, and his demeanor was one of ease. When he spoke of the people with whom he had difficulty, his voice as well as his facial muscles hardened and his body state was tense.

Peter wanted to find a way to get some personal space in his life. He ran a successful business and he worked almost without a break from the time he arrived in the morning to midnight each day, taking work home with him. Sometimes he even worked until one or two o'clock in the morning. When he thought of how he wanted to spend his time with his family, his whole body relaxed. His speech slowed and he paused between sentences. Also when others asked him questions he paused thoughtfully before he answered. When he started to think of the problems, which was often, he began to interrupt others, leaving no space between sentences, either his own or those of others. His speech accelerated. His patterns in behavior, especially his spoken behavior, were his patterns in life.

Our every move, every gesture, every intonation, every speech pattern reveals the patterns we run in our lives as a whole. The lack of space in Peter's speech was a perfect metaphor for the lack

Every action reveals a pattern

of space in his life. We cannot not communicate our issues to the world at large, but we can learn to listen to these issues so that we can coach ourselves and others.

THE GROOVE IN THE WELL

At our home in France we have a well that dates back to the seventeenth century. There is a groove in the front of the well where the rope to lower and raise the bucket has been pulled for all these years. It would be difficult to get the rope positioned in any other place than in this groove – the rope naturally defaults to the groove.

The rope defaults to the groove

It is the same with our patterns. Once the groove is cut, the easiest choice is for us to do what we have done before. Unfortunately, this is not a recipe for success in business. You may be familiar with the expression "If it ain't broke don't fix it." Today it is more likely that if it ain't broke it is probably redundant! We don't get many second chances; we take our chances or our chances pass us by.

What we need increasingly to be able to do is to cut new grooves for ourselves, and to do so daily, so that we are continuously making new connections in our behavior and our thinking. To do so we need first of all to find the behaviors that we want and then practice them until they become a natural choice. We already have these alternative choices in our repertoire. We just need to note when we are behaving in a way that is in line with how we want to be and mark it out (anchor it) so that we can access it when we choose.

A delegate on one of my courses who had lived a fairly depressed life and was often in a down state said, "If there is one thing that I have learnt with NLP it is that if I ever experience a resourceful state, anchor the bugger!"

CODING STRATEGIES

Before I started to write this morning, in my head I saw the title of the chapter I was going to work on. I pictured any writing I had done to date on this subject. I asked myself what was important to me about this subject right now in the world and how I was using it for myself today. I thought of how this topic would help others in the world experiencing the crises that are challenging them today and how it would help them turn these crises into opportunities. I remembered images of situations where I had used this topic to make a difference for myself and I also began to imagine (by picturing them) situations that might occur during the day that would be helped by my paying attention to this theme. I began to feel associated and experienced a sense of satisfaction. As I allowed that to develop, it became a feeling of eager anticipation of what I could say when I sat down to write. I started to create some of the sentences and examples I would use.

The above is a strategy. I have refined it over the years so that I have taken out the redundant parts. What I have now is the essence of what really works for me so that I can accelerate the process of writing in the way I want. My first book took six years to write; the last one took 12 months.

We can discover the essence of what works

Yesterday I was feeling tired. My husband used what I considered to be an emotive word in something he said to me. It was an emotive word because for me it was an anchor for feelings of inadequacy. I heard the word and started to repeat what he said to me over and over in my mind. I told myself that he "should" not have said that and began to imagine ways in which I make a point to him in conversation. I imagined him avoiding this indirect feedback and started to feel annoyed. I remembered (by picturing them) situations in the past that didn't involve him at all in which I had had similar feelings. The feelings intensified. He spoke to me again. I snapped back.

The above is also a strategy. This is an example of an unproductive strategy, but by knowing it consciously I can begin to make new choices.

The ability to stand back and recognize our strategies is the ability to transcend limiting states of mind. Strategies consist of much more than thinking patterns; they consist of the way we structure our beliefs, our values, our sense of purpose, our sense of identity, and more. However, if we start with a simple approach to modeling our thinking strategies, we can code the elements.

We have the ability to transcend limiting states of mind

For example, we can have any of the following elements in a strategy:

* An image that we see externally – Visual/external: **Ve**
* An image in our mind that we remember – Visual/internal/remembered: **Vir**
* An image that we create in our mind – Visual/internal/construct: **Vic**
* A sound that we remember – Auditory/internal/remembered: **Air**
* A sound that we construct – Auditory/internal/construct: **Aic**
* An inner dialogue – Auditory/Inner dialogue: **Aid**
* A feeling that we experience physically – Kinesthetic/external: **Ke**
* An emotion that we feel – Kinesthetic/internal: **Ki**

I have frequently used my cycling as an example of modeling and one of the significant elements for me was to learn how to match my husband's hill-climbing techniques. To model a skill we have to want to do it and believe we can do it. I most certainly wanted to learn this skill as I so frequently got left behind on the hills – and some of the hills in France are very long! I also believed that I could do it. I had learnt to cycle on the flat as well as my husband and I firmly believed that at a minimum I could at least learn to keep up with him.

The strategy I had been using was to see a hill approaching (Visual external), tell myself "Oh no this is going to be a problem" (Auditory internal dialogue), picture how difficult it was going to be (Visual internal construct), start to feel frustrated with myself (Kinesthetic internal), and go round that loop until I got off the bike or lagged behind, feeling pretty fed up!

So the sequence was:

$$Ve \rightarrow Aic \rightarrow Vic \rightarrow Ki \rightarrow$$

Then I decided to model my husband's strategy and started by watching him. I noticed that he didn't look up at all, he looked down at the pedals or the ground all the time (Visual external, although a different Visual external to the one I had been using).

He maintained a regular rhythm with his pedaling (Kinesthetic external). That was all I could get by watching him. I tried these bits of the strategy and it made a difference. I got up the hill at a consistent speed, but it hurt! I was aware of the pain in my thighs all the way up.

So I then asked my husband about his strategy (I didn't use those words). I told him what I thought I had discovered about his strategy and he confirmed that was what he did. However, he added some new pieces that I could only get by questioning or by watching his eye movements. When he looked down he said he did indeed watch the pedals but only fleetingly, he listened to the regular rhythm of the pedals as they turned (Auditory external), he said something to himself like "That's good" (Auditory internal dialogue), and he felt satisfied (Kinesthetic internal). So I asked him about the pain and he said that yes, he felt pain (Kinesthetic external), but he told himself that the more pain he felt the fitter he was getting (Auditory internal dialogue) and he felt good about the pain (Kinesthetic internal).

I have to admit that this process took longer than it needed as I had made some wrong assumptions about what he did and I asked "unclean" questions. (See Chapter 6, Clean questions.) The more neutral and unassuming we are, the more likely we are to discover what the other person's strategy really is.

This was quite a different strategy from the one I had been using and there were some key pieces I had not picked up the first time round. His strategy coded was:

Ve➜Ae➜Aid➜Ki and anywhere in there if he became aware of pain he would insert a loop (Ke➜Aid➜Ki)

I have used and refined this strategy for some time and we are of similar ability now on most aspects of cycling, but (importantly for me) we cycle the hills together!

> We discover strategies by watching and listening, rarely by having the subject just tell us what they do

WHY IT IS IMPORTANT TO LEARN HOW TO MODEL

Modeling is the way we discover the essence of excellence in ourselves and others. If our work depends in any way on our ability to influence others, to do this with excellence we need to

> Modeling is the way to discover the essence of excellence

know how to model. We all have strategies for how we learn, for how we make decisions, for how we buy, for how we motivate ourselves… the list is endless. So if we want to influence ourselves or others, we can only do so if we use the relevant strategy. If we are already good at influencing and we have never come across the concept of modeling, then we probably do this unconsciously. However, we cannot leave these skills to chance and intuition – we need to be masters of our trade. The more skillful and respectful influencers know how to detect the strategy of the person with whom they are dealing and how to use that strategy to adapt their communication to suit the individual.

For example, if you want to help someone make a decision and you have learnt that their strategy for decision making involves them creating an internal image, then asking themselves a question in order to get an internal feeling that lets them know the decision, you can adjust the way you summarize your discussion with them. To match their strategy you can say, "Imagine the scenario in the future (you might be more specific here if it is appropriate) (Visual construct), and ask yourself how is this going to make a difference to you (Aid), and you will sense that this is the decision that fits for you (Ki)."

At the end of Chapter 21, High performance coaching, I describe a very elegant use of a learning strategy by Robert Dilts (one of the leading creative developers of the use of NLP) to help a boy who had been described as learning disabled spell complex words and regain his belief in his ability to learn. If you are a manager you need to know the strategies of the people who work for you to enable them to reach their true potential. If you are a parent you need to know the learning strategies of your children to help them be the individuals they are meant to be. If you are a salesperson you need to know the buying strategies of your customers. If you are a member of a team you need to know the motivational strategies of your fellow team members. There really is no end to the contexts in which this is important in your dealings with others.

This also applies to you personally. If you want to write you need to know your best writing strategy. If you want to motivate yourself you need to know your motivation strategy. I have just started coaching a friend who is using NLP to help herself find a strategy for full recovery from a stroke. When you know your

Parents need to know their children's strategies

own strategies you can use them, modify them, develop them, transfer them to other contexts in your life, and if you wish replace them.

TOTE

You may be thinking that I am introducing the concept of gambling to modeling! Far from it – modeling is a way of ensuring certainty and consistency in the results we achieve.

The TOTE I refer to here is not the betting kind but stands for:

Test→Operate→Test→Exit.

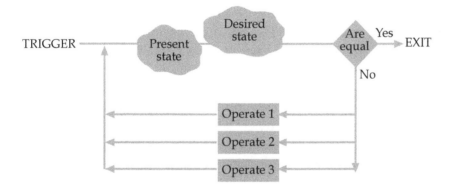

I sit at my desk in my study in France. The sun comes out and shines through the window, warming the room. I have an ideal comfortable state, which includes the temperature in which I am working. As the room warms I check if I have the wall radiator on or not and if it is on I switch it off. If it is not on, then I open one of the windows. I keep unconsciously testing if the temperature I am feeling is my ideal. If it gets too warm in my office with the both the radiator off and the window open, then I may move to a cooler part of the house to work.

I run the same structure for my mental state. To do the work I do and for the sheer pleasure in life, I have an ideal state of confidence and inspiration where ideas and my writing are flowing. If that takes a knock, I become aware of the change in my state and I do something about it. For example, I remind myself of how I feel when I am confident. If that doesn't fully restore the state, then I read books that I know inspire me. It might be just a passage or two, but it's enough to get me back on track and, depending on how fully that restores my state, I might go for a cycle ride, as that invariably clears my head and allows me to think objectively. I have these options and more to achieve the state that I know is best for me.

Both of the above are examples of the TOTE in practice. The principle is that our behavior is driven or motivated by an outcome and we recognize when we have achieved our outcome by a unique set of evidence criteria (i.e. what we will be seeing, hearing and feeling when we have achieved that outcome). We are continually comparing our present state to our desired state to find out if they match. When they do match we know that we have reached the exit; we have achieved our outcome. If the present state does not match the desired state, we have to do another operation to discover if that makes a difference.

We are running TOTEs throughout our lives comparing where we are with where we want to be and taking actions to bring us closer to the exit and eventually to the exit itself. What we have learnt from modeling leaders in business over many years is that they keep going until they have reached a successful exit, whatever it takes, whereas others who do not naturally emerge as leaders exit, but at an earlier point than their original outcome determined. Leaders have more choices (operations).

In effect, when I was modeling my husband's cycling I was running a TOTE. I knew what the exit was: for me to reach the top of the hill either at the same time as my husband or before him. And I wanted to have enough breath to keep on cycling at the same rhythm. After my first pass at cycling my state did not match the desired state, so I knew that some of the operations in the TOTE were missing. That prompted me to question my husband.

The key here is not just to ask the person you are modeling. What they think they know and what they really know are two very different things. It is key to have the subject imagine that they are doing the act you want to reproduce. Alternatively, you can have them actually do the thing you want them to model. In my case I could not keep up with my husband long enough to ask the questions and talking while cycling was not a part of his strategy. So by questioning and watching for clues as he talked about his strategy later, I got the remaining operations that enabled me to exit the loop.

What they think they know and what they really know are two very different things

Essentially, the TOTE is a feedback loop designed to prompt you to find what you need to achieve your desired state. Key skills for successfully navigating the TOTE in order to be able to model are the ability to set a well-defined outcome, sensitivity to what is happening, a willingness to learn from feedback, the flexibility to do or learn something different when what you are doing is not working, and the ability to access and anchor resources within yourself. If you are not achieving what you want in life, the chances are that one or more of these fundamental skills is in need of development.

TOTE is a feedback loop

Our days are a series of TOTEs. Some repeat every few moments, some every few hours, some perhaps every few days or weeks. And there will be some TOTEs that only repeat every few years or maybe longer. The value of knowing someone over time is that we are in a position to learn about the TOTEs with a longer time frame.

Our days are a series of TOTEs

By modeling we discover the structure by which we and others are getting results. By choosing qualities that we admire and that get results we value, we are able to model how we or others get those results. And in the process of doing that, we are valuing the structures that we uncover, even if some of them are currently being used unproductively.

SHORTCUT TO DEVELOPING A STRATEGY

When my son was younger and at school he was reprimanded for unofficially getting himself down to Southampton on a school trip to join his friends. To do this he had to think of a way to get there and find somewhere to stay with very little money in his pocket. He was in trouble for not doing this through the official channels and for not letting anyone know where he was. He was suspended from school for a week for his actions. However, what he was doing was showing great initiative and determination to get to where he wanted to be. This same son was awarded the Military Cross last year for his initiative in leadership in the Marines.

I discussed earlier in this chapter the concept of cutting a groove. We cut grooves that result in resourceful states and we cut grooves that result in unresourceful states. Given that the states to which we give our attention are the ones most likely to be strengthened, this exercise is about identifying a strategy that leads to a resourceful state, so that you increase the likelihood of having consistency in your ability to choose this state when you wish.

1   Identify a resourceful state that you would like to experience when you choose, one that you have experienced before. It might be a state of confidence, enthusiasm, or motivation.
2   Wait until the next time you have this state. (You could alternatively go back in your thinking to associate into a time when you had this state previously.)
3   Be aware of what it is like to be in this state: what are you seeing, hearing, saying to yourself and feeling?
4   What was the trigger for the state: what set you on a sequence of getting to this state?
5   What happened next: what did you see/hear/say to yourself/feel? (If you are not sure, keep the question "What am I doing in my thinking?" in your mind each time you experience the state.)
6   Write down the sequence of thinking patterns so that you can check it out again the next time you experience it.
7   Test to see if you can create the state without the usual trigger. If it doesn't work, keep tracking what happens when you do get the state so you can find the missing pieces.
8   Keep the question "How am I doing this?" in your mind.

SUMMARY

One definition of NLP is that it is the study of the structure of subjective experience. We all experience external events, but what we do with them is subjective. If we want to reproduce the results that we recognize in ourselves or in others, then what we can study is the structure of that subjectivity. Not only can we then learn how to reproduce those skills, but we are respecting the uniqueness of our individual interpretations of life. If we can learn how to respect individual culture, maybe we can begin to do the same in the world at large.

THOUGHT PROVOKERS

1 Write down what you think is your thinking strategy for each of the following:
   - How you get up in the morning.
   - How you respond to feedback.
   - How you decide when it is time to stop work.
   - How you decide to buy something.
   - How you learn.
2 Identify any TOTEs that you recognize you often run successfully (familiar behavior or thinking loops for which there is an exit that matches your original desired state).
3 Identify any TOTEs that you recognize you often run unsuccessfully (familiar behavior or thinking loops for which there is an exit that does not match your original desired state). This will be something that you recognize you consistently try to achieve, but where you frustrated in the process of doing so.

REFERENCES

Robert Dilts (1996) *Strategies of Genius*, Meta Publications.
Robert Dilts (1998) *Modelling with NLP*, Meta Publications.
Stephen Wolinsky (1991) *Trances People Live*, Bramble.

Two monks came upon a girl struggling to cross a river. One of the monks offered to carry her across and the girl accepted, so he picked her up and waded to the other side of the stream, where he put her down safely.

When the other monk joined him he remonstrated with the first monk. "I cannot believe that you carried that girl. It is against all our principles. You know that we are not allowed to touch or even think about women. And yet despite that you carried this young girl in your arms!"

The first monk looked at his brother and replied, "Yes, I did carry the girl. The difference between you and I is that I put her down when I reached the other side. You are still carrying her!"

Part II
Model Yourself with NLP

Once you have explored the elements of NLP, the exciting part is putting those skills together in many different ways to achieve the results you want. One of the principles of the way NLP is taught is that it starts with you.

A woman took her son to see Mahatma Gandhi, who asked what she wanted. "I'd like you to get him to stop eating sugar," she replied.

"Bring the boy back in two weeks' time," replied Gandhi.

Two weeks later the woman returned with her son. Gandhi turned to the boy and said, "Stop eating sugar."

The woman looked surprised and asked, "Why did I have to wait two weeks for you to say that?"

"Two weeks ago I was eating sugar," Gandhi replied.

With NLP you can learn to recognize the structure of your own strategies – you can model yourself. By first learning to model yourself with NLP, you become a model of the principles that influence those around you. For example, once you have learnt how to set compelling goals for yourself, you are more able to facilitate compelling goals for others.

"Example is not the main thing in influencing others. It is the only thing."

Albert Schweitzer

WHAT WORKS?

The techniques in this section are derived from modeling people who are excellent in their ability to lead themselves. By learning these skills you will reinforce the self-leading skills you already have and develop new ones that suit your unique circumstances.

More and more, it is entrepreneurial style and skill that are emerging as significant for this new age. Whether we work for ourselves or an organization, we need more than ever before to be able to lead ourselves. NLP is a way of creating your own sense of direction, of harnessing the resources that are naturally yours, and of influencing others to collaborate with you.

The topics included in this part of the book follow a natural sequence for self-leading.

The first of these is Chapter 12, Tap into your inner potential: Anchoring. This is an approach for enabling you to access your personal resources when you want them. In particular, anchoring is a way of managing your emotional state. The ability to choose the best emotional state to suit your circumstances is one of the most powerful and yet most overlooked skills you can have. When you can choose your state you can choose your techniques and the kind of influence you want to bring to any situation.

When – and only when – you have the state you want, you can build on that by ensuring that you are the example you want to be. You may not be able to control external events, but you can control the way you respond to them. All of us have values and beliefs that drive every move we make and every word we utter. Sometimes those beliefs and values are what we want them to be and sometimes they aren't. Before we can ever think of how we might influence others, we need first to think of how we want to influence ourselves. And it is not just beliefs and values but our sense of identity and purpose in life that provide the example that unconsciously influences others to want to be a part of what we represent – or not.

Chapter 13, Align yourself: Levels of influence deals with all the elements of influence. By thinking through not only how you are but what you might want to change at each level, you can generate an aligned state where every part of you is working toward the same outcome. When you achieve this state of coherence, you can achieve your maximum state of success, influence and satisfaction.

Tap into your inner potential: Anchoring

Align yourself: Levels of influence

Write your own life script:
Beliefs of excellence

When technical skills are equal, it is the person, the team or the company who has the greatest belief in themselves that will win through. The quality and nature of our beliefs override our technical knowhow. If we believe we can, then we can. Those people who have mastery in their ability to lead themselves share certain core beliefs. Chapter 14, Write your own lifescript: Beliefs of excellence explores these beliefs, their increased significance today, and ways in which you can try them on for size to influence yourself.

Achieve what you really
want: Well-formed
outcomes

People who consistently achieve their goals have a way of imagining those goals as if they already have them. They are able to harness the power of their unconscious mind to work for them to realize goals in ways that are compelling. You can learn how to do this for yourself by following the steps in Chapter 15, Achieve what you really want: Well-formed outcomes.

It is interesting to contrast the elements of this approach with some of the standard objective-setting approaches used in business. The difference between NLP approaches and many of the techniques that have been taught previously is that NLP provides you with the tools to find out what really makes the difference. How often have you learnt techniques on training programs only to return to work and resume your normal practices after a day or two? If the techniques worked, then you would probably continue to use them. If you apply all the elements of outcome thinking, as with all other NLP techniques, you will begin to achieve what you really want.

Carpe diem: Time

Chapter 16, Carpe diem: Time is a new chapter on how the way in which we relate to time affects everything we experience. It explores how you can use your perception of time to make your experience in the present increasingly closer to how you really want it to be.

The above skills and ways of thinking are at the heart of self-leading. By starting with yourself, your example is in line with your words and your actions. Although I would say that you could dip into this book at any point, when it comes to applying the principles *you* are the beginning and the end.

STANDING ON THE SHOULDERS OF GIANTS

The beauty of the time that has elapsed since NLP was first coined is that we have accumulated years of learning from models of excellence in all walks of life. I have modeled sportspeople, inspirational leaders, people who have recovered from injury, motivational speakers, monks, vicars and priests in all faiths, stall holders in the local French market, world-class restaurateurs, my husband, my children, my cats, delegates on programs, the fishermen on the beach in Kerala in southern India, traditional Keralan storytellers, outstanding NLP trainers, world-class psychotherapists… The list is endless. I have modeled qualities – commitment, the ability to show emotions and grieve, Booker prize-winning writing styles, mountain cycling, the way to move with speed and elegance on crutches, captivating speaking skills, grace and energy in old age, the ability to work with passion no matter what age… And that is just my experience. You can see what some of my students have modeled on my website, www.sueknight.com.

So we have years of research on what constitutes the essence of excellence in thousands of spheres. I offer you some of the results of those years of modeling in this book: how to hold on to the best emotional state for the moment, how to think about your outcomes in such a way that you are most likely to achieve them, the beliefs that support these states of excellence, how to create an instant state of trust and respect, how to use laughter to heal, how to manage the way we experience time. These are not NLP processes, they are the results, the discoveries of those processes. And we can try them on for size to explore how they work for each one of us. We can then tailor them, adjust them and reinvent them to make them work in a unique way for us personally.

Some of the discoveries have been reapplied to enhance the process of modeling; the fertile compost is returned to nourish the very plants from which it came. And so NLP and the study of excellence in this special way continue to develop and grow.

What you will find in Parts II and III are the results of modeling the qualities that make the difference in leading yourself with excellence and leading others. The world has never been in more need of true leaders. Perhaps you are one?

12
Tap into your inner potential: Anchoring

Let the foundations thereof be strongly laid. -Ezra 6:3

As I write in France with my son sitting outside in the sunshine, the song "Dancing in the Moonlight" is playing on the radio. That music has become a regular part of our time here together. I suspect that particular track will be a reminder to me for years to come. The music is now an "anchor" for a very special time and the good emotions I have attached to this period. The value of associating the music to this time is that I will not only be able to recall the events we have experienced when I hear it, I will also re-experience the emotions I feel right now.

We need to be able to manage our emotional state

Leading starts with the ability to lead ourselves. To do this we need first and foremost to be able to manage our emotional state. Not only is this the first step, it is probably one of the most important and yet surprisingly, it is omitted from many leadership models. Any glitch in emotional state leads almost inevitably to a less than resourceful response to any situation. If we feel irritation, guilt, anger, frustration, doubt or self-consciousness, the result will be less than we are capable of and is unlikely to be a win/win. In contrast, feelings of ease, confidence, forgiveness, acceptance, inspiration and amusement are states that are much more likely to lead to us giving of our best, whatever the context. Anyone who achieves excellence in any form undoubtedly has the ability to manage their emotions, to choose them according to the situation and do so with consistency.

Different states lend themselves to different circumstances. For example, a state of relaxed concentration is the best in which I can cycle. A state of thoughtful meditation is the best for me to write, and a state of amused self-assurance is best for me when giving a talk at a conference. We can learn to recognize and choose which states work best for us in those situations when we want to give of our best. And once we have the state we want, the challenge is to hold on to it when it is threatened by circumstances outside our control, particularly if those circumstances are less than desirable.

When presenting ourselves to others, we need to be able to stand firm and hold on to our convictions and our beliefs, even if everything around us may seem to be changing. As I am writing this chapter, many comparisons are being made between the world's current and aspiring leaders. Gordon Brown is not coming off too well in the comparisons! Excellent leaders are typically people who have the capacity to stand firm and stand alone. Successful people intuitively know how to anchor the emotions and the confidence in themselves that they need.

Excellent leaders have the ability to stand firm and hold on to their convictions

Anchoring is a process of learning to hold on to the states that are crucial to success. It is a process of associating an internal response (a desirable emotion) with some external or internal trigger so that the response may be quickly, and often covertly, re-accessed. It is a way of choosing the emotional state we want and finding a way of accessing it when we choose. An anchor is a stimulus: it may be a sound, an image, a touch, a smell, or a taste that triggers a consistent response. Calling this process anchoring relates to the way that ships down anchor to keep themselves in a specific place to avoid drifting away. And so it is with our emotions. We can choose where we want to keep ourselves to avoid drifting into feelings of tension, stress or worry, for example. At a time of economic and global turmoil there is a huge market for people who can help us do this!

People would benefit from being able to anchor their state right now

Very simply, anchoring involves associating two experiences, one a desired emotional state and the other very often a physical touch. For example, we could ask someone to recall and vividly re-experience in their imagination a time when they felt very confident. As they do so, we might touch them on the elbow. By repeating this process the touch will eventually become linked to the feeling of confidence, so that eventually just by touching their elbow the person will automatically experience this confidence.

The ability to use anchors in NLP enables us to:

* Access the resources (feelings and states) that we want when we want them.

+ Replace unwanted feelings and thoughts with desirable ones.
+ Gain control over our emotions.
+ Transfer and accelerate learning experiences.
+ Keep on course when going through periods of intense change.
+ Positively influence the response we trigger in other people.
+ Experience the day as we want to, no matter what is happening in our work and life.

You already have anchors that work for you. For example, think of the associations you have with:

+ A favorite piece of music.
+ A special perfume.
+ A specific touch.
+ The taste of a memorable meal.
+ The view of a special place.
+ Someone who is close to you.
+ The memory of a particular time in your life.
+ The anticipation of a future event.

We have anchors that work for us as well as anchors that are counterproductive

It is also likely that you have anchors that are counterproductive.

ANCHORS CAN MAKE OR BREAK OUR DAY

Consider this scenario.

You get up and look out of the window. It is cloudy and wet and your heart sinks a little. You think about the day ahead and anticipate your first meeting. You know the person you are meeting and you start to feel a bit heavy as you think about how you expect this meeting to go. You think about the journey you have to make and you begin to imagine how difficult that can be and the sort of delays you might experience. You wish it were still the weekend and slightly dread the week ahead. En route to the meeting, you get stuck in delays and begin to feel tense and irritated. You can feel yourself fidgeting as you wait for the delays to clear. You get to the meeting with little time to spare and it goes much as you expected.

You arrive at your place of work and there is a stream of messages to deal with, some of them marked urgent. You start to feel stressed. The phone rings and you hear the voice of a colleague whose calls you dread, as he seems only to tell you problems. The day continues in a similar way and you arrive home in the evening with a headache and feeling tired.

Now consider this:

You get up and look out of the window. It is cloudy and wet. You are glad you didn't have this weather over the weekend; you can let yourself concentrate on your work now. You think about the day ahead and anticipate your first meeting. You know the person you are meeting and you decide to pay more attention than usual to the outcome you want to achieve. You start to get quite excited about the possibilities for the future. You think about the journey you have to make to get to this meeting and establish some contingency plans in case there are any holdups. You also plan how you can use the traveling time to good effect.

En route to the meeting you get stuck in delays, but you realize there is nothing you can do about them, so you use the time as you had planned to consider other things. You think about the weekend and how good it has been and how resourceful you feel now because of it. You get to the meeting with little time to spare and it goes much as you expected: you are well on your way to achieving not only the outcomes you set yourself but also ones you had not anticipated.

You arrive at your place of work and there is a stream of messages, so you decide to work through the urgent ones and put the rest out of your mind until you have got through the other high-priority issues for the day. This helps you to focus your thinking. The phone rings and you hear the voice of a colleague who seems to talk to you about his problems quite often; you are privately amused at how someone can center his attention on the negative aspects of life so consistently. You listen with empathy and he seems to become more positive over the duration of the call. You feel very fortunate to have the work you have and to be surrounded by people who make your days so rich and entertaining. You arrive home tired but satisfied with the day and ready for a relaxing evening.

Our days are governed by the associations we have chosen (often unconsciously) to make with the various kinds of events we encounter. We make associations throughout our lives; the question is whether they lead to the kinds of outcome we want for ourselves, or whether we are making our lives a misery because

We make associations throughout our lives

of what we are choosing to think about our circumstances. Given that what we choose to think is one of the single most powerful influences on the outcome of a situation, this is one of the most significant ways in which we can influence how we experience our lives and what we get as a consequence of our thinking.

"There is nothing either good or bad, except that thinking makes it so."
William Shakespeare

The anchoring process is a vital way in which we influence how we lead ourselves from within. We can choose the experience we have in life, irrespective of our external circumstances.

MAKING ANCHORS WORK FOR YOU

The previous examples demonstrate how we sometimes use anchors in ways that trigger unresourceful states, such as depression, anger, frustration or unhappiness. These are states that typically limit our subsequent behavioral choices.

Let's suppose you are a person who sometimes gets stressed. Many people are likely to ask themselves either "Why do I get like this?" or, slightly better, "How do I get like this?" Both of these questions are likely to lead a deepening of the undesirable state. It would be more useful to ask "What do I want instead of this state?" and, following on from that once you have the answer, "How do I do that?" Asking "how" in relation to the desired state raises awareness of the structure of the desirable experience, as opposed to reinforcing the reasons for the state and consequently the state itself. It helps to appreciate that most of our limitations are self-taught.

We were invited by a manufacturing company to explore the staff's resistance to the new appraisal scheme. We discovered that previously the only time a manager typically sat down with a member of their staff was when they perceived a problem. Any discussion between a manager and a member of staff was usually a critical one. It was no surprise, then, to understand that the staff would be reluctant to welcome any scheme that promoted a discussion with their manager! The managers were unwittingly linking (anchoring) discussions about problems with the appraisal scheme.

By using anchors hand in hand with outcome thinking, we can begin to take control of the effect we have on ourselves and others. For example, we can decide first of all how we want to feel in key situations such as:

We can take control of the effect we are having

- At the start of a presentation.
- Being on the receiving end of aggression.
- When we have to tell someone they have been made redundant.
- When delegating an area of work to a new employee for the first time.
- In a meeting when our point of view is different to that of the majority.
- When we get some tough feedback.
- When we are faced with unexpected change.
- When all the technology we rely on fails us.

Similarly, we can decide what effect we want to have on other people, when for example:

- They are entering a discussion with us.
- We are delegating jobs to them.
- They have feedback to give to us.
- We are asking them for a decision.
- They receive an email from us.
- They check into our website.
- Someone makes contact with our company.
- They receive a call from us.

We have the ability to influence our own and others' responses in a way that is resourceful, one in which we have confidence and choice about what we can do.

ANCHORING A RESOURCEFUL STATE FOR YOURSELF

Let's start by considering how to generate the state you want for yourself. The process of anchoring involves linking a specific sight, sound or touch with an experience that is present; that is, a situation into which you are associated. The linking process subsequently enables you to use the anchor to reaccess that same experience when it can benefit you in another context.

Procedure for anchoring a resourceful state

1 Choose a place that is free from distractions and make yourself comfortable.
2 Decide on a state/a feeling that you have experienced in your life that you would like to be able to access when you choose.
3 Choose an anchor that you can use whenever you want to access this feeling. It must be something precise and easy to use. For example, you could press the little finger and thumb together on your left hand.
4 Now recall the memory of a time when this feeling was strongest for you. Check you are associated into this experience, experiencing it as if in your own shoes and not as an outsider.
5 When you are completely associated, allow yourself to experience what it is like to be in this experience, seeing, hearing and feeling it. As you do so, touch your little finger and thumb together for as long and only as long as you feel these sensations intensely. When you have experienced the feeling and the touch of your finger to thumb, release that touch. Shake yourself or move in some way so that you bring yourself back to the present, which is called *breaking state*.
6 This touch becomes the anchor for the feeling. Repeat the process several times until you have a strong connection between the touch and the feeling.
7 Test the anchor. Think of something else and as you do so, touch your little finger and thumb together in precisely the way you did when you were setting up the anchor. This is called *firing the anchor*.
8 What happens? If you have set up the anchor effectively, you will recall the scene, the sounds and the feeling of the memory as if you were there. If this doesn't happen, keep practicing. It may be that you weren't fully associated when you set the anchor. Check that you use exactly the same anchor to recall the experience as you used to set it up in the first place. The sensations in an experience tend to rise and fade. Set the anchor just as the experience is reaching a peak, and remove it as soon as or just before the feelings begin to fade.
9 Now think of a future situation where you would like to have the feelings you have anchored. This time, as you imagine the

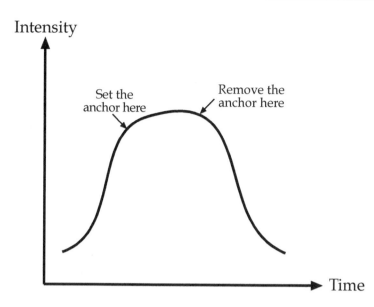

Intensity

Set the anchor here

Remove the anchor here

Time

situation in the future, fire the anchor. What do you see, hear and feel now? When you do this successfully you are transferring your desired feelings, your resourceful state, to another and in this case future context.

10 Learn first to do this for yourself so you can recall the resources you want when you want them. Then you can coach others.

Remember the key factors in anchoring:

* Fully associate into the experience before you set the anchor.
* Make the anchored experience intense.
* Use a distinct and specific anchor that is easily reproduced.
* Set the anchor just prior to reaching the most intense part of the experience.
* Use exactly the same anchor to recall the experience.

In this example we used a touch as an anchor, but an anchor can be anything as long as it meets the above criteria.

Natural anchors are related to sensory preferences. For example, a visually oriented person is more likely to be sensitive to visual cues, someone who is aurally oriented is more likely to respond to sounds, and some who has a feelings preference is more likely to make associations with tactile cues. Smell is a powerful primitive anchor for many people.

Natural anchors are related to sensory preferences

Exactly the same process works for anchoring others as for yourself. You cannot easily know exactly when the point of greatest intensity has occurred for someone else in order to know when to set the anchor. You rely on your ability to detect from their external behavior exactly when this occurs. By building rapport, you will learn to detect when this peak state is occurring. Otherwise, the process is exactly the same as it would be if you were anchoring yourself.

STEPS FOR COACHING OTHERS

1 Ask the other person what state they want to have in a particular situation. Ask them to identify a time in the past when they had that state.
2 Ask them what anchor they want to use to anchor the desired state.
3 Ask the other person to step into the time when they had the state they want now. Help them to associate fully into that experience by asking them rhetorically what it is like to experience this state in this way.
4 Invite them to experience fully all the sensations of being there so that they intensify the experience. "As you experience this state, you might allow yourself to experience it even more intensely than before... "
5 Pay attention to them so that when you know they are reaching the peak of that experience, invite them to set the anchor.
6 As soon as the intensity of the feelings begins to diminish (again, you need to watch them carefully to establish when this occurs), invite them to step out of the state and bring them back to the present. You can repeat these steps a few times if you want to ensure that the anchor and the state are associated.
7 Test by asking them to imagine a time when they would want the desired state that they have just anchored, but they might not typically access it. As they imagine this time, invite them to use (fire) the anchor. As the anchor works, you will see the person reproduce all the characteristics of the desired state. If the anchor needs strengthening, go back and repeat the

process, checking for full association, intensity of the experience and accuracy of the anchor.

BUSINESS ANCHORS

You are anchoring other people all the time. The question is, are you anchoring them in resourceful or unresourceful ways?

We are anchoring others all the time

When I worked in ICL, we often invited external consultants to join us on some of our projects. They invariably brought different perspectives and new ideas. One consultant, Peter, brought much more than that, however. He was always positive and invariably arrived with a smile on his face. When Peter was around everyone felt a good energy and was in high spirits. If there was a choice, we would invariably choose to work with Peter in preference to anyone else.

Can you imagine how different work meetings would be if managers were measured by the state in which they left their staff at the end of the discussion?

The examples of anchoring we used earlier in this section, such as touch, aren't always as available in a business setting. It isn't always part of the culture to touch others in this way. It is necessary to be a little more creative with the anchors you use to enable others to access resourceful states.

Examples of anchors you can use in business are:

- A word or words that you would not use regularly in conversation, said with a specific volume and tonality.
- Space, which can be employed to good effect in a presentation, where you can anchor different information and responses to you by standing or moving to different parts of the room.
- A posture or movement that you would not naturally make in discussion.

My experience is that using anchors in this way only works if you use them with integrity, in a way that fits with other people's outcomes. I believe if you attempt to use them manipulatively, in a way that is out of line with the other person's outcomes, the other person will sense this, often intuitively, and block the anchor.

STEPS FOR ANCHORING A RESOURCEFUL STATE IN A MEETING

1 Identify the state you want to anchor in the other person that will support the achievement of your mutual outcomes. This might, for example, be a state of confidence, decisiveness or happiness.
2 Decide what anchor you will use, a particular word, a specific gesture or a posture that can be noticed by them in some way (very likely unconsciously).
3 When the other person naturally demonstrates the desired state, use your anchor. You will probably need to do this four or five times.
4 If the discussion gets to a stage when this state would be valuable and it is not naturally occurring, fire your anchor. Notice what happens. If you have been successful in setting the anchor, then the other person will demonstrate the state.

SWITCHING STATES

There are many different ways of using anchors. One easy way is to use a technique called *collapsing anchors*. This is a way of reconciling two states, for example an unresourceful state and a resourceful one. You could do this when you want to lessen an extreme negative state and achieve one that is a blend, so that you don't lose the unresourceful state but experience it in a way that is manageable. The consequence of collapsing anchors is that you will achieve a third different state to the original two that is in someway a mix – a cocktail of the two with a uniquely new flavor.

One of the simplest ways to do this is to use the knuckles on one hand. With the extreme end of your right-hand index finger, touch specific knuckles on your left hand. If it is easier for you, reverse the way you use your hands in this exercise.

STEPS FOR COLLAPSING ANCHORS

1 Decide on an unresourceful state that you want to change. It might be, for example, a state of anxiety, stress, lack of confidence or frustration.

2 Associate into this state so that you are re-experiencing it and anchor it by touching your index finger to the first knuckle on the other hand. Test the anchor until you know it works. Only access this state briefly.

3 Choose a different state altogether, a break state. This might be thinking about something funny or just something that requires thought, like saying your phone number backwards.

4 Choose a resourceful state, one of confidence, calm or security for example. Associate into a time when you had this feeling. When you experience the intensity of this feeling, anchor it by touching your second finger to the second knuckle on your other hand.

5 Test the anchors in the following sequence:
   a Break state.
   b Fire the first anchor.
   c Break state.
   d Fire the second anchor.
   If either of the anchors fails to work, repeat the sequence of resetting them.

6 Now apply both anchors simultaneously. You will feel some confusion as the two states sort themselves out into a new, integrated state. If the less resourceful state is still a strong part of the subsequent state, go back to choose and anchor an even stronger resourceful state. Repeat the process. You may also find that it helps to fire the anchor for the resourceful state for a second or two before also firing the anchor for the unresourceful state.

7 Now think of a future situation, one that typically in the past would have triggered the unresourceful state. What happens as you think of this situation? If the collapsing anchors technique has worked, the unresourceful state will not exist any more.

Some of these techniques may seem quite formal at first, yet these processes are ones that we are slipping into and out of through a typical day. What we are doing here is breaking them down into their constituent parts in a similar way to how we might learn to drive a car. However, once you master the skill, you can begin to use it more informally. For example, if you find yourself slipping into a state of unresourcefulness, you can learn to step quickly

You can learn to step quickly into a resourceful state

into a resourceful one. Recall a time when you felt particularly resourceful and reaccess those feelings by associating yourself once more into that situation.

Eventually you will find that even the process of switching from unresourceful to resourceful state becomes automatic. Your unconscious mind makes the switch for you without you even having to think about it consciously. You will have "hard wired" the strategy for resourcefulness by learning to chain anchors.

CHAINING RESOURCES

Sometimes the gap between the unresourceful state and the resourceful one that we would like in its place can be too wide to step from one to the other in one go. In such cases it is useful to learn to move through a series of anchored states in order to lead ourselves gradually from the least resourceful to the desirable state. It is worth emphasizing that it is also important to know when to stay in what might at first seem to be an unresourceful state. The risk of always creating a pathway out of what we believe to be "unresourceful" states is that we fail to value the richness of diversity, the beauty of all emotions.

There is a beauty in all emotions

Staying in a state or moving to another is a choice. If the gap is a wide one – from, for example, a state of extreme stress to one of total relaxation – you might want some interim steps. You might choose to go from stress to concern, from concern to neutrality, from there to mild amusement, and then finally to relaxation. In this case you would be *chaining anchors* so that you are creating a pathway for yourself from one state to anther. By learning the chain each time you experience the first undesirable state, you will automatically move down the path you have created for yourself.

STEPS FOR CHAINING ANCHORS

1 Decide on an unresourceful state that you want to work with in this exercise. Choose a state that you want to replace with another much more resourceful state, but one that you recognize is a significant distance from the first undesirable state. You might choose an initial state of something like

anxiety, stress or depression. The replacement state might be something like calm, relief or ease. Check that the replacement state is one that is truly desirable as a replacement whenever you experience the first.

2   Associate into the first state so that you are re-experiencing it and anchor it by touching a part of your thigh. (You are going to use places in line down your thigh to access each of the subsequent states until you get to the resourceful one.) Only experience this first state briefly (there is no need to stay there too long). Break state.

3   Choose a next intermediary state, for example irritation, but something much less intense than the first state. Experience this state and when you are fully associated into it, anchor that to a point a little further down your thigh. Break state.

4   Choose a more resourceful state, one of confidence or security, for example. Associate into a time when you had this feeling. As you experience the intensity of this feeling, anchor it by touching a point further down your thigh again. When you have done this successfully, break state.

5   The number of intermediary states you need will depend on the intensity of the first state and the gap between the first and the destination state. Repeat this process until you have anchored all the intermediary states and the final destination state.

6   Test the anchors to make sure they all work, being sure to break state between each one. If any of them is not yet fully anchored, return to experiencing and anchoring them until they are.

7   Now fire the first anchor and, when you are fully in that first state, fire the second anchor simultaneously; as you experience the second state approaching its peak, remove the first anchor and, continuing to hold the second one, fire the third one. (You are always linking each state with the next one in this way.) As the third one builds, remove the second anchor and fire the next one. You should experience yourself moving through each state in turn and as you do so, you are connecting them together in a chain.

8   Do this until you have reached the destination state. When you have the destination state, fully remove the previous anchor and fully experience this final resourceful state. Break state.

This is important so that you when you repeat the whole process to check that it works, you want to ensure that you end on the destination state and don't loop it back to the unresourceful state that you started with.

9 Repeat step 7 until you have the states chained together.

10 Now fire the first anchor. If you have chained the states together successfully, you will go through the chain you have created for yourself and automatically move through the states, finishing at the destination state.

It is not that we don't do this already; we do. However, without thought and care we tend to create chains that either are not very efficient (e.g. it takes longer than it needs to get out of an unresourceful state), or we have created chains that take us to places potentially even less resourceful than the one with which we started. How often have you begun a day feeling a little gloomy and then got frustrated with yourself for doing that, which led to your getting annoyed and then stressed and so on? How much more desirable is it to find that if you do get into a state of confusion, you can lead yourself to state of curiosity, inquiry and finally understanding and insight?

I believe that putting yourself into a resourceful state is a vital precursor to most situations. You can learn to recognize which state is most useful to you, for example in:

- Giving and receiving feedback.
- Solving problems and being creative.
- Achieving balance.
- Listening.
- Tackling work you would not naturally be motivated to do.
- Spending time with your family.
- Making a presentation.
- Dealing with customers.
- Writing.
- Going on holiday.
- Starting the day or the evening when you arrive home.

More traditional training will teach you what structure to use, for example how to structure appraisal, how to handle objections, how to plan a presentation. NLP teaches you how to generate the state that triggers the resources and the style you need to achieve what you want.

SUMMARY

Anchors occur naturally. You have many associations already established: some individual, some connected with other people. Most of these will have occurred by chance without any forethought. Some association anchors will be helpful, supportive and rewarding for you; some will not. The process of anchoring enables you to choose the associations you want both for yourself and for others. Mastering the skill of anchoring means learning to lead yourself by managing your state of mind. It also means taking responsibility for the effect you have on other people.

This chapter has set out a few of the ways in which you can apply the anchoring techniques, but you will find that anchoring is part of everything you do. Begin to explore how you can use these anchors creatively as a way of enriching your day-to-day living and making your involvement with others a continually rewarding experience.

THOUGHT PROVOKERS

1   What state do you typically have in the following situations and what state would you like to have?

Situation	Current state	Desired state
Giving a presentation		
Saying what you want		
Refusing personal requests		
Appraising or being appraised		
Going for an interview		
Exercising		
Dealing with aggression		
Having your ideas challenged in public		
Add your own situations		

Choose one of the above situations and use either the self-anchoring, the collapsing anchors or the chaining anchors technique.

2 Write down the state you would like to generate in yourself and in others in the following situations.

Situation	Own state	Desired state in others
Appraising others		
Giving feedback		
Explaining what you want		
Clarifying technical information		
Running or contributing to meetings		
Add your own situations		

3 Write down the states you would like to have when dealing with each of the following people and the state you would like them to have:

Person	Your desired state	Desired state for them
A member of staff		
A colleague		
Someone in your family		
Your best friend		
A friend		
A customer		
A supplier		
Your partner		
Someone else		

Use either of the anchoring techniques to experiment with achieving these desired states.

4 Develop a list of anchors that you could use in your everyday situations. Check they meet the outline for an effective anchor; that is, that each one is precise and easily reproducible, and that it can be used uniquely to anchor a specific resource.

5 How has your day been so far? What anchors have you used that have worked for you/worked against you?

6 Read *An Evil Cradling* by Brian Keenan as an example of someone who chose what he made of extreme circumstances.

Many years ago there was a sailor who had traveled to many different countries around the world. He had been to many places and seen many different sights. One day as he was sailing across the seas, he came upon an island and decided to rest there for a while. He moored his boat on the shore and began to look around. All around the island was a beautiful white beach and behind the beach was dense tropical jungle.

All was quiet until...

He thought he could hear a faint noise in the distance and tilted his head to listen. He sensed it came from within the jungle and walked closer. Sure enough, once again he heard this faint noise in the background. He started to hack his way through the foliage in order to make a pathway. The more he moved inland the louder the noise became. He continued to cut his way through, until eventually he reached a clearing and there in the middle of the clearing he saw an old man sitting cross-legged on the ground.

The old man had his eyes closed and was chanting "Mo, Mo, Mo" in long, soft tones. The sailor stood and watched and listened. "Mo, Mo, Mo," continued the old man. Eventually the sailor approached the old man and tapped him on the shoulder.

The old man turned slowly around and smiled.

"Excuse me," said the sailor, "I think you have made a mistake. I think you should be saying 'Om, Om, Om.'"

"Oh," said the old man, smiling. "Thank you so much," and began to chant, "Om, Om, Om."

The sailor felt pleased with himself and made his way back to his boat. He began to sail away, and when he had sailed for a while he felt a tap on his shoulder. He turned around, surprised to see the old man, who said, "Forgive me for interrupting your journey. Could you please remind me what the chant should be?"

The sailor, in a state of shock, said, "Om, Om, Om."

"Thank you so much," said the old man, and walked back across the water to the island.

13
Align yourself: Levels of influence

Conscience is that ability within me that attaches itself to the highest standard I know, then continually reminds me of what that standard demands. If I am in the habit of always holding it in front of me, conscience will always indicate what I should do.

Oswald Chambers, My Utmost for His Highes

W e live in a complex, unpredictable world. We can no longer rely on plans and predictions. We are called to work in ways that are entirely different to the ways of the past. The only part of the system on which we can potentially rely is within us. And yet this is the part of the system that for many people lies largely untapped. We have to trust and believe that if we are true to ourselves, our outcomes unfold in line with that truth.

Our outcomes unfold in line with our truth

When I wrote the first edition of *NLP at Work*, I said that to achieve our goals we need to be able to imagine and feel them, and this still holds true. However, I have seen a new and different style of achievement develop in the last few years. This relies more and more on our ability to allow outcomes to unfold. We have to be able to walk forward with faith into a world that is chaotic and abstract and allow the opportunities to present themselves. And we need to be so aligned, so true to what we believe, that we are in a position to seize these opportunities when they occur. Our example is our reputation.

We don't know where the next ball will come from

It is as if we are sportspeople playing a game. We don't know where the next ball will come from or how it will come. But we manage ourselves so that we have a strong sense of the outcome we want to achieve and are always in a state of readiness and flexibility to seize the chances as they present themselves.

"Mastering complexity means not letting complexity get the better of you. I means having a coherent viewpoint to guide action in spite of the confusion uncertainty, and ambiguity that are introduced by the swirl of events and interactions going on around you. The mastery we are alluding to is that o

the craftsman and not that of the M in MBA. The ability to act coherently in the face of complexity, and to do so on an ongoing basis, is the hallmark of a true master."

Michael Lissack & Johan Roos, The Next Common Sense

At the time of starting up the NLP open courses branch of my business, I acted in faith that it was the right thing to do. It was something I had wanted for a long time. I had realized the connections between the NLP I had seen used powerfully in therapeutic scenarios and its potential for excellence in the workplace. I met with resistance not only from other consultants but from my own associates, who said that I didn't stand a chance of succeeding. And for the first two years when I struggled to create a profitable business, I almost succumbed to their doubts. Nevertheless, my belief and my desire kept me on track and I am very glad that they did.

Only recently I advised a colleague who was launching an open program who wanted to see what the number of potential attendees might be before committing to the schedule. "It doesn't work that way. Only you can commit and when you do, you find out who is then drawn to what you propose," was my advice.

"Build a field and they will come."

Field of Dreams, *starring Kevin Costner*

Build a field and they will come

They didn't say "See if they come and then build a field"! And yet that is how many people expect business to work.

To support people in achieving their personal best is one of my main aims in my NLP training and consultancy. By having a personal sense of direction, resolving inner conflict and managing personal change, we can move toward a state of coherence. When we have this state we are at one with who we are: there is little or no conflict or stress. We are approaching the best we can be.

When I first wrote this chapter, I was watching the Tour de France cycle race in which Lance Armstrong was taking part. He outcycled all the other cyclists in the field to take the yellow jersey (worn by the overall leader at any point in the three-week race).

Only a few years previously, Lance Armstrong had been diagnosed with cancer in just about every part of his body and given a negligible chance of survival. Not only did he fight his way through the cancer, he regained his fitness to cycle and win the Tour de France, one of the most grueling sporting events in the world, not once but twice. He eventually won it seven times, an all-time record.. When he started on his cycling career he was not a popular rider; because of his arrogance and aggressive tactics, he became a target for the French press. However, through his illness and astonishing recovery, he has realized his purpose in life. He cycled to raise awareness of cancer and the possibilities of overcoming it.

Armstrong's cycling style has influenced other cyclists worldwide. On one occasion his key adversary, Jan Ulrich, crashed off the side of the road. It is the custom not to take advantage of the misfortune of a fellow competitor and Lance Armstrong followed this custom to the letter: he took one foot out of its pedal to wait for Ulrich to catch him up. As he overtook the leading cyclist, Laurent Jalabert, a French favorite who had shown great courage in leading through the mountains all day, Armstrong indicated for Jalabert to accompany him to the finish line. Jalabert indicated that if he could have, he would have. The following day the headline in the French press was "Armstrong – Ace of Spades – Ace of Hearts." They described his performance as that of a virtuoso.

Lance Armstrong cycled with purpose, with a total sense of his identity as a world-class cyclist, with principles and beliefs not only about his sport but also about what is possible when everything seems to be lost. He showed integrity in the way he took part and demonstrated a skill in cycling that was artistically outstanding – he danced in the pedals. His influence is assured for posterity, not only in cycling but in the world at large.

Just as a company can work more effectively if each of the teams within it cooperates and works toward the same goal, so an individual can function more effectively if each of the "parts" is cooperating with the others. This kind of aligned state can be achieved by paying attention to different levels.

THE DIFFERENT LEVELS

You can use this model to clarify your thinking about yourself, your team, and your company. I recommend you start with yourself. Change comes from within; once we have a coherent mental model our environment follows suit.

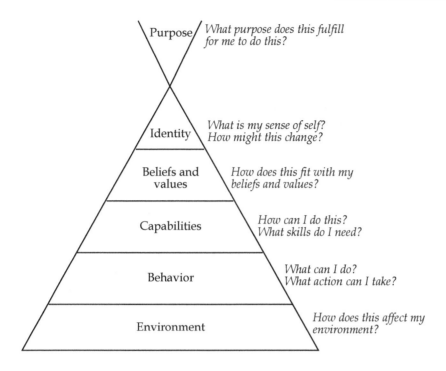

PURPOSE

The level of purpose or spirituality relates to what we hold as being "beyond self." That might include bigger goals than those of self-interest, legacy, contribution to the bigger systems of which we are a part, faith and our sense of the supernatural. At this level we are thinking about our relationship with those bigger systems. These might include:

- Our family.
- Our marriage or partnership.
- Our team.
- Our community.
- Our company.
- Our faith.
- Our world.

Or it might relate to a temporary bigger system like:

- The group we are meeting today.
- The client with whom we are interacting right now.
- The dynamic between us and the staff in the restaurant in which we are eating.
- The people around us on the train.
- The people next to us in a queue.
- The family members around us.

This is the highest level of unconscious influence

By paying attention to this level, we can become aware of the way we are always adding value by being who we are, no matter which system we happen to belong to at that time. This is our highest level of unconscious influence. This is the level at which most people make decisions about whether we are someone with whom they want to do business, live, collaborate, make a long-term business commitment and so on. Having goals at this level is more likely to ensure their sustainability. This is about everything that is beyond self.

There are companies with missions that are ecological; that is, they cooperate and contribute to the bigger system. For example, a travel company that pays attention to its effect on the culture of the countries with which it does business; an information technology company that thinks about and plans the impact it wants to have on the future culture and world at large through the development of technology; a consultancy that is concerned that the work it does supports the environment and the culture in which it is working.

What we have witnessed in the financial world in recent times is the result of greed and self-interest. And what we are all experiencing with its repercussions is what happens when the goals held by the people in power do not encompass or contribute to the bigger systems – the communities of which we are all a part.

Paul Smith is a fashion house and as such works to impossibly tight and demanding schedules, holding several fashion shows every year. Despite that, the people in the company are open, warm and dedicated to their learning and growth. Their attitude to learning and change resembles the cultures I experience in Asia, where delegates are nonjudgmental about learning. They take it in, check that they understand and try it out before deciding how they will use it. In western culture it is more likely for delegates to judge at an intellectual level before trying something on for size. So the people in Paul Smith have a universally different approach to learning than many western organizations. And they are simultaneously creative, loyal and passionate about what they do.

The unconscious value you add to the bigger systems of which you are a part is your most significant form of influence. Stephen Covey, in his book *Seven Habits of Highly Effective People*, refers to it as your legacy. Your legacy does not have to be only what you leave when you die; it is what you leave when you leave a meeting, leave a room, leave a company.

IDENTITY/MISSION

A company's mission statement defines the identity of the organization, the unique nature of its business, and it encompasses purpose, what the company does for others. For example:

To support and develop the leaders of today to make a positive difference in the world.

This is a visionary mission and expresses the uniqueness of the business and the person who is running it. It is different to the mission statements that appear on so many financial statements: We want to be number one in the car hire business. We want to be the best web developers in Europe. These are self-based mission statements and are generally meaningless to both the employees of the business and their potential clients.

Our personal purpose is lived out through the kind of person we are. Identity/mission defines our sense of self and contains statements describing how we think of ourselves as a person, "I am" statements, such as:

+ I am a successful person.
+ I am an optimist.
+ I am a shy person.
+ I am practical.

What we have "coded" within ourselves in this way is central to who we are. In my experience, there is a huge difference between saying "I write articles and books" (a behavioral statement) and saying "I am an author" (an identity statement). An author is so much more central to who I am in all contexts. It was several years of writing before I described myself this way.

This level can also provide a means of thinking about the key roles we fulfill in our life, such as parent, provider, sportsperson, consultant.

What role were you born to fulfill in the world?

"The problem is not in what we do but in what we become."

Oscar Wilde, De Profundis

BELIEFS AND VALUES

Our sense of identity informs our beliefs and values. A compassionate leader, for example, will very likely believe that it is the quality of our relationships that inspires people to work together toward a cause. A talented engineer will believe that there is a solution to every problem.

Our beliefs are emotionally held opinions about ourselves, other people and situations we hold to be true. They are not fact. For example:

+ I believe that people in general can be trusted.
+ I believe that we can learn from any experience.
+ I believe that meeting customers' needs is at the heart of success.
+ I believe that there is excellence in everyone.
+ I believe that integrity is the key to a successful business.

Coherence results from feeling that the actions required of us are consistent with our own sense of purpose and identity and that of the organization of which we are a part. This feeling can only occur when the values and guiding principles embodied by the corporate purpose and expressed identity align with how we define and embody our sense of self.

Our values are at the root of life's decisions

Our values, derived from our beliefs, are at the root of our decisions in life. These are the qualities that we hold to be important in the way we run our business and live our life. For example:

* Honesty.
* Openness.
* Integrity.
* Fun.
* Learning.

Some very interesting new values are emerging as important, such as:

* Generosity.
* Charity.
* Abundance.
* Relationships.
* Spontaneity.
* Selflessness.
* Freedom.
* Humility.

Each of us has our own interpretation of what these values mean and how we know they are met. It is important not only to have values but also to know specifically how you will recognize that they are being satisfied.

Companies with coherent values that are lived out in their daily practice are what Peter Senge (author of *The Fifth Discipline*) refers to as "transparent." Transparency translates to certainty: an attractive quality to others, especially in times of chaos.

Certainty in times of chaos

Taking time out to clarify purpose, mission, beliefs and values, and subsequently a code of practice for all employees, has to be one of the best investments a company can make. It is also a sound foundation for established companies that have lost their way and want to inject new life into the business.

CAPABILITIES

Our capabilities describe *how* we do what we do. Many organizations are paying increasing attention to competency-based training and development. It is important to recognize that this is only one of the levels in this model. What we can learn to do through modeling is to recognize unique capabilities, not only those that happen to be on a company's appraisal list. No matter how comprehensive this list, it can only serve to box people into predefined categories.

The opportunity for forward-thinking leaders is to recognize and celebrate everyone's unique talents. More than that, it is a characteristic of leaders that they can and do recognize the unique qualities of the people who work for and with them, as well as the people with whom they do business outside the company. Natural leaders model naturally! And they can detect qualities such as the ability to:

- Ask multi-level questions.
- Achieve instant rapport.
- Observe and comment on his own behavior (and joke about it) while he is in conversation with someone.
- Scan a screen of code and intuitively detect the bugs in a program.
- Take a new idea and identify with the people who need to learn this idea in the business.
- Take time in the most critical situations to make a balanced decision that is most likely to benefit all involved.
- Build trust in endangered wild animals to be able to get close to them and nurse them back to health for release back into their natural habitat.

When I was working with people in the stores of one company, I noticed that whenever I asked a question, one of the packers, Mike, looked consistently left and to his side. It was a very marked preference in his eye-accessing cues. I had the opportunity to talk about the group's social interests and this eye-accessing cue became even more pronounced. I was able to comment on this (I had explained eye-accessing cues as part of a company-wide training program) and I discovered that Mike had a great interest in music. Not only that but, rather bashfully, he said that he could hear a piece of music and remember it exactly. (His eye-accessing cue was auditory remembered.) I commented on what a remarkable skill that was and he looked astonished, and explained that he had always thought it was weird so had kept quiet about it!

I wonder just how many skills are buried in this way. Excellence involves discovering and releasing these natural talents.

When Goran Ivanisevic entered the Wimbledon tennis championships in 2001, he was not considered to have any chance of doing well, let alone winning. However, his belief in his purpose and himself gave him the influence to persuade the panel to let him enter the tournament on a wild card. His passion was intense. His purpose was to give something to a country that had been torn apart with conflict. Even during the war in Croatia, he believed that his best contribution was not to take on the identity of a soldier but to inspire through his identity as a tennis player. He played every point as if it were match point. And he won the Wimbledon title in a final that will be remembered as one of the best in the history of the game.

BEHAVIOR

All of the previous attributes – purpose, identity, beliefs, values and capabilities – show themselves in everything we do. Our behavior is what we do and say. It is what the world around us can see and hear us doing. All of my beliefs and values are apparent in every word I write.

Think of behavior as the tip of the iceberg, the bit of us that is above the surface, whereas purpose, identity, capabilities, beliefs and values are our internal thoughts and feelings.

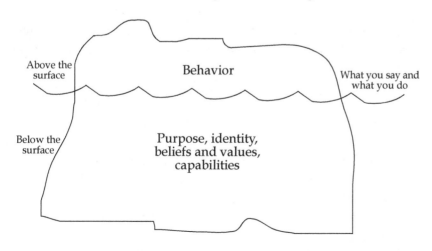

Examples of behaviors include:

* Asking questions.
* Saying what you want.
* Losing your temper.
* Writing out your goals.
* Giving feedback.
* Folding your arms.
* Smiling.
* Blushing.
* Running.
* Making eye contact.

Most people have characteristic patterns of behavior that support what they really want and also patterns of behavior with which they sabotage themselves.

Martin is a very caring leader. He is open to feedback and acts on what he hears. He laughs a lot, especially at himself. He is skilled at creating visions for the future and when he does this, he looks very definitely up and to his right. He asks precise questions to be sure he has understood what others are telling him.

However, Martin can also sometimes dominate the conversation by taking much more airtime than anyone else in the meeting. He does this when he is feeling angry and his upper lip pulls back taut across his teeth. At the same time his behavior becomes muddled: he starts to answer his own questions and run different kinds of questions and comments into each other without a gap. He looks down and to the right when he feels this way. He interrupts others and he will not be interrupted.

Behavior can also be reflected in the personal development plans you set yourself. For example, committing to:

* Write down your priorities at the start of every day.
* Read about a new aspect of technology every week.
* Smile at everyone you meet today.
* Stop, pause and ask a clean question before replying to questions.
* Learn a new skill by practicing it every day.

* Ensure that you listen by summarizing each meeting you attend.
* Agree and write up on the flipchart outcomes for each meeting you hold.
* Check that all emails you send have the effect you want.

The characteristic behavior of a company defines its culture. For example:

* The sales support team handles customer queries efficiently and promptly.
* Staff keep you waiting and blame others in the company for any mistakes.
* Employees in the company take initiatives and make decisions on the spot.

Behavior can also be represented in the style of development plans, for example to aim to:

* Respond to phone calls within three rings.
* Build quality into everything you do.
* Empower people to make their own decisions.
* Update web pages every day so that they are always current.

It is as important to know how to be specific with behavioral plans as it is to know when and how to "chunk up" to the higher levels for strategic thinking. What is most important is to know the difference between the levels.

ENVIRONMENT

Finally, our environment defines the contexts in which we demonstrate all of the above elements. Environment refers to everything "outside" ourselves: the place we work, the economy, people around us, our business, our friends and family, our customers, it even includes what we wear. What we think about as being in the environment is also a measure of how much we take responsibility for what happens to us.

For example:

◆ If we say "It's a tough world out there," this suggests that we put some of the power and influence outside ourselves.
◆ Equally, talking about "they" ("They won't let me" or "They don't tell me") gives the same impression.

"All travel is, after all, a journey in time and in mind. Like many people I believe that physical landscapes are a mirror of, or perhaps a key into, our inner landscape, It wasn't simply chance or good luck that brought us to Chile. The silent messages from the images on the hillside and those unearthed from the desert had assured me of that."

Brian Keenan, Between Extremes

THE INFLUENCE OF THE LEVELS

There is a natural hierarchy of change

There is a natural hierarchy in the processes of learning, change and communication. The rules for changing something on one level are different to those for changing on a lower level. Changing something on a lower level could, but would not necessarily, affect the higher levels. However, changing something on the higher levels would always change things on the lower levels.

For example, if I want to influence my own or someone else's behavior, I would need to make an intervention at least at the level of capability. So if someone says that they can't do something (at the level of behavior), and I respond at the level of behavior by saying something like "Do it this way," I may have fixed the issue but that is all; no learning or cure will have taken place. To effect lasting change I would need to intervene at a higher level, which might be to show the person how to do what it is they can't do (at the level of capability) or challenge their beliefs about their capabilities.

Businesses often make the mistake of attempting to resolve an issue by taking action to deal directly with a deficit, for example the loss of a customer prompts cost-cutting exercises, shortage of business triggers skills training, and so on. We need to learn to shift levels so that we intervene at a different and higher level than the one at which the issue presents itself.

"We won't solve the problems in the world with the thinking that generated the problems in the first place."

Albert Einstein

SUSTAINABLE CHANGE

Our thinking about ourselves at the higher levels will determine our thinking and behavior at the lower levels, whereas our behavior may or may not influence our beliefs at the higher level. As in the examples of behavior earlier in the chapter, companies that only pay attention to behavior when trying to introduce a new culture of quality, for example, typically find that the change isn't sustainable unless they also address the higher levels of beliefs and values. In order to bring about change, it is necessary to work at least one level above the one you want to influence.

The government in the UK has recently invested millions of pounds in the banking system. It is already apparent that money alone does not make a difference. What matters is that we learn to change and *do* change at all the other levels too. We are in the process of experiencing a complete identity change in the world of finance and possibly in the world as a whole.

We are experiencing a complete identity change in the world

If you have someone in your organization who does not manage their time effectively to enable them to do their job well, sending them on a course to learn how to use an organizer may not be the answer. One manager realized that for one of his team the issue was not just a behavioral one; the person did not value or believe in the use of time in the same way as the manager.

Characteristically, NLP training works at the higher levels. Many change models are to do with beliefs and identity. Although NLP does include teaching of techniques, the emphasis is on using capabilities such as sensitivity and flexibility to make these techniques work. Much NLP work can be done without knowing the content of the problem or the issue at hand. This distinguishes it from many other forms of training. NLP training operates on the philosophy that:

People have within them all the resources they need to achieve what they want.

With NLP we learn how to learn and how to think in ways that tap into our unique personal excellence. We can learn how to create a personal formula to manage our work and our life.

The shift in the teaching of mathematics is to teach mathematical thinking rather than techniques. And so it is for me with NLP – it is not the techniques that matter but the thinking that generates those techniques in the first place.

REACTIVE OR PROACTIVE?

Imagine yourself in the following situation.

You have been working on a new project for your company for the last six months. It is now nearing completion and all the results have been achieved to plan. You believe that the results of this project are an important contribution to the future of the company. You are pleased with the contribution you personally have made and expect that the launch of this project will boost your promotion prospects.

Two weeks before the launch, the directors announce a major company reorganization. All projects started within the last year are to be put on hold, awaiting any further decision by the board. You and the rest of the project team feel very disappointed and disheartened.

Which of the following would you be more likely to do?

+ Accept the situation and feel upset.
+ Get annoyed.
+ Complain to others about the way you have been treated.
+ Hope that someone else takes action to change the decision.
+ Ask for a meeting with your manager to discuss the decision.
+ Accelerate the completion of the project so that you can announce its readiness for launch.
+ Leave the company.
+ Wait to see what happens.

What else might you do? Are you reactive or proactive in the way you respond to events in your life? Puppet master or puppet? What is it that distinguishes those who influence their own destiny from those who leave their fate in the hands of others or to chance?

Puppet master or puppet?

Steve's conversations centered around what he and others did. For example, he would measure the strength of people's friendships toward him in terms of what they would do for him. Equally, he expected them to judge the level of his friendship by the type of actions he undertook on their behalf. He was self-employed and considered himself lucky each time a new large contract "turned up." He was never entirely sure what the source of the next contract would be, however. He was influenced a great deal by the climate. When the weather was sunny and warm he generally felt more optimistic, whereas when it was cold and cloudy he often felt depressed.

Linda is quietly self-assured. She is very skilled at listening to other people and reflects before she answers or acts on what they say. Her posture is very upright, balanced and symmetrical. She knows what is important to her and has strong beliefs, but does not impose these on anyone. In fact, she has a very nondirective style of being with other people. She is flexible in her behavior, so if what she is doing is not working she tries something else until she finds a way that is effective. If things go wrong, she takes stock of the situation and decides what she really wants to do. She gives the impression of being at peace with herself most of the time and she is an attractive person to be with. People enjoy listening to her speak.

If your attention is directed mainly to the lower levels of change, you will be thinking about how you and others behave in the environment. You will be affected by changes in other people's behavior and changes in the environment. If the weather is sunny it may cheer you up, if it is dull and wet you feel down. This tends to lead to a more reactive way of dealing with life. A company that concentrates on the lower, behavioral and environmental levels will be more likely to respond to "the competition," rather than moving toward its own vision of the future.

Carla has a very clear sense of identity and mission. She knows what she wants to achieve and what is important to her. She believes that people can be trusted and that if anyone behaves aggressively toward her, it is not meant toward her personally but is more a statement of what they are feeling inside. She believes that she can learn from whatever happens. She treats times of recession as an opportunity to learn how to approach work and customers differently.

Proactive behavior requires you to focus on the higher levels of spirituality, mission and identity, beliefs and values. This is characteristic of those who operate independently of others (not without regard for them, but making decisions in line with what they believe to be important).

"You carry your own weather around with you."
    Stephen Covey, Seven Habits of Highly Effective People

Consider these examples:

- "Overall I think I've been very lucky, both in my career and in my personal life. I've always been employed and now self-employed; amazingly, work always seems to turn up. My personal life has been less smooth and though I have many regrets, especially with regard to my children, I have experienced much happiness. I enjoy being and feeling fit, and I enjoy my work, demonstrating skills that I have and spending time with my kids."
- "I know what I want and how and when I am going to get it. I have decided to become a physiotherapist. I have researched into this and had some experience in it. This work is right for me and I'm right for it. I'm a happy person who loves helping people. I get along with anyone and everyone, a feature of myself of which I am proud."

- "I find it very hard to talk about myself, maybe because I am quite a shy and inward person. I don't really like to let people know how I am feeling. I also know that I am a very negative person. I lack confidence in myself, so therefore I never believe in what I do. I would like to be more positive in my attitude toward life and I wish I had the ability not to worry and to be more relaxed."

Consider what you know now about the levels at which these people are thinking about themselves and how their thinking is likely to be influencing their behavior and the results they achieve.

How do you think about yourself?

The level at which you think about yourself affects how you are

WHEN WE GO OUT OF ALIGNMENT

I don't know anyone who has a coherent state of alignment at all times. What matters more is that the incidence of this state of coherence is increasing for you and that you know what to do to regain it if and when you lose it.

You may recognize you are out of alignment when your circumstances affect you adversely, when you are preoccupied with a negative internal dialogue, when your focus is on problems, or when you feel stressed, tired or upset.

Are you experiencing any of the following right now?

- A family disappointment or upset.
- An unexpected downturn in finances.
- A shake-up in the economy.
- An unexpected change in your work circumstances.
- An uncooperative colleague or friend.
- A change in health.
- Gloomy predictions for your business, your country, the world.
- A surprise in the market sector in which you operate.
- A personal conflict.
- An unsatisfactory outcome in your work.
- A home move.
- A major work challenge.
- A relationship problem.

The more familiar you are with what is important to you, the more able you are to hold on to a state of alignment

It is possible that you have one or several of these issues. It is when these kinds of problems occur that your alignment is most challenged. Often the combination of such difficulties can trigger an unproductive pattern of thinking and behavior. At these times it is of most value to be able to hold on to a state of alignment. It is when you are tested that your true values and principles come through. The question is whether they are the ones that you want to come through.

The more familiar you become with what you want to be important for you at each of the levels and the more you remind yourself of this, the more likely you are to be able to regain your alignment (and maybe hold on to it) in times of challenge and stress.

STEPS TO PERSONAL CONGRUENCE

First become aware of your thinking, and then decide what you want for yourself at each level.

Here are some questions to help you to do this.

- **What is the system of which you are a part or would like to influence?** What contribution do you make to the bigger systems of which you are a part? What contribution do you want to make? (Other ways of thinking about this question would be to ask: What legacy do you want to leave? What added value would you like to give? What is your purpose in life?)
- **What is your identity/mission?** How do you describe yourself? When you say "I am..."what do you follow this with? What roles do you fulfill in life? How do you describe yourself?
- **What are your beliefs and values?** Be honest with yourself. Write down the beliefs and values that you actually operate to, rather than the "good," textbook words. Think about the decisions you make on a day-by-day basis. What are the factors on which you make those decisions? What beliefs do you hold about yourself, other people, your family, your job, your life? Ask other people who know you what they believe you stand for. What do you *want* to stand for?

- **What are your capabilities?** What are your natural talents? These are demonstrated not only by what you do in your work but by what you do outside work. You may not be the best judge of your capabilities. Elicit other people's views on what they might be. What unique set of skills would you like to be able to realize from within yourself?
- **What do you do?** What is your everyday behavior? It is often others who can give this feedback most accurately. Do a self-perception and contrast it with others' perception of how you behave. Identify the behaviors that are characteristic of you, the things you say and do. What is characteristic of you when you are at one with yourself and when you are not? What would you like to be characteristic of you at all times?
- **What is your environment?** Where and when do you do the things identified above? What would you say are the external influences on you and your life? What does your appearance say about you, today? Every day? How is your physical environment a metaphor for who you are? In what contexts would you like to be able to make a difference?

The mere process of becoming aware of what these things are for you will give you more choice about whether you hold on to them or not. Awareness leads to choice.

The person who wrote the third description on page 203, describing himself as a shy and inward person, has subsequently experienced significant shifts in his self-perception. He felt that the process of writing out the paragraph highlighted some of the patterns in his thinking about himself that he didn't like and wanted to change. He has developed confidence in himself, has been appointed to a position of responsibility, and is generally much happier with life and himself. The way forward may not always be as straightforward as that, but it is surprising how often it can be much simpler than we let ourselves believe.

Life is often simpler than we make it

SHORTCUT TO PERSONAL ALIGNMENT

1 Choose something that you know to be true of you when you are aligned and that you can imagine easily. It might be a behavior, a value, a belief, or something that makes you

feel good when you wear it. It helps if you have anchored this aligned state previously, but this is also a way of doing that.

2 Imagine that the levels are stretched out in front of you. In effect, imagine that you can see the diagram on page 189 set out before you. You can do this sitting down or you might find it easier to walk through the levels as if they were marked out on the floor.

3 Start at the level that you can imagine most easily and begin to walk up the levels, allowing yourself to imagine how you are and how you want to be when you are at one with yourself.

Awareness leads to choice

Take whatever time you need to do this and allow whatever comes to mind to do so. This is not something you can do absolutely consciously or intellectually. Allow your unconscious mind to guide you. Awareness leads to choice.

You may find that the higher you go in the levels, the more abstract your thinking becomes. You may be thinking in metaphors.

4 Once you have reached the level of spirituality, turn around and look back down the levels with this sense of overall purpose. Now walk back down, bringing the sense of purpose with you and explore each of the levels again, reminding yourself all the time of how you want to be.

SUMMARY

Knowing our own or others' thinking at each of the levels described here enables us to get an in-depth awareness of how we are doing what we are doing. So when we are excellent, we can use this model to unpack what is going on. Equally, when we are not doing as well as we would wish, we can compare the two and find out what the difference is. In this way, by adopting the thinking we have when we are at our best, we can increase the consistency with which we achieve this.

We can use the levels to study others too. So if we want to know how someone is achieving the results they do, either because we are coaching them to develop or because we are modeling someone we admire, then the levels give us a framework with which to do this.

Think of sport as a metaphor for business. What creates outstanding performance in cycling or tennis or any other sport is what creates personal and business success.

There are many NLP techniques designed to bring about change at each level and some of these changes may be best brought about with the help of an external facilitator. However, by becoming aware of your thinking and beliefs at each of these levels and by beginning to question and challenge those you want to change, you will begin to achieve the state of balance that you want for yourself.

THOUGHT PROVOKERS

1   Consider the following aspects of your life. How close are you in each of these areas to the way you want to be? In the column headed "Ideal" give each a mark out of 10, where 10 signifies this is exactly as you want it to be and 0 indicates it is not at all as you would want it. In the column headed "Reactive/proactive," rate yourself in terms of how actively you are influencing each area. 10 indicates you are, in your view, entirely proactive in the way you are influencing this area to bring it up to the ideal. 0 indicates you are waiting and hoping (or you've just given up).

Ideal   **Reactive/Proactive**
Your job
Your social life
Your friends
Your skills

You will be building up a picture of where you lie on the reactive–proactive scale. Even if you have what you consider to be an ideal situation, or close to it, you may find you actively influence that situation to keep it that way.

It can be useful to get other people's feedback on how they perceive you on this scale. It is easy sometimes to delude yourself, for example into thinking that being busy is the same as being proactive, when in fact what you are doing is having little influence.

2   Take a few moments and imagine you are applying for the work you really want to do. Write a paragraph about yourself which, in your view, describes what makes you uniquely you.

3   Ask a colleague or friend if they will answer the following questions in the order given.

   a   What is characteristic behavior for you? (Behavior)
   b   What does your environment say about you? (Environment)
   c   What unique skills do you demonstrate and might demonstrate? (Capabilities)
   d   What is important to you about what you do and what values do you communicate to others by doing what you do? (Values)
   e   What do you believe is true about you and those around you that enables you to do what you do? (Beliefs)
   f   Who are you? (Identity)
   g   What value do you add to others by just being you? (Spirituality)

What was it like to answer these questions? The ease with which your partner answered the questions can be an indication of how familiar they are with that level of thinking about themselves.

REFERENCES

James Collins & Jerry Porras (2000) *Built to Last: Successful Habits of Visionary Companies*, Random House.

Stephen R. Covey (1999) *Seven Habits of Highly Effective People*, Simon & Schuster.

Paul Z. Jackson & Mark McKergow (2008) *The Solutions Focus: Making Coaching and Change SIMPLE*, Nicholas Brealey Publishing.

Brian Keenan & John McCarthy (2000) *Between Extremes*, Black Swan.

Michael Lissack & Johan Roos (2000) *The Next Common Sense: An E-Manager's Guide to Mastering Complexity*, Nicholas Brealey Publishing.

Peter Senge, Richard Ross, Brian Smith, Charlotte Roberts & Art Kleiner (1994) *The Fifth Discipline Fieldbook: Strategies and Tools for Building a Learning Organization*, Nicholas Brealey Publishing.

Gilbert Kaplan was an American millionaire publisher. He had achieved all the key business goals he had ever set himself. He was also a Gustav Mahler enthusiast. His obsession began in 1965, when as a young Wall Street economist he heard Stokowski conduct the Second Symphony. From then on he attended every live performance possible of that symphony, avidly studied every recording, and eventually at the age of 40 conceived the wild idea of conducting the work himself. The experts sniffed. Kaplan's only musical training lay in childhood piano lessons.

When he eventually gave his first public performance, people attended out of curiosity and disbelief. They had heard of his obsession but knew what sort of training it took to develop the ability to conduct, in particular to conduct the music of Mahler. As the performance began, Kaplan realized that he could not synchronize his conducting with the sound of the orchestra. He was unfamiliar with the acoustics of the hall. The audience were not surprised; after all, it was to be expected. The performance was a failure.

Kaplan, however, was undeterred. He believed in his ability eventually to conduct Mahler. He continued to study and was particularly obsessed with Mahler's Resurrection Symphony. *He memorized this complex score and traveled to hear the work whenever it was performed. He decided he was ready to give a performance in 1982 and did so with the American Symphony Orchestra. His revealing interpretation confounded the critics and won him worldwide requests to repeat the performance.*

Kaplan now devotes his spare time to Mahler research, financing in 1986 a finely documented and superbly produced facsimile of the Resurrection Symphony, *whose original score he now owns. He has conducted this piece over 50 times.*

14
Write your own lifescript: Beliefs of excellence

Since we are destined to live out our lives in the prison of our mind, our duty is to furnish it well.
—Peter Ustinov

O ur beliefs influence and shape our behavior. They form our life script, in the sense that whatever we believe dictates how we respond to the situations and people we meet in our life. If I believe that I will always find a way to succeed no matter what I do, I am more likely to do just that than someone who believes they can never have what they really want.

Most of our beliefs are formed by the age of seven and are shaped by our parents or the equivalent of parent figures. In most cases we don't realize what our beliefs consist of and yet they influence every moment of every day. Every belief has a structure to it, which we can influence if we choose. It is a little like carrying round a recording in our head. If the recording is working for us we can keep it, maybe updating it to refine it from time to time. If, however, the recording is limiting what we think about ourselves, we can take it out and re-record it so we have one that does work for us. It is a basis of NLP that if we understand the structure of what we hold in our thinking, we can change it if we choose.

If we want to model excellent performance, we need to be able to "step into" the beliefs of the person we are modeling in order to influence the way we behave. Equally, to tap into our most resourceful state for a specific context, we need to be able to "step into" the belief that supports us in this (to model ourselves). For example, if I want the confidence to talk with ease at a conference, it helps me to model those times when I fully believe

Our beliefs influence every moment of every day

that I do have something of value to share with the conference delegates. In reminding myself of this belief, I tap into a resource that I already have but may temporarily have shelved.

Beliefs can be expressed as statements. These are not factual statements, but are emotionally held opinions that we have reinforced over time. So what are the beliefs that are so vital today? We have available the result of years of study of people who exhibit excellence in the way they are. We can shortcut the road to excellence for ourselves by assuming and trying on for size any or all of these beliefs.

They are as follows:

- **Everyone has a unique perception of the world**. It will be different to our own. It is not right or wrong. To accept this belief is to accept and understand people as they are.
- **Everyone makes the best choice available to them at the time they make it**. By believing this we can learn how to understand, coach high performance, and forgive.
- **There is no failure, only feedback**. We can take in and learn from changing situations. Consequently, we need to be able to learn continuously and this belief is central to our ability to do this.
- **Behind every behavior is a positive intention**. This belief is fundamental in our being able to take whatever happens to us, no matter how detrimental it might be initially, and turn it into personal learning and growth.
- **The meaning of the communication is its effect**. We may not be able to control our environment, but what we can do is be aware of the effect we have on it. In holding this belief we take full responsibility for the effect of our actions.
- **There is a solution to every problem**. This belief is characteristically held by people who find new ways of working through or round obstacles and challenges. It is the source of creativity and characteristic of leaders.
- **We have within us all the resources we will ever need**. By believing this we can learn how to tap into every resource (skill, attitude, belief) that we will ever need to achieve what we want.
- **The person with the most flexibility in thinking and behavior has the greatest influence**. If what we are doing isn't working, then the more choices we have, the more likely we are to find a way that does work.

- **Mind and body are part of the same system**. Our mind and body are totally interconnected. What affects one affects the other.
- **If one person can do it, anyone can do it**. If one person can do something it is possible to model it and teach it to others. In this way everyone can achieve excellence in their own way.
- **What we recognize in others is true about ourselves**. To recognize a quality in someone else, we have to be able to represent it in ourselves. If we can represent it we have the capability of reproducing it. If you can spot it you've got it.
- **Knowledge, thought, memory and imagination are the result of sequences and combinations of ways of filtering and storing information**. If we learn what those sequences and combinations are (the programs), we can influence what is and isn't working for us and do something about it.
- **The way to understand is to do**. We learn by doing and being open to feedback. This belief underpins the style of most NLP training (or should do!). We learn NLP not by theoretical study, but by experiencing it.

If you can spot it, you've got it

These beliefs form an ethical set of principles for life. However, they are not just "nice to have," they support the best of who we are. Take any influential leader. Take any successful independent. Take any top sportsperson. Take anyone who successfully facilitates the development of others – and behind their actions you will find beliefs like these. Take anyone who is thriving and making the best of their life, no matter what the circumstances. Equally, take anyone who has managed themselves through turbulent physical and emotional times and you will also discover that their actions are based on such beliefs.

These beliefs form an ethical set of principles for life

These beliefs are central to NLP. They are often referred to as presuppositions, as you do not have to believe them. They are not claimed to be true or universal and they are certainly not fact. They are called presuppositions because you presuppose them to be true and then act accordingly and discover what happens as a result of that. In my experience, anyone who does that ends up doing more than merely holding them as assumptions, they come to believe them – because they work.

These are beliefs, not facts

HOW BELIEFS ORIGINATE

Jane struggled to make her opinion known in meetings. Unless she was asked she kept her views to herself; even when asked she would rarely elaborate on what she thought. She found this increasingly frustrating and left meetings exasperated, overwhelmed by her feeling of inadequacy and a determination to say what she thought the next time. But nothing changed. She just could not overcome the feeling that she could not say what she really thought.

Finally, she asked for help, and her coach helped her to trace the source of this experience. She remembered that when she was young and in the presence of her mother, her mother would always speak on her behalf. So if someone asked her a question, her mother would jump in with the answer, even when the mother didn't know the details, only Jane did. What Jane realized was that over time, although her mother was well meaning, she had come to believe that she could not speak for herself. This belief was still unconsciously haunting her as an adult and a very capable manager.

This is an example of how beliefs are formed. We experience situations and accept opinions from influential people in our lives and hold them as facts. Jane's mother wasn't literally saying that Jane could not speak for herself, but that was how Jane was (not surprisingly as a young girl) interpreting her actions. So beliefs aren't facts at all. They are perceptions formed through our own experience and the views of others.

We experience others' behavior and opinions and believe them to be true

Beliefs are emotionally held opinions that we assume to be fact. For example:

+ "I wants" don't get.
+ You can achieve whatever you want in this world.
+ People close to you will abandon you.
+ You always get what you want and you always will.
+ You'll always land on your feet whatever happens.
+ You're lazy.
+ You have to work hard in this life to get what you want.
+ You're a grade A student.
+ You're stupid.
+ People can't be trusted.
+ Children should be seen and not heard.

- Feelings don't count.
- You're a liar.
- You're the "good" child in the family.
- You're a born artist.
- You're a lousy mathematician.
- People will always look after you.

We can create our own set of principles

The nature of NLP is that we can change our beliefs so that we create our own set of principles to support the way we want to be. We need not carry around redundant or even destructive belief systems belonging to someone else. We can create our own empowering set of beliefs instead.

How many of us carry around baggage that really belongs to someone else? Because our beliefs are principles that we hold entirely within ourselves, they are completely under our influence. We do not have to be limited by patterns of the past; we can write our own lifescript.

There are several ways to do this. One way is to presuppose that we do hold beliefs that, although new to us, are more in line with the way we want to be. Alternatively, NLP gives us the techniques to rewrite our own history. Because our unconscious mind does not know the difference between what is real and what is imagined, we can imagine the past we would prefer to have had and rewrite our memories. This comes from the belief that knowledge, thought and memory are the result of sequences and combinations of ways of filtering and storing information. By knowing what sequences and combinations of thought patterns we are using, we change how we represent the memories we hold. We can influence our memories to support us in the way we would like to be now, as opposed to the way we happen to be. This is a mental agility that can be learnt.

HOW BELIEFS WORK

Top sportspeople believe that they have the potential to win every match they play. This belief works for them in this way:

The less consistently successful players are more likely to think as follows:

Beliefs are self-fulfilling
prophecies

Our beliefs act as a self-fulfilling prophecy. We act in a way that proves the validity and value of our beliefs to ourselves. If our beliefs are self-limiting we limit our performance, thus proving the belief to be "true." Over time, the beliefs become more and more entrenched as we continue to live them out each day.

However, if we hold empowering beliefs such as the beliefs of excellence outlined below, we act and behave in a way that releases our potential and allows us to be the best we can be.

THE BELIEFS OF EXCELLENCE

Have you ever wondered how some people achieve success? For example:

◆ How Christopher Columbus held on to his vision of discovering a new route around the world and maintained the courage and tenacity to cross waters that no one had sailed before?
◆ How the Americans managed to break through the limits of what seemed possible to land a man on the moon?
◆ How British hostage in the Lebanon Brian Keenan retained his sanity and self-worth when held in solitary confinement bound, blindfolded and threatened with death?
◆ How previously unheard of entrepreneurial companies such as Google and Amazon became household names overnight in markets that hadn't existed a year before?

Many people would have given up after a fraction of the journey. What made these and so many more achievements possible? These people succeeded because they believed they could. Once Roger Bannister had run a mile in under four minutes, within months many other athletes did the same. Once he had broken the barrier, he created a belief in others that it was possible.

Let's consider what each of the beliefs of excellence means.

EACH PERSON IS UNIQUE

This belief is sometimes referred to as "the map is not the territory." We do not know what reality is. Our senses, beliefs, and experience contribute to a map of the world that we use to find our way through life. A map can never be perfect – it would otherwise be the same as the territory that it represents. So the map is not the territory; it is a representation. Some maps work better than others for some people. The question is, how does your map of the world work for you?

Consider this conversation:

"I really enjoyed the film last night."
"It was rubbish."
"No it wasn't, the photography was beautiful."
"Yes, but the story line was nonexistent."
"That's ridiculous."
"No it isn't!"

Recognize that? Neither person in this conversation is right or wrong, although they may not appreciate this. However, each has their own way of experiencing life, their own "map of the world."

How often does your map of the world bump up against the map of someone else? And what happens when it does?

Once you accept that everyone has a unique map of the world, you begin to understand and accept difference.

> We can learn to understand and accept difference

"When I think about other cultures I think about what they represent in terms of human possibilities: a whole set of ways to see and hear and feel about the world that could potentially resonate with my neurology, a place where news of difference is waiting to be discovered."
> Judith De Lozier, Turtles All the Way Down

Imagine a world where this understanding and acceptance existed – how different our daily lives would be. How would the press survive? What stories would they print? Can you imagine how different the headlines would be?

How often are you party to the following kinds of situations?

Jim was explaining how he saw his future and the sort of obstacles he wanted to overcome.

Jane listened to him for a while and then said, "You know, Jim, what you really ought to do is to leave this job and move into sales, you'd be much more suited to that."

"But that isn't really what I want to do, Jane."

"You may not think it is," replied Jane, "but believe me, I know it's the right move for you."

Jim sat back and folded his arms. He disagreed.

Diane could not understand why staff were complaining about the new appraisal scheme. She was a member of the human resource development team who were instrumental in its design. The design involved managers rating their team members on a scale of 1 to 5, 1 being "subject to disciplinary action" and 5 meaning, more or less, "the sun shines out of every orifice." The staff were very unhappy about the form, particularly the rating system. Diane found all these complaints very frustrating and considered the staff to be "difficult."

Both of these illustrate what can happen when someone doesn't presuppose "each person is unique" to be true and consequently doesn't value others' "maps of the world." This means we all have our unique perception of the world, the way things are, the way people behave, our own experience. And that perception is only a view of those things, an interpretation. It's not an exact representation of reality. Just like a map is only a representation of a territory, highlighting some features and ignoring others, so your personal experience leads you to highlight some features and ignore others.

Accepting this presupposition means that you respect difference.

"Difference is the difference that makes the difference."

Gregory Bateson

The table opposite compares what it would be like to hold the belief that each person is unique with what it would be like not to do so.

EVERYONE MAKES THEIR BEST CHOICE

When your colleague argues with you and refuses to see your point of view, at that moment it is the best choice available to them. And the way you react to them is your best choice at that time.

	People who do believe that "each person is unique" is true	People who don't believe that "each person is unique" is true
Have this sort of approach	Cooperative, respectful, and open to difference and feedback	Rigid, inflexible and dogmatic
Hold these sorts of beliefs	Difference is valuable	Their own opinion is right. They know best
Have these capabilities/limitations	Listening skills, sensitivity to and respect for difference	Determination and singlemindedness
Do and say	Look interested, cooperate, ask questions, are curious about others' experiences and explore differences. Ask for clarification when they get feedback of which they were previously unaware and had not seen in themselves.	Speak in terms of what others "should" or "ought" to do. Disagree and interrupt. Dismiss. Do what they have always done. Defend themselves and rationalize away feedback.
Feel	Relaxed and curious	Frustrated, irritated and stressed
Experience	Find new talent, cut new ground	Stagnate

If you had learnt the most elegant and cooperative ways of achieving what you want, life would be very different. But you didn't. You learnt healthy and unhealthy ways of getting what you want. When a child cries and shouts in the middle of the supermarket, that child has learnt that is the way to get the attention they want; not the best way for those around, but the best choice for the child. You do what you do because at some level it works. If what you are doing didn't work, you wouldn't do it.

If you run away from potentially painful situations, that is what you have learnt to be the best choice. This does not mean it is the "best" choice overall, but it is the best you can come up with given your experience to date and your emotions and state at the time of making the decision. It is a measure of your flexibility.

However, one thing is for sure:

The best is a measure of your flexibility

If you do what you always did you will get what you always got.

Think for a moment about anyone you have felt frustrated with within the last month. For example:

- The colleague who gave a boring presentation.
- The person who dominated a meeting.
- A member of your family who made an insensitive comment to you.
- The support person who was abrupt with you.
- The car driver who cut in front of you.
- The salesperson who wouldn't answer your questions.
- The receptionist who kept you waiting.
- The person who took their time in the queue in front of you.

Now step into the belief that "everyone makes the best choice available to them at the time." Imagine what it would be like if you were to believe that. As you imagine what it is like, how does that affect your feelings toward the people you have listed? Would that colleague really have chosen to give a boring presentation if he had a choice? Would the colleague have dominated the meeting if she had other choices about how to influence you?

This may not be your belief, but you can experience the results of holding it by presupposing that it is true for you. If you don't hold this to be true, you might respond to the deliverer of the boring presentation with disdain. By presupposing that this is their best choice, you will be more likely to give them constructive feedback and suggestions for other ways they could present their ideas. It doesn't mean that you have to accept what they are doing in the way they are doing it. It does mean that you are more likely to be in a state where you can influence it.

Beliefs of excellence give us resourceful ways to respond to less than ideal scenarios

The beliefs of excellence give us more resourceful ways of responding to less than ideal situations in ways that are most likely to lead to a win/win outcome. The focus shifts from blame, disdain and frustration to curiosity, understanding and concern, particularly in terms of how to enable ourselves and others around us to have more choice, so that the best choice for one or a few becomes the best choice for many.

How many people do you know who live their life with regrets? Do you? Knowing what you know now, there may very well be decisions you would change, places you would have gone, people you would have treated differently. But this is you now, with different skills, different knowledge, different experience. At that time the choices you made were the best available to you. Once you can accept this, you can let go of regrets; they clutter the places reserved for other more self-fulfilling choices.

THERE IS NO FAILURE, ONLY FEEDBACK

Christopher Columbus, John F Kennedy, Brian Keenan, Roger Bannister are all people who persevered to get what they wanted against all odds, people who held the belief that "There is no failure, only feedback." I'm sure if we interviewed Christopher Columbus today he would not say, "Actually, I put it all down to this belief, 'No failure, only feedback'"! However, for him to do what he did, this must have been what he believed in order to find the courage and tenacity to carry on with his exploration.

Experience and acceptance of failure = defeat and resignation
Experience and review of feedback = learning and choice

Imagine that you hold this belief to be true. How would it influence how you respond to:

* Your acceptance of feedback from others?
* Your confidence in giving feedback?
* Your self-esteem when presenting ideas?
* Your willingness to take risks?

Try it on for size: What would it really be like for you? Imagine the learning potential this can unleash. This is a very powerful belief in the context of self-development. When we truly hold this belief, we can learn from everything that happens to us.

This belief is taking a new and even greater importance day by day. We live in a world where feedback is ever more available, in real time. The people and companies that are able to take advantage of this are the ones who do believe that there is only learning; there is no failure, only feedback, in many more forms than we have ever before experienced.

BEHIND EVERY BEHAVIOR IS A POSITIVE INTENTION

This belief can be mind-blowing. It means that we choose to believe that behind every action there is a positive intention toward us. The key thing to remember here is that it doesn't have to *be* true. The benefits come from *believing* that it is true.

I can choose to believe that if someone behaves aggressively toward me, the positive intention behind their behavior is for me to learn a greater independence of state. The person being aggressive does not consciously have this purpose for me; I choose to believe that this is behind their behavior.

By believing this I have choice in how I respond. Without this belief I am more likely to become either submissive or even aggressive in response. I might start to lose self-esteem and confidence because of how I am feeling about the way they are with me. People who are able to maintain choices in the way they respond to the behavior of those around them are typically people who hold this belief or something very similar.

Ian and his teenage son had almost come to blows. His son stood in one corner of the kitchen and Ian in the other. They shouted, but neither listened to the other. To Ian his son was being a demanding, inconsiderate teenager. To the son his father had a closed mind, was inflexible and completely out of touch. Ian stopped himself from rushing forward and hitting his son and in that moment he gave himself the time to stand back and think about what he was doing. He moved toward his son, put his arms around him and said, "I'll always love you, no matter what you do."

That moment enabled Ian to express what he really felt. That moment would also imprint itself on his son's mind in such a way that when he had a teenage son of his own he had this memory, this role model of how a father can be.

At that point Ian was not consciously thinking, "What is the positive intention behind my son's behavior toward me?" But at a more unconscious level this principle was in operation. It certainly wasn't in his son's mind to think, "How can I be so disagreeable that I cause my dad to give me a role model of parenting for my future?" Far from it! But by acting as if this were the case, Ian turned what might have been a damaging situation into a special one.

This is the sort of influence you can have. If you choose to believe that there is a positive intention toward you in the following kinds of circumstances, you can transform the way you respond to the situation. For example:

◆ Your boss criticizes you for your incompetence.
◆ You could choose to believe that the positive intention toward you is to provide you with the opportunity to learn how to stay calm and confident when faced with aggression.

◆ A colleague misunderstands what you tell her.
◆ The positive intention is to teach you how to be more flexible in your communication so that you find a way of explaining that she does understand.

◆ Your business takes a nose dive.
◆ The intention is for you to make a new start and learn how to pick yourself up when things go wrong.

These examples may or may not work for you. It is important to generate your own ideas of what the positive intentions might be, ones that make sense of the behavior for you. This is an opportunity to let your creativity generate some ideas. When you find a positive intention that works for you, you will find that the behavior takes on a whole new meaning. More than that, it will free you from giving a compulsive response: It will change your state so that your response is one of choice and not of inappropriate habit.

When you find a positive intention the behavior takes on a new meaning

THE MEANING OF THE COMMUNICATION IS THE EFFECT

The principle operates at many different levels. For example:

◆ Have you ever experienced a moment of frustration when you have carefully explained an idea to someone and they have misunderstood you? Or have you ever given feedback to someone with the intention of helping them to learn and develop, only to find that they felt angry about what you said?
◆ Have you ever heard a teacher say things like, "This particular class are a difficult group to teach, they aren't good listeners.

They've got to learn to pay attention." How does this reflect on where that teacher puts the responsibility for the learning?

+ Have you ever appraised someone working for you in a way that devolved all responsibility for their performance from the way you were managing them? How do you think they felt? Have you ever been in the same position? How did you feel?
+ Has an audience come to you and praised you for moving them with your performance? How is that an expression of how you play?
+ If you have a colleague who won't cooperate with you, how is that is a reflection of your influencing skill?
+ If you have a child who won't "behave," how is that a statement about your ability as a parent?

Of course, the other people in these situations play a part in what happens. And *you* are a part of the system. Something you do is allowing and even encouraging the response you receive. The power in this way of thinking is that you take responsibility for the responses you receive. If you don't get the response you want at first, you can find new ways of communicating until you do. For example, if someone doesn't understand you, you find a way of explaining your thoughts in ways they do understand.

To believe that "the meaning of your communication is its effect" means that:

+ If you have people working for you who give their all to their work, it is an indication of how you manage them.
+ If you explain a new concept to a colleague and they don't understand, it is a measure of lack of flexibility in the way you explain.
+ If you have a warm, loving family around you, it is a reflection of how you are.
+ If you give feedback to a friend and they are offended, it is a result of how you gave the feedback to them.
+ If people choose you as their main supplier, it is a measure of how you have related to them in the way you conduct business.

Someone who holds this belief is less likely to experience customers, staff, managers, friends and family as problems; they are much more likely to experience a "problem" as an opportunity to change themselves. Holding this belief means that you take responsibility for the reactions you get and take them as feedback on how you are doing. By holding this belief you do not consider others to be a source of problems. You seek to develop your own flexibility so that you find new choices that elicit new responses.

THERE IS A SOLUTION TO EVERY PROBLEM

What happens for you when something goes wrong? Do you down tools? Do you sulk or shout? Do you take your frustration out on others? Do you perhaps try to conceal a problem for fear of recrimination or blame? Indeed, do you try to lay blame at someone else's door? Or do you take what has happened as feedback and persevere till you find a way forward?

Imagine what it would be like to believe that you could find a solution to every problem you ever encountered. You would probably spend much less time worrying about how you are going to get on in life. You would have confidence that somewhere, somehow you will find a way to achieve what you want.

That is what it is like to hold this belief. This belief is characteristic of people who find new solutions to old problems. They do because they believe they can. This is the belief at the heart of all creativity. There is a solution to every problem and believing this opens the mind to the possibilities, to innovative solutions. What might frustrate you are people who do not hold this belief; people who give up when they encounter a difficulty. However, if you truly hold this belief then the chances are that you will find a way to influence them as well.

WE HAVE ALL THE RESOURCES WE NEED

We have all the resources we will ever need within ourselves already. The most self-sufficient people recognize that the place to look for resources is within themselves. (And that includes the ability to ask for help.) Most of us have largely untapped reserves of qualities, skills and attitudes that we have never learnt how to use. It is not unusual for people to either be ignorant of or play

A "problem" is an opportunity for change

Somehow you will find a way to achieve what you want

Who are we to play small?

down their talents for fear of seeming arrogant. Nelson Mandela in his famous speech (quoting a poem by Marianne Williamson) said "Who are we to play small?" And yet many of us do.

From the day we are born we are experiencing, learning, experimenting and growing. En route we develop a huge repertoire of talent that works for us uniquely. Even if we only demonstrate a talent for a brief moment in time, we still have it in our memory banks just waiting for when it might be needed again.

When I need confidence to say what I want to say fluently, but instead I doubt my abilities, then I can look within myself for resources. If I believe that I have all the resources within me, I can search until I find a time in my life or a context in which I had the very resource I want now. By asking myself the question "Where do I have this resource (self-confidence, amusement, determination, detachment...)?" I trigger my unconscious to search for the very same thing. So by remembering and associating into a time when we had the resource we want now, we can access it in the present.

My mother had severe osteoporosis and struggled to walk or move without pain. Her back became deformed as a result of the decreasing bone density. One day she was talking about an officer she had met during the war and how whenever she came into a room he would stand to attention. She became totally immersed in this memory and, as she explained how the officer stood to attention, she sprang to her feet and illustrated exactly how he did this. She was smiling and amused by the memory. She was totally unaware of how she moved and how, in that moment, she had somehow forgotten and overcome all her physical disabilities.

I continue to be surprised by the abilities that we have within us all.

THE PERSON WITH THE GREATEST FLEXIBILITY HAS THE GREATEST INFLUENCE

At one stage in my career I worked for the training department of ICL. We ran a range of skills development courses for customers. At that time I was involved in an influencing skills course in which we taught the delegates choice in the way they expressed themselves verbally. We also taught them how to choose the most effective language to achieve the outcomes they wanted, particularly for meetings. We returned some highly verbally skilled people to our client companies.

Then we started to get complaints from the company sales teams. When a company salesperson was in a meeting with a client who had attended the influencing skills course, the company person was consistently being outmaneuvered by the client in the way they managed the meeting. Needless to say, the company changed its training policy. This course immediately became a key part of the training program for its sales teams!

With flexibility in our thinking and behavior, we have choice. If one choice doesn't work we can try another until we find one that does.

When Lance Armstrong won the Tour de France in 2001, part of his success was attributed to his high pedaling speed. Most other cyclists turn the pedals more slowly, often using a higher gear. The effect of this high speed is that the body uses different muscles to the ones used when pedaling more slowly. These different muscles have different capabilities: the former have greater endurance, whereas the latter have greater power.

Lance Armstrong had trained in such a way that he could use both. He could also cycle long distances in or out of the saddle. He could excel on the mountains and yet be unsurpassed in the time trials. What he had was immense flexibility in all domains in cycling: the attribute of a great champion. Ten years on he continues to perform at the highest level for someone of his age.

How does a sports player get flexibility? They train: they exercise the different parts of their body so that they can move freely, so that they can vary their style. Athletes undergo an extensive range of training programs. The most effective exercise is often the simplest but the most frequent.

By regularly practicing the skills and techniques explained in this book, you will develop your range of behavior and thinking and consequently your flexibility. You can achieve world-class status as a communicator as a consequence of the way you train your mind.

We can train our minds as athletes train our bodies

MIND AND BODY ARE ONE

Anything that occurs in one part of the system will affect the other parts.

Stand up to do the following exercise.

- Look ahead, stand feet apart, face forward, raise one arm horizontally out in front of you, and gently twist around, keeping your arm horizontal until it is pointing as far behind you as it will go.
- Keeping your arm fixed in that position, turn round and note the point to which your arm is pointing.
- Now look carefully at the scene behind you and decide how much farther you would like your arm to point.
- Fix that point in your mind as you turn to face forward again.
- As you face forward, twist again, moving your arm behind you as far as it will go. When you have pushed it as far as it will go, hold it steady, turn round, and see how far you have moved your arm this time.

Most people find that they have moved their arm farther the second time, often much farther than they expected. When you imagine yourself throwing a ball, the muscles of the body that would move if you were actually throwing a ball tense and flex in exactly the same way. Those of you with a vivid imagination probably recoil physically when watching something unpleasant on television or at the cinema. You can reproduce the feelings in yourself that are experienced by someone else. Your body becomes an expression of your thinking. Recent research has shown many connections between what we think and the wellbeing of our body.

What are the implications for you of believing that mind and body are part of the same system?

- You are independent, in the sense of believing that you have control and influence over your own experience.
- You believe that you can influence your state and health by the way you think.
- You are capable of generating whatever state you want in yourself: relaxation, excitement, peace, confidence.

- You take care of both your body and your mind and keep them fit.
- You recognize that it is others' body language that communicates with you as much if not more than what they say.
- You create the memories and imaginations that you want to have and you have the ability to do this.

Holding the belief that mind and body are one, you experience that what you do to one you simultaneously do to the other. As memory and imagination have the same neurological circuits, they potentially have the same impact.

Feldenkrais (named after Israeli physicist Moshe Feldenkrais) is a process of awareness through movement. It uses gentle, organized movements to awaken awareness and enhance the way someone moves as a whole person. Moshe Feldenkrais helped people who had lost the use of their limbs to find ways to make new neural connections in their brain, and in so doing to find ways to relearn movement they thought they had lost. He believed totally that mind and body are one – that by developing new choices in one we automatically create new choices in the other.

WHAT WE RECOGNIZE ABOUT OTHERS IS TRUE ABOUT OURSELVES

If you can spot it you've got it. That is the axiom and that is the principle here. If I can recognize a quality in you then I am able to represent it in my mind. If I can represent it, I am capable of it. I may not exhibit the same behavior, but I have that capability.

This belief underpins our sense of connectedness. Without it there is a chance that we might stand in inappropriate awe of someone else, feeling inhibited by their talent. Equally, we might be patronizing toward someone, believing that we would never be "like" them, when the very fact that we can think about them in this way suggests that we are very much "like" them!

KNOWLEDGE, THOUGHT, MEMORY AND IMAGINATION ARE THE RESULT OF SEQUENCES AND COMBINATIONS OF WAYS OF FILTERING AND STORING INFORMATION

This belief is at the heart of all NLP. With NLP we have discovered the details of the way we hold memories and thoughts. We know now that by developing our mastery of the way we represent these thoughts, we can change our experience in the present.

Remember your first day at secondary school. How do you remember this? What came to mind first? Was it an image, a memory of someone's voice, a feeling? What followed? Another image? Sounds? What are the qualities of the memory? Is it bright, dark, loud, gentle? Your memory and the way you hold that memory are unique to you. That unique representation is what gives the memory its quality. Without the representation in your mind it is merely a statement, "First day at secondary school." What makes it live as a memory is the way you think about it.

For me this is an exciting memory, also a slightly scary one. What I have illustrated below is the way I represent that memory and I can, if I choose, change any part of it in the way I think about it. I can turn up the brightness. I can imagine the teacher saying different words. I can change the order of the thoughts.

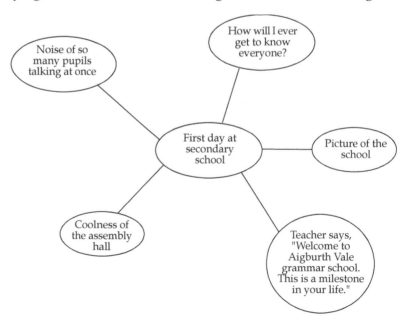

Now imagine tomorrow at work. What does your imagination conjure up for you? Successes? Problems? Satisfaction? Frustrations? Does your imagination create for you a representation of the "tomorrow" that you would like to have? It's all a "con trick" of the mind – so why not "con" yourself positively? You can change these representations so that you have the imagined day that you want to have.

Turn this:

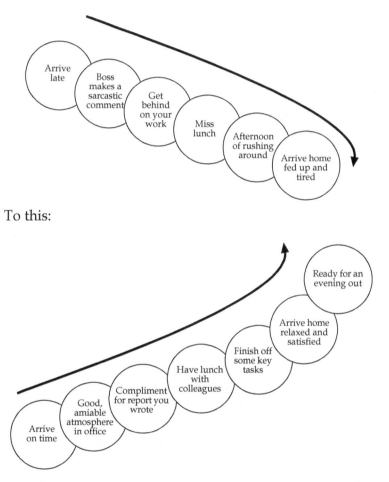

To this:

It may not happen exactly like this, but you have increased the chances that it will and you will feel differently in your anticipation of the day than you would if you thought the first way. Managing your thinking process is at the heart of being able to manage yourself.

THE WAY TO UNDERSTAND IS TO DO

This is the basis of NLP. We learn by doing, getting the feedback and finding out what works. We cannot learn what works through debate without action. The only way you can discover how what I have written in this book works for you is to try it out. Find out for yourself. If you ever find yourself on NLP training that trades in theory and discussion, my advice is to change courses.

BELIEFS IN THE WORKPLACE

A company culture is in part defined by the beliefs that underpin day-to-day work. Sometimes these beliefs are explicit and inform working practices. Sometimes they are implicit, learnt as you go along. You will usually find out in some way if you have violated a company belief even if it has not been made explicit. The clearer they are, the greater the likelihood that anyone working for the organisation will subscribe to them.

We communicate our beliefs in every behavior. For example,

- If part of a company appraisal scheme is to review performance against a manager's ability to discipline (as I experienced in one company), there is a belief that discipline will be necessary in the organization.
- When you see a van or lorry with the inscription "If you have any problems with the way this vehicle is driven please phone...," the belief is that there are drivers who will drive badly (and that it is bad behavior that is given the attention rather than good).
- In a holiday feedback form the question "Tell us any funny incidents that happened to while you were away" is going to communicate a very different belief to "Tell us about anything you didn't like about the accommodation."

Let's consider the beliefs that support some typical company practices.

APPRAISAL

- People have all the resources they need to achieve what they want. Leaders in business who hold this belief are likely to facilitate their staff's development through questioning and coaching rather than by telling them what to do. People are more likely to realize their true talents if this happens.
- People make the best choice available to them at the time that they make it. When someone underperforms there is a greater chance that they will be coached to learn and improve in the future. People are more likely to own up when they make a mistake.
- There is no failure, only feedback. A company in which all the employees hold this belief is a company with a climate of honesty, openness and learning: all keys to performance improvement.
- The meaning of the communication is its effect. For "the communication" you could substitute "the way you are" – the meaning of the way you are is measured by the results you get, the environment you have, the way people respond to you, the way your team performs. A complementary piece of thinking is: "If what you are doing isn't working, do something different."

The beliefs you want as the foundation for your business must be those that are truly held by everyone in that business. One of the most valuable things a top team can do is explore the actual beliefs held by the management team and decide if these are the ones that support their future vision. If they don't, start challenging them and the people who hold them.

As someone in one of the big financial consultancies said when asked what would happen to the people who did not fully share its newly published values and beliefs, "You are either living them, learning them or leaving"!

CUSTOMER SUPPORT

Whose business does not rely on the quality of their customer support? And yet despite that, there is so much room for improvement in many businesses. Unfortunately, many

Does the concept of delighting your customers run through your entire operation?

companies still rely on sending out a feedback questionnaire or teaching their staff to smile at customers and believing that is all it takes!

Does the concept of delighting your customers run through your entire operation or is it only surface deep? A specific set of beliefs that support caring and delighting your customers is:

- The response you get is a measure of the service you provide. Whether you have a surfeit of customer complaints or congratulations or possibly no feedback at all, whatever the scenario, it is a measure of how you are.
- Whatever your customer says and does to you has a benefit to your business (a version of there being an unconscious positive intention behind every behavior). Accepting this suggests you will turn any scenario into learning.
- There is no failure, only feedback. Knowing and acting on all feedback, no matter what form it is in and no matter how it is given, will most probably keep you in touch with your customers and ensure that your business meets and even anticipates their needs.
- Each person is unique. Understanding and relating to that uniqueness is most likely to earn your customers' respect.
- Whatever your customers' circumstances, by believing that there is a solution to every problem you will find new and creative solutions with which to move forward together.

By holding beliefs such as these, you will learn how to deal with your customers appropriately.

NEGOTIATION

The result of years of modeling skilled negotiators, those who are able to resolve conflict and bring situations to a solution that has the commitment of all parties involved, reveals that they are most likely to believe the following:

- There is always a win/win possible and available.
- The outcome is unlikely to be known in advance of any discussion.
- There is learning in every situation.

- We are all ultimately connected and therefore somewhere down the line have a common goal.
- If we are willing to forgive, forget, and learn to let go of the past, we will find a way to move forward.

The beliefs in each of the previous business scenarios are suggestions based on what has worked for others. More important than cherry picking those is to explore the beliefs that you hold for your business right now and identify which ones are the strengtheners for now and the future.

SHORTCUT TO STEPPING INTO A BELIEF

Imagine trying on a new outfit of clothes. You can have them for as long as you want, so that you can discover how they feel, whether they look the way you want them to look, what reactions you get from people around you and whether they fit. If you don't like them you can return them and wear your original clothes, or you might retain one or two items and wear them with some of your existing clothes. Or you can keep all of them and make them a part of your wardrobe.

Beliefs are like this. You can presuppose that they are true; you can "try them on." If they work, then it is likely that they will become a belief. If not, you can put them to one side. To help you do this, use the following shortcut.

You can try beliefs on for size

1 Think of a situation, A, where you would like more choice and where you believe that taking on one of the beliefs of excellence might encourage you to behave in a way that makes the difference you want. Pick the belief of excellence from the ones listed in this chapter that you think would be the most appropriate here.
2 Identify another situation, B, when you did hold this belief or one that was very similar.
3 Associate into this time B and associate into the feeling that you had at this time. Find a way to hold on to this feeling (anchor it).
4 As you hold this belief, re-experience situation A, doing the following as you do so:

- Being aware of where you are and how you are experiencing this environment.
- Knowing what you are saying and doing that demonstrates that you are holding this new belief.
- Realizing what skills and qualities you are bringing to this situation.
- Knowing what is important to you and how you are fulfilling those needs, both for you and for anyone else involved in the situation.
- Appreciating how what you are doing and the way you are feeling fit for you personally.
- Discovering how you are influencing bigger systems of which you are a part, both right now and at other times.

6 Reflect on what your experience has been of holding this belief as you re-experienced the situation.
7 How do you feel about the situation and others like it now and how you might approach them in the future?
8 What is your experience of the belief that you chose and how it can work for you now?
9 Repeat the process for two other situations that you know will occur in the coming week.
10 Decide what you will specifically commit to doing or believing in the future.

If we believe we can't, we won't. If we believe we can, we just might.

The pilot who landed a plane that had an engine failure and saved the lives of the majority of his passengers in doing so said, "It was belief that kept the plane in the air. I believed against all the odds that I could get the plane safely on the ground."

SUMMARY

You can spend your life being busy. But if deep down you don't believe you will succeed, then no amount of work is going to make a difference. If, however, you believe you can succeed no matter what the situation, then you are likely to act in a way that will lead to success. And you will find the behavior you need at the time you need it.

Operating on the basis of belief is a very different way of going about work and life than operating on the basis of do... do... do... People who have achieved excellence have beliefs that support that excellence. Finding and accessing those beliefs is the shortcut to excellence for us all.

THOUGHT PROVOKERS

1   Identify someone to whom you do not relate as well as you would like:
    * In your family.
    * In your work.
    * In your social circle.
    For each, list what you believe about them. Think of an occasion when you communicated with them and it was not the way you would really like it to have been.

    Now think of someone in each of these groups with whom you have a good/excellent relationship. Identify one of the beliefs you hold about them. Imagine holding the belief that you have about the family member with whom you have a good relationship for the family member with whom you would like to improve your relationship. Imagine having an interaction operating from that belief. What are you seeing, hearing and feeling? How are they responding to you? If they are not yet responding in the way you would like, re-experience the belief of excellence until you have it more firmly or strongly in your mind.

    Repeat the process. Now repeat the whole process for the person in your work and then the person in your social circle.

2   Think of a goal that you want for yourself but have not yet achieved and you are not sure why not. What beliefs do you hold about:
    * Your ability to achieve this goal?
    * Your right to achieve this goal?
    What beliefs might be limiting you in the achievement of this goal? What beliefs might you hold instead of the limiting ones?

3   Which of the beliefs of excellence do you already hold?

4   Which beliefs of excellence would you like to hold?

5   Which one belief of excellence would make the biggest positive difference to your life if you held it? What do you imagine would be the effect of holding this belief for you?

REFERENCES

Edward de Bono (1990) *Lateral Thinking*, Penguin.
John Grinder & Judith DeLozier (1996) *Turtles All the Way Down: Prerequisites to Personal Genius*, Metamorphous Press.

Once upon a time there was a young prince who believed in all things but three. He did not believe in princesses, or in islands, or in God. His father, the king, told him that such things did not exist. There were no princesses or islands in his father's domain, and no sign of God. The young prince believed his father.

One day, the prince ran away from his palace to the next country. There, to his astonishment, from every coast he saw islands, and on these islands, strange and troubling creatures whom he dared not name. As he was searching for a boat, a man in full evening dress approached him along the shore.

"Are those real islands?" asked the young prince.

"Of course they are real islands," said the man in evening dress.

"And those strange and troubling creatures?"

"They are all genuine and authentic princesses."

"Then God must also exist!" cried the prince.

"I am God," replied the man in full evening dress, with a bow.

The young prince returned home as quickly as he could.

"So you are back," said his father, the king.

"I have seen islands, I have seen princesses, I have seen God," said the prince reproachfully.

The king was unmoved. "Neither real islands, nor real princesses, nor a real God, exist."

"I saw them!"

"Tell me how God was dressed."

"God was in full evening dress."

"Were the sleeves of his coat rolled back?"

The prince remembered that they had been. The king smiled. "That is the uniform of a magician. You have been deceived."

At this the prince returned to the next land, and went to the same shore, where once again he came upon the man in full evening dress. "My father, the king, has told me who you are," said the young prince indignantly. "You deceived me last time, but not again. Now I know that those are not real islands and real princesses, because you are a magician."

The man on the shore smiled. "It is you who are deceived, my boy. In your father's kingdom there are many islands and many princesses. But you are under your father's spell, so you cannot see them."

The prince returned pensively home and when he saw his father he looked him in the eyes. "Father, is it true that you are not a real king, but only a magician?"

The King smiled and rolled back his sleeves. "Yes my son, I am only a magician."

"I must know the real truth, the truth beyond magic."

"There is no truth beyond magic," said the king.

The prince was full of sadness. He said, "I will kill myself."

The king, by magic, caused death to appear. Death stood in the door and beckoned to the real prince. The prince shuddered. He remembered the beautiful but unreal islands and the unreal but beautiful princesses.

"Very well," he said. "I can bear it."

"You see, my son," said the king, "you too now begin to be a magician."

The Magus, © John Fowles, Jonathan Cape, 1977. Reprinted with permission.

15
Achieve what you really want: Well-formed outcomes

Imagination and faith are the same thing, giving substance to our hopes and reality to the unseen.
—John V Taylor

How sustainable are your goals? At the time of writing we have experienced one of the most turbulent periods in stock market history. Just how much more evidence do we need to realize that focus on profits, income, self-interest and material gain is the most fragile way to set goals for ourselves? They may seem to work in the short term, but what we are seeing is the inevitable result of trading this way. How robust are you in times of turbulence – in fact, how robust are you at all?

Here in rural France, and particularly in the south of India where I work much of the time, the locals probably have no idea that the flashing lights of the financial markets even exist, nor are the numbers likely to change their lives significantly in the next few years. The fishermen who live in palm leaf-roofed huts by the beach in Kerala are more likely to be devastated by a tsunami than a stock market crash. So how do we create these panics in the western world? And how can we personally rise above it?

It was Einstein who said that in order to affect the world's problems we need to think (and act) differently: that we won't change the issues with the thinking that generated those issues in the first place. So the question is: What have we learnt from our models of excellence about the way they think about and set their goals? How can we find a way to discover what we really want (which may not be what we think we need) and do so in a way that supports this beautiful world in which we live?

What we have learnt is that those who have a way of life that is in line with how they *really* (this is important) want to be are a

To change this madness we can learn to think differently

very small percentage of the population. Statistics suggest that only 6 percent of the population thinks strategically, and this includes the ability to set and hold compelling goals. Yet thinking in this way is available to all of us. Some people inherit this influential way of thinking from their parents or parent figures. Some people learn through adversity. The key is that they learn!

The key is to learn

Surprisingly, most company training schemes do not teach the most vital elements that make the difference with respect to goals, even though they might spend millions of pounds on objective-setting programs and appraisal schemes. As we frequently find when we use NLP to model excellence, the critical pieces are so often either taken for granted or so subtle that they are omitted from training.

Many training programs concentrate on formats such as SMART goals (specific, measurable, achievable, realistic and time bound). Do you really think that the high achievers in life, the people who act as the inspiration to the rest of us, sit down and wonder if their goals are realistic? The high achievers act out of passion and a love for what they do. It is their belief that they can achieve what others might consider to be unrealistic that makes them outstanding.

High achievers act out of passion

The difference between those who succeed and those whose goals last as long as a house built on sand lies in their willingness to pay the price. For example, are you willing to let go of everything you think you hold dear to achieve what you really want? The things we believe we cannot live without are often the very same things that we need to let go of if we are to realize our deepest desires.

People who live their lives the way they really want and who have fulfillment in what they do have a structure to their thinking that we have modeled over the years.

Pete Goss is a British sailor who took part in the Single-Handed Round the World Yacht Race at the beginning of 2001. I was tempted to describe him as the person who won the race, but in fact he came second to a French competitor. However, many people do believe that he won the race, such was the influence he had with the way he took part. Not only did he potentially sacrifice his place by diverting his course to rescue another sailor in distress, he also made major repairs to his damaged boat in high seas and treacherous weather. He stood by his values and principles no matter what the circumstances to achieve a position in this race that no other man of his age had achieved before Although British, Goss attracted the passionate support of many other nations, especially the French, who gave him a bigger homecoming than even their own competitor.

Pete Goss is the epitome of all that constitutes successful outcome thinking. The joy of what we see in him is that we each have our equivalent achievable success. What we will explore in this chapter is what success can mean for each of us individually and how we can think and act in a way that makes that success possible, not only in the future but also the present.

"All men dream: but not equally. Those who dream by night in the dusty recesses of their minds wake in the day to find that it was vanity; but the dreamers of the day are dangerous men, for they may act their dreams with open eyes, to make it possible."

T E Lawrence

PROBLEM THINKING

Let's consider some contrasting examples, ones that are all too familiar.

Kevin was continually searching for success. He'd had eight different jobs in five years, but all had failed to meet his expectations. Every time he'd fallen out with his manager or the market conditions for each business had not been "quite right." "Customers just aren't coming through the door," he stated frequently. Lack of success certainly wasn't due to lack of effort. Kevin tried very hard. He was constantly busy; he rarely had time to spare for anything else. He regularly talked about it being "a tough world out there" and yet each new challenge resulted in the same familiar disappointment. He talked about not wanting to make the same mistakes again, particularly in terms of his choice of business and manager, but somehow he always did.

Jay worked for a large organization. He had fulfilled his particular ambitions by continuing in the family tradition of engineering. Although he had developed quickly within the organization, he somehow felt that the job he had wasn't quite what he wanted to do, but he wasn't really sure what that was. He felt as though he was continually searching for what his future might be. Initiative and ambition, particularly in younger managers, were generally frowned on, although Jay's own manager had been supportive toward him. His family, however, were pleased with what they considered to be his success. In their terms he had done well.

Mary managed a sales team. They had been given new sales targets. As the company had decided to grow, it had changed the way in which it set the targets. Wanting a greater volume of sales, it decided to use unit sales as the measure of sales performance. To reach their targets the salespeople, who lacked an overall empathy with and understanding of the company's goals, practically gave the products away! Unit sales soared, but profits plummeted.

These examples are not unusual.

Ask yourself: "What do I really want?"

- Today?
- Tomorrow?
- This year?
- Next year?
- In the next five years?
- In my career?
- In my life?

This is not about what you must, should or ought to do. Nor is it about what you don't want to do or what you will try to do. Those kinds of thoughts tend to be the legacy of the goals that others want for you rather than the outcomes you truly want for yourself. Either that or they arise out of your fears of what you don't want to lose. Outcome thinking is to do with what you really want. That might seem selfish, but you cannot make others' goals come true for them, although you do influence others by what you achieve for yourself.

Thinking about what you don't want is problem thinking. What is happening when you are thinking this way is that what you are imagining in your mind is how things are today – that is, what you want to change – even though you might be saying how

Outcome thinking is to do with what you do really want

you want to change it. This leads to an *away from* motivation, in that you are motivated away from what you don't want. For example, you might change jobs to get away from what you don't like about your current one. You might leave your partner because you are not happy with your relationship, or you might go away on holiday to get a break from the stress you are feeling in what you are doing. The following are examples of this kind of goal:

- I want to lose weight.
- I don't want to have another argument with him.
- I want to give up smoking.
- I want more spare time.
- I want less stress in my work.
- I must clear my desk.
- I should go to that meeting.
- I want to finish off the decoration on my house.
- I want to be happy when I retire.

The language in all of these indicates that what the person is thinking about is how things are at the present, even though they want to change them.

OUTCOME THINKING

Goals expressed in outcome thinking mode indicate that the person is imagining what they really want as if they have stepped forward in time and have got it. The motivation generated by this way of thinking is towards, in that the owner of the outcomes is motivated towards what they do really want.

Imagine what you really want

For example, they might change jobs because they are so attracted to a new job opportunity. They might exercise because they want to be really fit, and they might go on holiday to a particular location because it is a country they have always wanted to experience.

Outcomes expressed in this way are as follows:

- I want to be really fit.
- I want to achieve agreement about how we go forward.
- I want to be in good health.

- I want to have balance in my life.
- I want to achieve a state of peace and wellbeing.
- I want to be someone who makes a difference in the world.
- I want to have a really attractive, state-of-the-art office.
- I want to make a key contribution to my community.

Jill works for a large organization and is clear that although the organization is slow and bureaucratic in its style, she wants to stay and make a difference. She wants to be a key player in the management of change toward a culture that is open, supportive and honest. She recognizes that her level of influence in her current role is limited and has mapped out the future roles she wants that would increase her influence to introduce the changes she believes to be important. She knows that if she waits for others to make this happen she might wait for ever. One thing that strikes you about Jill when you meet her is that she wants passionately to achieve this future. Her whole presence is captivating as she talks about what is important to her. She talks positively of what she wants and she is always respectful of other people's views and opinions. People are attracted to her.

What precisely is the difference in the way Jill thinks about her outcomes and the way Kevin and Jay think about theirs? Jill certainly seems to be on track to achieving her outcome and is enjoying the journey toward it.

You can enjoy the journey

How is it that some people are satisfied, highly motivated and consistently achieving the sort of success they want? What exactly is the difference? Let's explore this in a way that will enable you to set compelling outcomes for yourself and to support others to do the same.

"Until one is committed, there is hesitancy, the chance to draw back, always ineffectiveness. Concerning all acts of initiative and creation, there is one fact, one elementary truth, the ignorance of which kills countless ideas and splendid plans. That the moment that one definitely commits oneself then providence moves too. All sorts of things to help one that would never otherwise have occurred manifest themselves. A whole stream of events issue from the decision, raising in one's favour all manner of unforeseen incidents and meetings and material assistances that no man could have dreamed would have come his way."

W H Murray

Consider this statement: "Don't think about kangaroos!" Can you not do that? I doubt it. Your unconscious mind cannot recognize negatives. When you tell yourself not to worry or not to make a mistake, you are actually programming yourself to do just that. However, if you program yourself to think about being calm or getting things right, you are dramatically increasing the chances that this is how you will be.

The truth is that we are brainwashing ourselves all day long by what we choose to think about and more especially how we choose to think about it. What we get with NLP is the recognition and awareness to program ourselves in a way that will not only work for us but for others too.

My husband used to manage a team of software developers who had been very successful in winning business with their contribution to the sales pitches for new systems. Then they were taken over by a bigger company and they reported to a new director. The bigger company asked the development team to pitch for the software business for some of their existing accounts that they had been at risk of losing. Normally this team's style had been relaxed and confident and this was how they approached the new challenges, until the director instructed them "On no account lose this business." He followed this up with "You just can't afford to go wrong here." After several days of these problem statements, the tension in the team began to mount and they found themselves feeling unusually stressed by the prospect of the presentations. They did not get the business.

Manage your thinking to achieve a "personal best"

Successful top sportspeople know exactly how to manage their thinking to achieve a consistent personal best. They know that if they start worrying about hitting the ball out of court or off the green, that is what they are programming themselves to do. Even if the bulk of their thinking is positive, they know that a fleeting negative thought can make the difference between winning the point and losing it. They have modeled themselves on excellence.

How often have you said to yourself "I mustn't do that" only to find yourself doing it? Just this morning my husband said he wanted to be sure that no one dropped his new kitchen knife as it has a fragile ceramic blade. He was indirectly telling the rest of our household to take care if we used it. But those weren't the words he used. Within an hour of saying this, he had dropped the knife! What we think is what we get.

What we think is what we get

Two teams had been given the job of identifying ways in which their business could pull itself out of recession and achieve new business objectives. The teams had been asked to develop their ideas and come back on a specific date to present their conclusions. They returned with new proposals as agreed. One team looked dejected. They presented their ideas: how to cut costs, reduce overheads and rationalize the workforce. They felt this was the way forward. An air of gloom hung around them. The rest of the room was silent.

The second team presented their ideas. They looked delighted. This team was made up of people from the manufacturing side of the business. Previously they had looked at ways of improving quality and reducing wastage. This time they had decided to take a different stance. They had thought about the future they really wanted: the number of plants they would like to build, the amount of research they wanted to do and the people they wanted to employ. They were fired up with their ideas and their passion for the future. They had decided it was time to turn the company around. It should be they who were telling the salesforce how much business they needed to support this program, instead of them responding to whatever the salesforce sold, as had been the case in the past.

The difference in the enthusiasm and sheer energy of these two teams was dramatic. One had thought about what they had to cut back and lose and the other about what they really wanted. It is almost inevitable that if you think about what you don't want you become disheartened. You will develop the feelings and responses that are triggered by being in an environment of circumstances, people and events that you don't like. It is no surprise that if you think about what you really want, if you imagine what it is like to have what you really want, then you will be committed, you will be motivated, and you will be influential because your enthusiasm will be infectious. This is one of the reasons visionary leaders are compelling.

Enthusiasm is infectious

I recently worked with a group of trainers and was with them as they met the groups they were going to train. One of the trainers, who had been nervous but excited and looking forward to the challenge, entered the room with their prospective delegates. This trainer believed that the delegates could really gain from the training program and was positive about everyone's potential to change. The group greeted this trainer with warmth and acceptance.

The second trainer had doubts about the abilities of the members of his group, particularly their ability to change. He had a tendency to talk in problem-centered language: "I won't let the group get out of control," "I'm not worried about how the group will react." When this trainer entered the room the atmosphere seemed to change from fun to confrontation. The group asked challenging questions and wanted proof of how the program would help them personally.

Desired state thinking is linked to charisma

A team of researchers set out to quantify the relationship between the speaking styles of US Presidents and the inspiration felt by citizens. They measured charisma and greatness, charisma being the emotional bond between leaders and followers, and greatness measuring perceptions of actual achievements. Then they studied the inaugural addresses and key speeches of US Presidents. Examples were taken from speeches by John F Kennedy and Jimmy Carter.

John F Kennedy, a clearly charismatic President, used phrases like "Together let us explore the stars, conquer the desert, eradicate disease, tap the ocean depths, and encourage the arts and commerce." Jimmy Carter's 1977 address, in contrast, included "Let our recent mistakes bring a resurgent commitment to the basic principles of our nation, for we know that if we despise our own government, we have no future." The differences are striking. John F Kennedy's speech is an example of communication based on outcome thinking, whereas Jimmy Carter's is almost entirely problem centered. Barack Obama's style is increasingly likened to that of John F. Kennedy. The hypnotic language patterns (see Chapter 9) in both evoke very different unconscious responses. Compare "let us explore the stars, tap the ocean depths" with "despise our own government, we have no future." It is in the words.

Some things lend themselves to outcome thinking and some things very definitely do not. There is good news and bad news. The bad news is that goals that include the following are not achievable with this way of thinking:

- To be number one.
- To win the race.
- To cut the legs from under our competitors.
- To be managing director of this company.
- To achieve the profit target.
- To make my children happy and successful.

That might surprise you, as it is very likely that some of your goals do fall into some of these categories. The point is that some goals are indeed outside of your control, or they are not ecological for other people. You will see the significance of these goals as I go through the other conditions for well-formed outcomes in this chapter. The only part of the world for which we can set outcomes and hope to achieve them is in the kind of person we want to be.

So the kinds of outcome that you can expect to achieve with this way of thinking include:

Keep it within your control

- To be an example of a caring, entrepreneurial leader.
- To achieve my personal best in whatever field I choose.
- To work in a way that is supportive of others.
- To achieve a role in life that is a position of leading others in a high-tech business.
- To create a climate of learning and fun in all or most of my interactions with others.
- To be sure to be a parent who can support my children emotionally and practically.

One of the top salespeople in a telecommunications company has targets to achieve and does quite naturally want to achieve them. However, when he considers his existing and potential customers, what he thinks about is not how much he is going to make out of each of them, but rather how he can make their time with him valuable and enjoyable. To do this he thinks about his state and how he wants to be when he is with them. He puts his attention on what is within his control, his way of being in the world. He achieves all his financial targets with remarkable consistency.

In the example at the beginning of this chapter, one of the reasons Kevin did not achieve his goals was that those goals depended on others and on external circumstances. When he didn't achieve what he wanted it was because his manager or the business climate or his customers weren't quite right. He had not asked himself how he could be different whatever the external circumstances. He wanted *others* to be different. A useful question here is to ask, "What kind of person do I want to become?"

Where is your attention in relation to your outcomes? On yourself or on others? Do your outcomes depend on someone else being there or responding in a certain way? If so, they are not self-maintained. In a story in *Waiting for the Mountain to Move*, Charles Handy describes a traveler who, journeying around the world, came to a road and across this road was a mountain blocking the way. The traveler sat down and waited for the mountain to move.

When Lance Armstrong recovered from cancer and was considering entering the Tour de France, his goal was not to win the Tour, it was to cycle competitively again. He won. When David Hemery took part in the final of the Mexico Olympics as potentially the slowest candidate, his goal was not to win the race but to do his personal best. He won.

What will it be like to have what you really want? If you can imagine it, it is virtually yours. The more you step into this imagined future, the more you are programming yourself to get there. Think again about one of the outcomes you really want for yourself. Imagine having achieved what you really want. What is it like?

- **What does it look like?** What do you see? What is around you? Is there anyone else in the picture? Look around, take in the details.
- **What does it sound like?** What do you hear? What are you saying to yourself? What are others saying?
- **What does it feel like physically?** What can you touch and what sort of feeling is that? What textures do you experience?
- **What does it taste like?** What sort of taste do you get in your mouth? What is that like?
- **What does it smell like?** What is the aroma of achieving what you really want?
- **What does it feel like emotionally?** What are the emotions that you feel in achieving what you really want? What is the quality of those emotions and where do you feel them?

Are you waiting for the mountain to move?

Know how you will know when you have arrived

Your unconscious mind does not differentiate between what is imagined and what is real. The more vividly you imagine yourself achieving what you want, the more your unconscious mind believes it already has it and will program you to act as if you do. And of course, the more you act as if you have it, the more likely you are to get it!

Once you have established your outcome in all your senses in this way, it begins to take on a momentum of its own. This ability to step into your outcome is characteristic of NLP. The difference comes from being able to imagine yourself (associate) into the future that you want. Although planning to get there is important, the steps in the plan will almost begin to present themselves to you automatically because you will begin to recognize opportunities when they occur.

Watch a player take a goal kick in rugby. You may be able to begin to determine how he prepares his thinking. I watched Jonny Wilkinson playing for England against France in the Six Nations Rugby Union Cup. The camera zoomed in on his face as he prepared the kick. He looked at the ball and then tracked the trajectory that he wanted the ball to take up and through the goal posts. He repeated this three times, then very quickly, almost without looking this final time, kicked the ball. He converted every goal kick.

Sometimes people say to me, "Won't I get disappointed if I imagine what I really want and then I don't get it?" I have found that those people who consistently achieve what they really want, often against the odds, also hold a belief that whatever happens is learning. In this way they are happy with the journey toward the goal as much if not more than arriving at the destination. This outcome way of thinking is a way of influencing the way we journey through life.

It is likely that you will want your outcome in some situations but not others. For example, if you want a feeling of certainty and self-confidence, this could be very appropriate when giving a presentation or planning your future, but inappropriate in a situation where you had some partly formed ideas and wanted your colleagues to develop their own thinking about these ideas.

So ensure that you put your outcome into context. Where, when and with whom do you want your outcome? If your

Your unconscious mind doesn't know the difference between real and imaginary

We can influence the way we journey through life

Put it into context

outcome does depend on someone or something else, sometimes this can be the painful part. Can you let go of that need to have someone or something else change? Once you can, then in a strange way you increase the chances that you can have what you really want.

Is your goal in the interest of others?

When our goals are in the interest of others and beyond self, then they begin to defy the challenges of time.

"Think not of what your country can achieve for you but what you can achieve for your country."

John F Kennedy

These key others might be family members and partners. They might be colleagues and other employees. They might increasingly be suppliers and competitors. If the outcome is a win for the bigger system, then that bigger system may very well support you. If the outcome is a loss for the bigger system, then those significant others will either consciously or inadvertently block its achievement.

Business has been locked into a win/lose mentality for some time now. One of the most cut-throat markets has been the travel industry. Each company has fought with the others to the point where they have all lost business. There has been an annual battle for the release of the next year's holiday brochures, with each travel organization attempting to release its brochure ahead of the rest. This competition has come to the point where the brochures are released so far ahead of the holiday periods to which they refer that they are almost irrelevant.

Forward-looking organizations find ways to collaborate

The more forward-looking organizations are not only finding ways to help their competitors succeed by promoting them, providing links to them through their website. They are also finding ways to collaborate so that together they promote the market to which they both belong. And it is those holidays that offer the chance to support communities in less well-off parts of the world that are beginning to climb the ladder in popularity. The greatest growth in travel is in the over 60s, who are now retired and want to see and make a difference in the world.

What will it take to achieve what you want?

- Risk?
- Feelings of discomfort?
- Giving up something you have now?
- Pain and sadness?

Is having the outcome worth what it takes? You may decide it is not, in which case you can give it up or decide to go for a part or a variation of the outcome. If you decide the outcome is worth what it takes, you are making a decision to commit and to proceed to the next step.

When I was thinking about leaving my full-time job at ICL, I was scared of leaving the team of people behind that I had worked with for the previous five years. I was also afraid of losing what I believed to be the security of a large corporate organization. However, I did want to run my own business, so to do this I had to decide if I was prepared to let go of those things I felt I must have. It wasn't an easy decision or a comfortable time. I remember having many panicky moments when I wondered if I was doing the right thing.

However, I decided eventually that what I wanted outweighed what I was afraid of losing. Ironically, many of my colleagues also eventually left and became independent consultants and I had more of their company subsequently than I would ever have imagined possible. And I have come to realize that nothing and nowhere is truly secure. Security is all in the mind.

Even though you have your outcome, your present state satisfies a need in you. If it didn't, you wouldn't maintain it. Think carefully about how your present state serves you. It may seem odd, but someone who wants to be fit and healthy may find that being unhealthy gets them sympathy and attention. Equally, someone who is nonassertive but who wants to be assertive may find that being nonassertive is a way of avoiding risk and responsibility.

What does your present state do for you?

It is important to consider these needs and either how you will challenge them or meet them in different ways in the future to leave you free to achieve your outcome. Once you have identified what it is that you get out of your present state, you explore how you might satisfy that need but in a different way through your outcome.

Have a higher purpose

Having a higher purpose makes your outcome significant. It also puts your outcome into context and opens up options for ways you might achieve it. If, for example, your goal is to be healthy and fit, the higher purpose of this might be to be the kind of person who can play and join in with what your children are doing. If your outcome is to reach agreement in the meeting, it might be so that you are able to negotiate collaboration for a future way of working together. And if your goal is to run your own business, it may be that your outcome is to create a balance between your work and your personal life. Knowing your higher purpose keeps your outcomes in perspective and ensures that you stay on track with what is important about what you achieve.

What positive influence do you want to have?

Another way of thinking about your higher purpose is to consider the contribution you want to make to the bigger systems of which you are a part. We all have an influence in the wider systems to which we belong – the question is what positive influence you want to have. Another way of thinking about it is to consider what added value you will bring to those bigger systems by achieving what you want.

Peter had achieved great success in developing a professional presentation style on a training course. When the group commented on how impressed his team back at work would be with his new skills, he responded, "You must be joking. I'd stand out like a sore thumb if I used this style back at work."

Having these skills did not fit with the person Peter considered himself to be at work. There was little likelihood that he would ever use them.

Ensure your outcomes fit with who you are

Check your outcomes against the kind of person you are or want to be. If they don't fit, forget them – find ones that do. Only by doing this will you ensure that every part of you is rooting for your success.

Ultimately, all goals are about how you are developing as a person. You might get so locked into thinking about shorter-term outcomes that you lose sight of what it is all about for you personally. Keep in mind the kind of person you are and the kind of person you want to become. In this way, you will make sure that what you achieve is a fit for you as a person.

One of my sons, who has worked for years in South America to build a sanctuary for wildlife, returned to the UK to earn some money. He took a job as a financial adviser working in the world of pensions and mortgages. It took him a year to acknowledge consciously that this was not the right work for him. He has resumed his studies and work with animals.

"Whatever you can do or dream you can do, begin it. Boldness has genius and power and magic in it. Begin it now!"

Goethe

You might be fiercely ready and passionate about your goal, but if you don't act on it all that passion will have been in vain. The sports company Nike was very astute to adopt the slogan "Just do it!" What are you doing to achieve your goals? I often see action plans on company appraisal forms that have grand statements such as:

◆ Improve managerial effectiveness.
◆ Develop better communication.
◆ Build an effective team.

Commitment takes the form of specific action steps.

"My brother who is ten years old was trying to get a report on birds written that he'd had three months to write and which was due the next day. We were out at our family cabin in Bolinas, and he was at the kitchen table close to tears, surrounded by binder paper and pencils and unopened books on birds, immobilised by the hugeness of the task ahead. Then my father sat down beside him, put his arm around my brother's shoulder, and said, 'Bird by bird, buddy. Just take it bird by bird.'"

Anne Lamott, Bird by Bird

Bird by bird

ORGANIZATIONAL OUTCOMES

What works at an individual level works at the corporate level too.

Problem-centered organizations are moving away from what they don't want. They are more likely to react to the competition and in so doing to become dependent on what the competition does next. They are *driven* by market trends and are *directly* affected by the economic climate. They step into a "fire-fighting," crisis-based way of working in which their actions are determined by the competition. The climate inside such companies is one of tension, worry and stress.

Outcome-oriented organizations, on the other hand, have a clear vision of where they are heading. This is an expression of what the employees in the company really want. Because of this there is a high level of motivation and commitment. People in the company enjoy their work. The vision is an inspiration both to those who work within the company and to those with whom they come into contact, their customers and their suppliers. This style of company sets market trends. It influences its customers to move forward with it to their vision of the future.

Outcome-oriented companies are innovative and influential. They do take account of market trends, the economic climate and competitors, but they do this in the context of having a clear, compelling outcome and business plan.

One of my clients, a family-run manufacturing business, took time out to ensure that they had a compelling vision for the business. The board members collectively imagined what future they wanted for the business so that they could see, hear, physically feel, smell, taste and emotionally feel what that was like. They did this individually and then shared their thoughts.

The measure of their rapport was that what they had each imagined individually was either identical to or complemented what others had imagined. Everything they imagined dovetailed with the outcomes of everyone else on the board. They each visualized the extent of the business, the culture they wanted, how the business looked, including its international premises, how they perceived themselves, the role they were fulfilling and the feeling of achievement.

What we measure is what we get. Measure the problems no matter whether they are falling or rising (as in the case of one company that measured the level of complaints) and problems are what you get. You presuppose problems. How about measuring compliments instead of complaints? Measure goods manufactured to compliance rather than scrap. Measure successfully operating installations rather than waiting times.

The company vision is an inspiration

What we measure is what we get

The situation in the UK National Health Service is a classic one. The decision to measure reduction in waiting times for an appointment has led to my local Health Centre only allowing appointments to be made on the day of the appointment!

Consider the following potential measures of customer satisfaction:

Reduction or absence of complaints	Amount of praise received for a job well done
Number of problems solved	Number of thank-yous for the service you give
Reduction in time taken to deal with customer calls	Voluntary feedback on the benefits of using your service or product
Extent to which you can keep customers off your back	Amount of repeat business
Amount of resource allocated to your customers	Evidence of improvement in customers' work processes
Number of system crashes	Amount of smiling and fun
Amount of downtime	Amount of business generated from visits to your website
	Difference made in the world

The column on the left contains some traditional ways of measuring customer satisfaction. They are typically problem based. If your customer satisfaction measures are expressed in terms of what you don't want, that is where you will put your attention and that is exactly what you will get. If you measure complaints, this presupposes this is what you expect and, sure enough, that is what you will get.

What we appreciate appreciates

I returned from a very enjoyable cycling holiday to find a "customer care" questionnaire waiting for me. In it I was asked to say not "What was my opinion of the overnight accommodation?" but "What problems did I experience with the accommodation?" What did I do? I immediately began to search in my memory for problems that might have existed. One well-known travel company has a whole floor of staff to deal with customer complaints. There is no equivalent floor to deal with customer compliments!

SHORTCUT TO ACHIEVING WHAT YOU REALLY WANT

1 Think of something you really want–not something you don't want or want less of or feel you should have.

2 Is it within your control? (To be the next Prime Minister is not, to have your partner behave differently is not. To be an example of professionalism is, to work with the people you enjoy is, to take part competitively is.) Find the part of the outcome that is within your control.

3 Imagine yourself having achieved what you really want. Let your unconscious do this for you – allow yourself to dream. Using your unconscious is a key part of the process. Be aware of what you are seeing, hearing, feeling physically, smelling, tasting, and feeling emotionally. Be sure to do this "from your own shoes."

4 In which contexts are you imagining yourself with this outcome? In which ones do you want to have this?

5 Imagine how this can be or is a real benefit to the significant people in your life. It is vital that it is win/win. If there is anything you need to do in your thinking to make it win/win, do that.

6 What sort of cost will you have to pay to achieve this? Are you willing to pay this price? If not, let go of the outcome and put your energies into something else.

7 What does maintaining your present state do for you (assuming you could have achieved this outcome before)? How might you build the benefits of the present state into the achievement of the desired state?

8 How does achieving this outcome contribute to a higher goal for you or an overall purpose that you have in your life?

9 In what way does achieving this outcome fit with who you are and who you are becoming?

10 What specifically are you going to do that demonstrates your commitment to achieving this outcome? When specifically will you do that? Be very precise here about your action plan. It need only be the first step, but it does need to be precise.

A SUMMARY OF THE CRITERIA
FOR A WELL-FORMED OUTCOME

And finally, a summary of the criteria for a well-formed outcome based on the study of those who are statistically more able than most to achieve the outcomes they hold.

1 Stated in the positive (what you do want rather than what you don't).
2 Expressed in the present tense (imagining it as if you have it right now).
3 Expressed in all senses. You can describe what you are seeing, hearing, feeling physically, tasting, smelling and feeling emotionally.
4 It is self-maintained (it is about your part of the system, not expressed in terms of others).
5 It is a win/win: it is a win for the significant others in your life as well as for you.
6 It is an end result not just a step en route (for example, dieting might be a step toward being fit and healthy, which is a step toward being a great healthy example and companion to your family).
7 It has a higher purpose (it is ultimately about making a difference in the world for others and is beyond self).
8 It fits with who you are. If you are an explorer at heart, there's no point having a goal about safety and security.
9 It satisfies the payoff that you get from your present state (if you get attention from being the way that you are and you like that, check that your outcome satisfies this need for attention in a healthy way).
10 You are prepared to pay the price to achieve it and this is demonstrated by your answer to the following question.
11 You are committed to taking the specific next step.
12 You are willing to act and do so.
13 You hold the belief throughout that whatever happens is feedback – there is no drawing back, only learning.

THOUGHT PROVOKERS

1 Are the following towards or away from?
   a I really want a job that involves working with other people.
   b The company I work for currently is very bureaucratic. I want somewhere else to work.
   c I have a clear vision of myself working abroad.
2 You ask another department to agree a level of service with you. When you have explained what you need, they say they will try to meet your requirements. How confident would you be that they would deliver?
3 What was the basis of your decision to take your existing job? Were you moving towards your ideal or away from something you didn't like? And your previous job?
4 Imagine yourself doing the type of work you would really like to do. What can you see/hear/feel?
5 Think of examples of action plans you have set yourself in the past. What is characteristic of the action plans that you have carried out compared with the ones you haven't?
6 How do you decide how to spend your holidays? How well does the reality match up to your expectations?
7 How often do you finish up with the things you don't want compared with the things you do?
8 Think about what you would really like to achieve by the end of this week. Pay attention to what is in your mind. Is it what you do want or are you imagining the problems of the things you don't want?
9 If you have lost sight of what it is that you want for yourself, start small and identify what you want for yourself by the end of today, for example, or by the end of the next meeting you have.

REFERENCES

Sue Knight, *Personal Selling Skills*, Sue Knight Books & Talks.

Once upon a time, there was a couple who had achieved many of their ambitions in life, yet there was one main goal outstanding: They wanted to swim to Japan. They reflected on this goal for a long time and one day they set off. They were not used to swimming, so they found it difficult.

They were aware of how heavy their limbs felt. They ached with the constant effort, especially when the strong current was against them. Gradually, however, their bodies got used to swimming and they developed a style that became effortless and rhythmical.

They began to notice the water around them, how it changed color as the days went by. In the early morning it would be clear and blue and in certain lights it sparkled emerald green. As the sun set it developed the rich warm colors of the evening sky. And they became aware of the creatures in the water, the small silver fish that swam with them in the day, the dark shadows that skimmed by them in the deep. They became aware of how the sound of the waves changed as the water lapped their ears and they felt the subtle changes of the weather as breezes turned into winds and died down again.

They learnt how to find food in the water, how to nourish themselves, and how to use their bodies effortlessly. They developed a refined sense of smell so that they could detect changes in the environment by the scent carried to them on the breeze.

They swam for days and weeks with no sight of land. One day, they saw the dark profile of land on the horizon. They swam on and they recognized the shoreline of Japan. As they approached, they became quiet and eventually they looked at each other and they knew. At that moment they turned back to the sea and swam on.

16
Carpe diem: Time

What some may call the process we call the end. If I can stay in the middle of the turmoil, calm and unperplexed, that is the end of the purpose. It is the process not the end.

Oswald Chambers

Do you love every minute
of life, rain or shine?

Do you do treat every moment as precious? Do you value the "now"? If so, it is likely that anyone in your company will feel very special and that you love every minute of life, rain or shine.

TIME IS A METAPHOR

The moment Charles wakes up he embarks on his list of tasks for the day. He knows exactly what he has to do and there is always "a lot"! Typical comments that Charles would make throughout the day are "I am really pushed for time," "I have got so much to do," "There just isn't enough time in the day," "If only I had a few more hours/days." If someone engages him in conversation, he is likely to cut them short by saying, "Can't stop now, must get on, things to do." It is unheard of for him to be the one who has to be curtailed in conversation – he expresses horror on the rare occasion that happens.

His days are mapped out in one-hour slots, so any interruption to this procedure is responded to with frustration and even anger. If he promises to deliver something, he will have it there on the dot, and he will expect others to be there at the precise time time too. "Just in time" is his motto and time spent waiting is time lost, in his way of being in the world. It is a joke in his family that they will put "If only I had a few days more" on his tombstone.

Contrast Charles' approach to time with Alan's.

Alan rarely plans ahead. Travel tickets are usually expensive for him as he has never considered them far enough ahead in time to get the early bird deals. Quite the opposite, he pays premium, last-minute prices. Although he promises to deliver on a specific date, it is rare if not unheard of for him to meet the target. There is always a good reason for the target date being missed.

However, Alan is great company – whatever you want to discuss, he gives his time freely. And if you ask for some of his time he invariably says yes, even though he might not arrive punctually for the meeting. His intention is always to be there for you. Alan loves to cook for his friends, but if he says that the meal will be ready in half an hour they know to expect to eat at least an hour later than that. Overall, Alan's friends would say that he is always there for them in spirit if not on time!

Do you recognize any, some or all of these patterns in yourself in the way that you relate to time? Are you someone for whom there is never enough time? Or are you someone for whom time just seems to expand for you to do whatever you really want? Think about your time this week. How would you describe the week ahead? Do you have things that "have" to be done? How many "'musts" and "got tos" are there in your thinking? What happens to your feelings as you consider the week: do you feel relaxed or do you experience a sense of pressure or something else?

"Time is what we want most but what we use worst."

William Penn

THROUGH TIME AND IN TIME

Consider for a moment how you know the difference between what you did yesterday and what you might do tomorrow. How do you know that one is in the past and one is in the future? Have you ever had the experience of not knowing if something you wanted to do has actually been done, like locking the front door, telling someone something important, packing your tickets and passport? I referred to this briefly in Chapter 2, Thinking patterns. Sometimes we confuse what we want to have done with what is yet to be done and we begin to have doubts.

How do we know the difference between the past and the future?

There are many ways in which we represent time, but one of the main differentiators is how we represent it in space. There are clues to this in the way we talk about time:

* The past is behind me.
* I am looking forward to...
* I was going to do that.
* I put that idea aside in order that I could go forward.
* That was back then.
* I am looking to be in a new home in...
* I can see myself being...
* Over time what has happened is...
* I consider myself to have been very lucky in the past.

We begin to get clues about where we hold time in space. Consider for a moment where you hold the past: is it behind you, to one side, in front of you? When you consider time, does the future stretch out in front of you, to one side, up towards the sky?

Someone I was coaching had great difficulty in "facing the future." When asked where the past was, she immediately put her hand to her forehead. I could begin to understand how she had difficulty moving away from some damaging memories in her life.

A distinction in the way we represent time is whether we can see our past, present and future in front of us. Some people see this as an arc, with the present the closest point to them on the arc. Whenever they consider themselves at any point in time, past, present or future, they can see and hear themselves as if they were an outsider. They have a dissociated way of experiencing themselves and time. People who code time this way tend to have their time mapped out. They are more likely to have schedules and they know the implication of one part of that schedule if any event changes, because they can see the relationship of one thing to another. They can become easily distracted by future or past events and it is likely that they are rarely fully present. This way of representing time is referred to as "through time." It is very likely the way in which Charles in the example at the beginning of the chapter represents time.

Alan, however, is much more likely to be "in time," in the sense that he is more likely to be associated into time and does not

Some people have an overview of time past, present and future

Some people are totally immersed in the present

have the kind of overview that Charles has. He is present and in the moment, now. And every moment is "now." In this way he is not aware of the impact of his actions or changes to his plans – if indeed he has any plans. The upside of this is that he dedicates himself to the moment and is 100 percent there for whoever is with him.

A colleague of mine who is most definitely "in time" can rarely be relied on to arrive at appointments at the time agreed. This is very frustrating for the other person, but fantastic when she is with you. Most of her friends and clients are prepared to pay the price!

UP TIME AND DOWN TIME

Yesterday a jazz band played at our local village fête. One musician in particular gave total attention to the music. His whole body moved with the rhythm. His attention was dedicated entirely to the music and the accordion he was playing (an unusual instrument to have in a jazz band). His performance was compelling. In contrast, the bass player was looking around, watching people in the crowd and engaging with passers by. The effect on me (and I suspect on many others in the audience) was completely different. Most eyes (and I assume ears) were fixed on the accordion player.

The way we relate to the time we have is a choice. We live in a world of high technology, filled with devices that can transport us from our immediate company and surroundings. I might be in rural France yet be speaking to someone in Australia. I can be in the heat of southern India and looking at a live broadcast from the US. I watch people walking down the road in London and see many with earpieces, presumably either listening to music or speaking on their mobile phone. There is much to tempt us away from what we have in our immediate surroundings in the "now."

The way we relate to time is a choice

Think of one of the most peaceful times of your life, when you were completely at one with yourself. Take a moment to think about what that was like. What happened to your attention?

You might have identified the time without any reflection. You might even have been able to describe the time to yourself with no thought whatsoever; it was a time that was so key to you that you carry it with you in your conscious thinking wherever you

There is much to tempt us away from the present

are. This is unlikely, however. It is much more likely that you will have gone into yourself to access the memory, an inner search.

Down time

This is what we refer to as "down time." It is unrealistic to expect that we can carry all our thoughts and memories and imaginings in our conscious mind. Our conscious is limited typically to between five and nine key thoughts; seven is the key number. This is why once we get above seven members in a team or in a group meeting, the dynamics and the ability to give the same kind of attention to each changes significantly. The rest we hold in our unconscious and going into down time is a way to access this.

We often discover our resources in our inner thoughts

Most coaching processes rely on us being able to access our unconscious mind in a down-time state. It is often in this deep, reflective state where we discover the resources we need, so coaches need to be able to elicit this state in their clients. There is more about this in the chapters on clean questions, hypnotic language and coaching.

It is equally important to respect this need for others to access a down-time state when we are interviewing or just having an everyday conversation. It is unrealistic to expect them to think and look at you at the same time. I once knew a manager who said that he would never employ anyone who did not look at him throughout an interview. I can only assume that he employed people who didn't think!

Up time

"Up time," in contrast, is when we are totally present, engaged in the moment with full attention on the people we are with and what is happening in our environment. This is an important state for coaches, trainers, salespeople, managers, leaders, sportspeople. The ability to maintain this state is a skill and for those who have this ability to manage themselves in this way it is a huge asset.

It is valuable to be able to dedicate our attention to others

In an up-time state our attention is outside of ourselves, dedicated to the people in our presence and to our surroundings. This is vital for successful trainers, coaches and people who rely on results through their ability to influence others. These people need to be sensitive to every nuance in behavior, particularly nonverbal behavior, and being vigilantly present allows them to do this.

So there are times when it is vital to be in up time, just as there are times when moving into down time serves our purpose well.

Issues arise when we mix the two in a way that does not serve our purpose or when we use one when the other would be more appropriate. To appear distracted and absorbed with your own thoughts when training would probably not be the most effective style to adopt!

MORE CHOICES IN THE WAY WE REPRESENT TIME

My time working for a company in the corporate world coincided with the emergence of time management systems. I had a grand, leather-bound organizer with an array of different colored pages. There were all sorts of supplementary accessories that you could buy at quite some cost. The name "organizer" is misleading, however. It suggests that the materials will do the organizing for you. Far from it. Only you can manage the way that you experience and use your time.

A member of my family has always had difficulty planning their time and keeping to that plan. I discovered that the future was to their side, which was not unusual, but whereas someone might say that a year out, say, might be some 2 or 3 metres to one side of them in the way they hold it in space, for this person 1 year on was only centimetres away from their face. That does not leave a lot of room for any detailed planning.

So space and distance are elements of how we code time. We are unlikely to change the way in which we use our time until we change the way in which we represent it.

We change our relationship with time as we change the way we represent it

Consider an old memory and a more recent one. What is different about the way you think about them? Ignore the content, just pay attention to *how* you think about them. For example, what image do you have of each? What is the color, focus, quality of sound, emotion? All or any of these factors affect the way in which we experience memories, thoughts and imagination. As you consider each of these memories, are you in them, reliving them, or are you watching and listening to yourself as an observer? This will be more likely if you have a preference for through time thinking. If your thinking is usually in time, you might also move yourself into the time that you are thinking about so that what was then becomes now, at least temporarily.

It is possible that the older the memory the paler it is in color or the less in focus, but your way of coding time might be

We internally code memories, thoughts and imagination

different to this. It might be that the older memories are clearer. Perhaps it is the sound of a memory that changes with time. What about future imaginings, dreams you may have? Think of something that you really want for next week and note the submodalities of how you think about this. Now think of something that you want farther into the future. What characterizes the way you think about this?

I look out over the valley and the hills beyond. There is morning mist hanging lightly above the distant village. I can see the church spire silhouetted against the hazy woods behind. I hear a harsh bird cry, intermittent, the rumble of a lorry away in the distance. From the open patio doors I feel the light breeze occasionally across my shoulders. There's more bird song. I feel at ease.

I believe I am present, that this is real, not a memory. How do I know that I'm not imagining this scene?

It is often the change in submodalities that enables us to differentiate between points in time, so any of the following may change:

+ **Visual** – color, clarity, position, moving or still, framed or unframed.
+ **Auditory** – volume, intensity, proximity, constant or intermittent.
+ **Feelings** – location of the feeling, intensity, nature.

In my office I have a means of finding the papers I want: I code them and have special places for different kinds of materials. We do the same with time, using changes in submodalities to differentiate between different points in time.

ACCESSING RESOURCES OVER TIME

We can learn to "time travel"

We can in effect learn to "time travel" in the way that we can access the resources that we have and have had at any time in our lives, and do so in a way that is independent of context. This is how you can do this:

1 Think of a resource that you would like to be able to access now, a resource that has been evasive of late. For example, if you have been lacking in confidence and would like that now, choose that.

2 Identify a quality that you do have intensely in the present. Even if this is a "negative" quality, for example stress, discomfort or boredom, as long as it is intense, that is all you need. Explore how you are experiencing this quality in the present. What are the submodalities? For example, how are you seeing, hearing and feeling the moment in this way? Note the submodalities of this intense experience.

3 Now ask yourself: "Where in my life have I had the resource (e.g. confidence) that I would like now?"

4 Allow yourself to drift or walk back in time with this question in your mind. Do this until you have identified several occasions when you have had this resource. Just let them come to mind rather than trying to work them out in your head. Move through the space that represents the past for you as you do so to engage your whole body in the search for the answer.

5 Choose the occasion where you had this resource in the best way in which you would wish to have whenever you choose. Take yourself into this point in time – associate into it.

6 Note the submodalities of how you are experiencing this moment: the distinctions in the way in which you are seeing, hearing and feeling this moment. When you have this state as richly as you would wish, choose a way to hold on to it (anchor it; see Chapter 12).

7 Bringing this resource with you, return to the present with the resource in place and explore how you experience it now.

8 You might even "dry run" a future scenario where you expect to want to hold this state. Move into a space that represents that time, bringing the resource with you, and explore how that is for you.

9 If that experience is a good one, then you can stay there for a while to wire it in. If you would like to improve on it, identify what further resource you would like and repeat the process.

In this way you can bring your desired resources from the past to the present so that you have them available to you now.

You can bring desired resources from the past to the present

MANAGING TIME WITH LANGUAGE

As part of my training, I often do a coaching demonstration. I expect the person who is my subject to get insight and learning that will help them to progress. Usually what they bring to the start of the demonstration is an issue of some kind from their personal lives or their work. I ask the rest of the training group to remain silent during the demonstration and I open it up for discussion at the end. Members of the audience can sometimes have a tendency to "backtrack," e.g. "I had a problem like yours and what I do with it is this..." By doing so the questioner is encouraging the subject to associate back in time to the problem with which they started. This can undo the coaching that has taken place.

So often we can be unaware of how our interest is affecting the other person. If I talk about the original issue at all with the subject, I put it into the past tense, for example: "The issue that you *had* back then... and the learning that you *have* now." We are always coaching.

We affect our state, our learning and our ability to progress through life by the way we use language on ourselves and with others. Consider these examples:

We are always coaching

- What would you like to achieve?
- As you imagine yourself achieving it, what is that like right now?
- Let's explore how you might have had this problem and the resources that you have available to you now.
- If I were to do that it might lead to that.
- Let's explore how this state of peace you have had is available to you right now and in the future.
- As you are sitting here, listening to what I am saying, you can begin to experience what it is like to be learning in ways that are already enhancing the way you can work and engage with others.

Our language can encourage an associated or a dissociated state

We can, through our language, encourage a dissociated state or an associated one. If we want to distance ourselves from our feelings and put an experience away from us in time, we can dissociate ourselves from our experience. Words like "would" and "might" and anything suggesting a different time frame to the present encourage a dissociated state. We might want to test a client's willingness to change and take on a particular learning, for example, before inviting them to commit to it. So we could say, "Would you be willing to take on that learning, do you think?" or "Can you imagine yourself with that learning in place?" If the answer is yes to both of those questions, we might then encourage them to make it present and associated: "OK, I would like you to step into your own shoes with that learning in place and do that now. What is that like?" Present tense – associated language.

BELIEFS ABOUT TIME

What other beliefs do you hold about time?

- Life is short and you must do everything you can in the time you have.
- Time spent not doing things is time wasted.
- You have all the time in the world.
- Time passes slowly.
- Time speeds by.
- Your time is not your own.
- Time flies.
- Time is short – you must get on.
- Time is a gift.
- Death is a remote concept.
- Death is ever present.
- Time is a metaphor and we can choose to experience it as we wish.
- The process is the end.

By changing your belief, you can change your experience of time. Follow this process to change your belief:

1 Do you experience time in the way that you would wish?
2 What is the belief behind your experience?
3 What might you believe instead?
4 What would you like to believe?
5 How might you presuppose or choose to believe what you want?

6   How would this belief affect your ability to be with time?
7   How do you expect this to translate into everyday behavior?
8   What do you expect the effect on others to be?
9   How does this fit with who you truly are and the person you want to be?

Remember, beliefs are a choice. We may have inherited beliefs about time from our parents or equivalent, but we can ultimately choose what we want to think about time in a way that enables us to achieve the true excellence of who we really are.

MY EXPERIENCE OF TIME

I have arrived in France for our summer holiday. Although we both work when we are here – typically I am in contact with clients and colleagues and often dedicate this time to writing – it has always felt like a holiday. This year seems different, however. I realized that my experience of being here had changed compared to previous years: it felt less like a holiday and more of a continuation of what I had been doing up to this point. And up to this point I have been very busy – exceptionally so. I began to recognize that I had not let go of the feelings of pressure that I had accumulated over the last month or two.

My strategy to deal with this had been to "do" some of things that we typically do when we are here on holiday – go to the local fête, visit our friends, garden – yet in doing those things I was still not feeling in my usual holiday mode. "Doing" was not working!

I had also spent some time wondering why my experience was different and came up with all sorts of answers based on comparisons of what had happened in previous years compared to this year. As interesting as that might be for me, it did not change my experience. So finally, I decided to pay attention to how I was representing time now compared to the way that I had represented time in previous years.

This is the learning with NLP. So often we engage in analysis and activity, believing them to be the answer to our issues. With NLP we explore *how* we are making our experience what it is. We study the structure of our thinking and physiology to see how we are creating our experience.

SUMMARY

Time is not a thing, yet it is something by which we are inevitably affected. Flowers bloom in the summertime. We sleep at night. Even when deprived of any daylight, we default to a wake and sleep pattern that approaches 24 hours. And we as human beings seek to control time in ways that no other creature on earth does or can.

It is what we believe about time and how we represent it that make our experience of time and life what it is. We have the opportunity to make each moment of our life count in the way that we would wish and we have the capacity to do so. By exploring our beliefs and our submodalities for how we think about time, we can make the best choice for ourselves and for those we influence.

THOUGHT PROVOKERS

1 Take some time at the end of a day. Reflect on what your relationship with time has been for that day. Is it what you would have wished? If so, what belief underpinned your day? If not, what belief underpinned your day and what belief might you choose to hold onto instead for tomorrow?
2 Think of someone with whom you have issues about time. For example, is there someone whose relationship to time frustrates you in some way? Knowing what you know now having read this chapter, how do you think that they have coded time? What do you think their belief about time might be that may be different to your own?
3 What would you describe as the best time of your life? What was it about the way that you approached that time that made it the best?

REFERENCES

Sogyal Rinpoche (2008) *The Tibetan Book of Living and Dying*, Rider & Co.

Eckhard Tolle (2001) *The Power of Now*, Mobius.

One day a fisherman was lying on a beautiful beach, with his fishing pole propped up in the sand and his solitary line cast out into the sparkling blue surf. He was enjoying the warmth of the afternoon sun and the prospect of catching a fish.

About that time, a businessman came walking down the beach, trying to relieve some of the stress of his work day. He noticed the fisherman sitting on the beach and decided to find out why he was fishing instead of working harder to make a living for himself and his family. "You aren't going to catch many fish that way," said the businessman to the fisherman. "You should be working rather than lying on the beach!"

The fisherman looked up at the businessman, smiled and replied, "And what will my reward be?"

"Well, you can get bigger nets and catch more fish!" was the businessman's answer.

"And then what will my reward be?" asked the fisherman, still smiling.

The businessman replied, "You will make money and you'll be able to buy a boat, which will then result in larger catches of fish."

"And then what will my reward be?" asked the fisherman again.

The businessman was beginning to get a little irritated with the fisherman's questions. "You can buy a bigger boat, and hire some people to work for you," he said.

"And then what will my reward be?" repeated the fisherman.

The businessman was getting angry. "Don't you understand? You can build up a fleet of fishing boats, sail all over the world, and let all your employees catch fish for you!"

Once again the fisherman asked, "And then what will my reward be?"

The businessman was red with rage and shouted at the fisherman, "Don't you understand that you can become so rich that you will never have to work for your living again! You can spend all the rest of your days sitting on this beach, looking at the sunset. You won't have a care in the world!"

The fisherman, still smiling, looked up and said, "And what do you think I'm doing right now?"

Part III
Lead with NLP

Perhaps love is the process of leading you gently back to yourself.
Antoine de St Exupéry

The world has never been in greater need of true leaders. In a state of shock, people look for someone to follow. The question is, are you a follower or a leader? We are all potentially leaders and the thinking in this part of the book can enable you to find the leader within, just as it can help you to refine the leadership qualities you may already recognize in yourself.

Great leaders are also great followers. And great leaders first learn to lead themselves. Lead with NLP is the last part of this book for that very reason. It is tempting to want to have a go with these skills on other people, but that is not the way they work – they work only because you are applying them to yourself. Make it a goal to be such an attractive example of what you have done with NLP for yourself that others want some of the same. That is the measure of success.

"You can preach a better sermon with your life than you can with your lips."

Oliver Goldsmith

One of the most important skills discovered in people who are models of excellence is their ability to influence and bring about change in ways that are far-reaching and sustainable over time. There is one common element in all their approaches: their ability to build immediate rapport with the people with whom they are working. I believe this is one of the most important skills in business. Without rapport, few management systems will work.

Develop a climate of trust with rapport

If you think you can get by with technical skills alone, you are wrong. You need cooperation, commitment, and respect to stand a chance of succeeding in anything you do. In Chapter 17, Develop a climate of trust: Rapport, I explore how to build and maintain rapport with the people with whom we come into contact face to face, in writing, and on the web.

All elements of NLP are complementary. Each adds another piece to the jigsaw of excellence. A more recent development in NLP thinking is experiencing situations from different perspectives in order to find a win/win, explained in Chapter 18, Negotiate your way through life: Perceptual positions. This approach complements outcome thinking and is a way of taking a balanced approach to situations and outcomes. Those who are most able to negotiate conflicts in work and life have the ability to appreciate situations from different perspectives. Some NLP techniques involve paying attention to the details of thinking and behavior; perceptual positions thinking provides a powerful shortcut to achieving the same results.

Negotiate your way through life with perceptual positions

Resolving conflict with parts integration

Chapter 19, Resolving conflict: Parts integration, covers a topic that has long been a part of the preliminary training I offer in NLP. It would be good to think that conflict would not exist if you put all the other principles into practice, but that would be unrealistic. Conflict also plays an important role in our lives: through it we can learn, heal and grow in ways that don't occur in other contexts. This chapter shows how to learn to deal with conflicts in your life – resolve the conflict within to resolve the conflict without.

Giving and receiving feedback

Giving and receiving feedback is becoming so important that it warrants a chapter to itself, Chapter 20. NLP is about how we elicit feedback from our minds, our language and our behavior, and the ways we use these together to achieve outstanding performance. And it is about continually testing to see how our discoveries work and continue to work. Nothing is static: we depend on feedback to maintain excellence. This is an important chapter; I encourage you to read and reread it, but above all to *do* it.

High performance coaching

Closely linked to our ability to give and receive feedback is our ability to coach ourselves and others. Chapter 21, High performance coaching, is what all of this book is about in a nutshell. We need to know how to coach ourselves and others if we want to grow our potential as individuals, as teams and as organizations. And we need to know these skills if we want to grow our relationships, our marriages, our families and our communities. Coaching is about learning and learning is about life. I have found NLP-based coaching to be life giving; I wish the same for you.

And finally a new Chapter 22 on Humor, one of those topics that is so obviously important that we often overlook it. I have put that right and I hope that this chapter will be the beginning of much more that I have to offer on this wonderful healing subject. I have drawn from my work with provocative therapy and included just a part of that, which I hope will enable you to explore more ways in which you can use humor for the benefit of yourself and others in whatever you do.

Humor, an overlooked topic

At the book fair in Roussillon, it took me almost half the day to figure out how to get the French to notice my author's stand. Some sort of "attrape-tout," or prop, would be needed... My current plan was bombing and, though the French allowed themselves to be lured over by an American-voiced command ("Pardon me! What is Your Favorite French Word?"), it was painful to watch as the Francophones struggled with their own language.

"Difficult, isn't it?" I sympathized, slyly handing over my card which read "French Word-A-Day."

"There are just so many wonderful words in the French language to choose from, n'est-ce pas?!" With that, I talked a little about my "mot du jour" blog and, when lucky, sold a book, based on the former.

By noon, I tired of pitching the unpopular "Favorite French Word" question out to the book fair traffic as it flowed past my stand. Then, just as enthusiasm began to wane, I had a stroke of good luck... one that corresponded with lunchtime. As I sat at my display table, eating three-cheese quiche, I began to notice something unusual: traffic began to slow – and sometimes stop – right before my very eyes!

"Bon appétit!" a French couple said.

"Oh... merci," I thanked them, covering my mouth, embarrassed.

Seconds later... it happened again:

"Bon appétit!" offered the man with a salt-n-pepper ponytail.

"Merci beaucoup!" I answered, in a muffled voice.

On and on the gastronomic wishes continued...

"Bon appétit!" chirped a woman in motorcycle jacket, and I quit chewing in time to give an enthusiastic nod of thanks...

"GOOD APPETITE!" a distinguished-looking Frenchman said, with cheer.

No matter the age or the outward appearance, the French were now noticing me!

For as long as that plate of food remained intact, each and every Francophone that passed my table paused in time to wish me a "Happy Meal!" So, that's that: at the next book fair I am ditching the "Favorite French Words" ploy... and getting smart – by bringing plenty of tarts!

Kristin Espinasse, *French Word a Day*

17
Develop a climate of trust:
Rapport

I am only through communication with the other. –Karl Jaspers

If you do not believe in the importance of rapport, then you may as well shut up shop now. Autocracies are dead. Hierarchies are crumbling. The only place for command-and-conquer management is in a museum. Relationships and influence are the only way to build the networks you need to succeed. And not only do you need rapport to build your business, you need it to succeed in life.

Rapport is the ability to connect with others in a way that creates a climate of trust and understanding. It is also the ability to appreciate one another's point of view (not always to agree with it), to be on the same wavelength, and to understand and accept one another's feelings. Rapport is essential for any form of communication to take place – unless, of course, you don't want to make progress!

I guarantee that most of your customers choose you because of the level of rapport you have with them. And more significantly, the customers you keep when things go awry are the ones with whom you have this kind of relationship. You are more likely to buy from, agree with, support and stay with someone to whom you feel connected than you are when this isn't the case. Hospital patients who build rapport with the nursing staff or carers have a greater statistical chance of recovery as a result of the superior care they get in return.

You can build rapport face to face, over the phone, via email, through text messages, through letters, or just in your imagination. And you can build rapport over time, shortly after you have met,

Rapport creates a climate of trust and understanding

instantly on meeting, or in advance of even making someone's acquaintance. No matter what the circumstances or who the people are with whom you want to build rapport, it is without doubt the quality of the rapport that makes the difference.

Near to our home in France is a restaurant, which was owned by an English couple when we moved into the area. We had sworn to ourselves that we would not become part of the English community in this part of France but rather part of the French community as far as they would allow us. So we avoided this restaurant – after all, why go to an English restaurant when we could do that back in England? However, one day we called there just for a drink and the way we were greeted was such that we felt our resolve soften. We could not avoid feeling welcome and well cared for, even though the service was not over-attentive. We decided to go back, such was the subtle influence of the relationship that was built in those few moments.

We learnt subsequently that the owners' approach had won the hearts of the local French people who also frequented the bar and the restaurant. We became regular customers. Imagine our disappointment, then, to discover that this couple decided to sell the restaurant, which was now a thriving business throughout the year. The new owner took over. He inherited an immense amount of goodwill and regular trade – and within six months he had lost it all. Nothing much had changed about the restaurant itself and the food was still good. However, this owner did not relate to the French customers and gave no impression of any rapport building. This once flourishing restaurant is now closed most nights of the week and is rumored to be up for sale again.

The skills involved in building and maintaining rapport were some of the earliest to be discovered with NLP and they have become essential to the networking economy. The people who were chosen as models of excellence, particularly in situations of influence or change, demonstrated that rapport is one of the most important factors needed for change to take place.

The new economy has three distinguishing characteristics. It is global. It favours intangible things – ideas, information, and relationships. And it is intensely inter-linked. These three attributes produce a new type of market place and society, one that is rooted in ubiquitous electronic networks.

Kevin Kelly, New Rules for the New Economy

If you think building rapport is just about matching people's behavior, then think again. The skill of building and maintaining rapport goes well beyond the level of body language. Rapport involves not only relating to people face to face but also remotely, by appealing to their style of communication and their expectations.

The skill of rapport goes well beyond body language

One of my clients received this email:

Jane
Have been looking further at the issue of your company's fees – which as you know, we are very concerned about. Your day rates not only equal those of the parent company but my investigations among my contacts have shown that they have increased exponentially in the last two years. I attach a comparison of your fees today compared with those charged in a previous proposal that you did for us a year earlier. Can you please justify to me:
1   Why you feel you can charge the same rates as the parent company?
2   Why there has been such a movement upwards in fees over the last two years please?
I feel very concerned about this. Thanks.
Wendy Smith

My client emailed back as follows:

Wendy
I have discussed the issues that you have raised with our parent company and internally with our fee department regarding company X. Please find attached a detailed explanation on both of the points that you have mentioned which I hope will serve to clarify our position on rates and illustrate that our rate increases are actually quite different to those you have indicated. Once you have had a chance to read this through I think it might be sensible for us to speak or even meet up to discuss the next stage.
I look forward to hearing from you.
Regards
Jane

To which, not surprisingly once you understand the principles of rapport, she received the following reply:

Thanks for the email which I read with interest; however I still feel that my questions are not fully answered... May I suggest that I meet with you at your office to clarify the matter of the fee rates so that I can be reassured that the fees do fit for the work that you are proposing.
Wendy

How would you have replied? Could you have found a way of replying that would have avoided the need for a meeting? We will come back to this email at the end of the chapter and see what Jane did eventually send after we had a session on rapport building.

Many people think that rapport is chatting about the weather

It is as important to know what rapport is *not* as it is to know what it is. Many people think that rapport is chatting about the weather, the family and the like. It may be, but only if the people you are talking to experience that as rapport. If not, then to chat about these things might have completely the opposite effect of rapport. If you are with someone who is aggressive, then although you may not want to be aggressive, you would certainly want to match the strength of their style in some way. There are some clues later in this chapter on how to do this.

Rapport is about connecting

Rapport is not about passing the time of day. Rapport is about joining people where they are in their style so that you connect with them in a way that supports all future communication. Rapport may be as much about being hard in your approach to someone as it is about being soft. And rapport is not about accepting what anyone says or does. In fact, by creating an environment of rapport you create the climate to discuss and influence those things that do present problems between you and others.

HOW TO BUILD AND MAINTAIN RAPPORT

Think of someone with whom you feel you have good rapport. What is true about your contact with them that isn't true for others? If you are in the company of other people, look around you. What would you say is your level of rapport with the people you see? Have you checked this out? What do you think your colleagues would say about the quality of rapport you have with them?

Consider some of the written communication you have with others. Who do you find it easy to communicate with? What is it about their style that you like? And whose communication do you find challenging? What is it about them and the way they communicate that you have found harder to relate to? If you are tempted to gloss over this question take care – you might be missing the very thing that will make a huge positive difference for you.

Pay attention to the physical mannerisms of the people around you. People in rapport typically adopt the same posture, move and gesture in similar ways, laugh together, adopt the same style and rhythm in movement and speech. They "match" each other. This happens naturally when two or more people are in rapport. They almost certainly aren't consciously aware of it happening. The result is that their thinking and feelings are similar.

People like people who are like themselves

How is your behavior similar to that of those around you now? Or not? Have you ever had that uncanny experience of having someone say exactly what you were thinking, or finding that you know exactly what someone else is feeling? When you adopt the same body language as someone else, you create the likelihood that you are engaging the same thinking and feeling circuits. So even if you are not thinking the same thing, you are very likely going to be thinking and feeling in the same way.

One of the core beliefs consistently held by people chosen as models of excellence in much of the research in NLP is:

Mind and body are part of the same system. What occurs in one part will affect all the other parts.

By modeling people who have deep levels of rapport, we discover that they adopt the same or a similar style of:

- Posture.
- Movement and gestures.
- Breathing levels.
- Voice tone and quality.
- Language content: visual/auditory/feelings, and key words.

They also hold similar or in some cases identical:

- ◆ Beliefs.
- ◆ Values.
- ◆ Sense of identity.
- ◆ Purpose in work and life.

When people demonstrate a similarity in any of these, we say that they are *matching* that characteristic.

Bill was a software developer who headed up a technical team. He dealt with many other departments in the company and frequently accompanied members of the sales team in meetings with clients. Technically he was highly skilled, but he didn't feel at ease in the company of others. He had attended many training courses on the techniques of running effective meetings, making presentations and communicating confidently, but he still didn't enjoy most situations that involved talking to other people, especially if it meant meeting people for the first time. He found these initial meetings extremely stressful.

Consequently, the clients in these meetings tended to direct their conversations away from Bill. Occasionally he met with someone with whom he seemed to "click" straight away, but this wasn't often. The emphasis in his role was changing. As his department grew he was expected to represent it more often, not only in sales meetings but in internal meetings with senior managers.

Rapport is essential for any meaningful communication to take place. You need rapport to be able to conduct a productive conversation, to engage someone's attention with a message, to run an effective meeting, or to expect others to follow your lead and want to buy into your sense of direction. Without rapport, very little communication of value will occur.

"Just because you are making a noise in my direction don't think you are communicating."

David Gordon

The skills are most needed when rapport does not occur naturally

So what happens when this connection doesn't naturally occur? This is when your skill of rapport building is most needed. The real test is whether you can build rapport when it is not returned in kind by the people with whom you are dealing. Let's explore the characteristics of people who do this.

Skilful communicators build rapport by:

◆ Seeking to connect with everyone with whom they come into contact in a way that demonstrates respect for difference. They respect the beliefs, values and styles of others even though these may be different to their own.
◆ Being aware of the degree to which they are similar (or not) in any of the following, recognizing that significant dissimilarity probably indicates lack of rapport:
  a Posture – Position of the body, position of the legs and feet, weight distribution; position of the arms, hands or fingers; shoulder tension or relaxation; inclination of the head.
  b Expression – Direction of the look; movement of the gaze.
  c Breathing – Rate of breathing; position of the breathing, in the chest, abdomen or low stomach.
  d Movement – Signature rhythm (overall tempo of movement), fast, steady, slow or still.
  e Voice – Pace, volume, pitch, tone, type of words, intonation.
  f Language – Visual, auditory, feelings patterns.

The more you can subtly get into the style of the person with whom you are communicating, the more you will begin to understand what their motives, attitudes, values, beliefs and feelings must be for them to be doing and saying what they are doing and saying.

And in written communication:

◆ Words used.
◆ Senses preferred.
◆ Values highlighted.
◆ Chunk size.
◆ Sequence of the communication, e.g. big picture first, details later.
◆ Problem or desired state orientation.
◆ Use of time during and between communication.
◆ Passive or active language.
◆ Use of metaphor or precision language.

This can be a long list to attempt to work on at one time. Some of these may come naturally to you. Choose one of the less natural ones and practice that until you can do it automatically.

Choose occasions to practice matching when you are an observer and do not have to engage in conversation. Using your written communication with someone is a good place to start, as you have time to analyze what they are saying and how they are saying it. You also then have the time to match your response to take into account their preferences.

Good rapport can often be silence

Be prepared for the consequences. One of my friends who sat silently matching the behavior of a manager who was engaged in conversation with a colleague was taken by surprise when the manager turned to my friend and said, "I'd really like to know what you think." It's interesting what happens when you actively demonstrate rapport, silent or otherwise!

RAPPORT AS A FORM OF INFLUENCE

Rapport is influence

Rapport is influence. As you communicate you engage in a system. The higher the level of rapport that exists between you, the greater the positive influence you have on each other.

This usually doesn't require much conscious attention. When you have rapport you know it, you feel at ease in the other person's company, conversation flows, and equally silence is comfortable. What occurs is like a dance: as one moves the other follows. It is impossible to tell who leads and who follows. Conversation flows as you understand the meaning and intention of what the other person says. You appreciate and respect each other's feelings. It does not mean that you necessarily agree with everything the other person is saying, but you understand what they say and why they say it.

Pacing is the next step. You can test the rapport by shifting the style of the communication. For example, if the other person seems "stuck" a problem state and you feel that the desired state would be a more productive place to be, you might test the willingness to move by making small steps in that direction. If the other person shifts with you, you probably have rapport and therefore influence. If not, you need to invest some more into matching where they are right now.

When you match and pace, you create an environment in which you can lead. This constitutes influence.

Examples of how and when you might want to use rapport to lead and influence are:

+ In a discussion or interview with someone who is nervous or hesitant, to help them to relax and open up.
+ When you want to attract potential customers to your company, either by face-to-face contact or remotely.
+ When you want to introduce new ways of working to an individual or department that has become fixed in their thinking.
+ When you want to encourage people to give you good support, service or care.
+ When someone is angry, to help them calm down.
+ When someone is worried and tense, to help them relax.
+ When you want to teach a new concept, by relating to what people know already.

Below are some examples of this kind of influence in conversation.

+ I can picture the new system that we want to develop.
+ So when you see this system and imagine what it looks like, what are you saying to yourself?

+ I feel uncertain about the customer presentation this afternoon.
+ I can understand that you feel uncertain. How would you like to feel?

+ My colleagues told me that they really valued the ideas I put forward at the meeting.
+ I can understand that–I value the ideas that you put forward too. What did you feel about them?

I recently received a text message from one of my friends in the following style:

Can you ring me wen u get bak I need 2 ask u a favour about nxt wk – Ta!

It would be inappropriate to send an eloquent, enriched language message back! It would be much more on the same wavelength to say:

Will do c u soon I hope 2 – Luv S

However, what about an email like this, which I received through my web page not so long ago?

Also a little story for your info-tainment.

A few weeks ago, I started a new role and during my lunch was strolling thru a mall (as you do) and there was a bookseller selling remainder books. Well, as I moved around the table ambling thru the various biogs, Ancient Greek tombs, and associated vegetarian cookbooks what should catch my ear but somebody talking about your book – NLP at Work. A fairly lively debate ensued between the woman thinking of purchasing your book and the bookseller justifying why he was selling it. Anyways to cut a long story to a small duplex, the woman put the book down and as I leant over to pick it up, she picked up the vegetarian book I was (past tense) planning to buy and said "I'll have this one, it's bound to be more useful – can't cook nuffin with NLP." So what am I to do – she's taken my book and here I am holding your baby – so to speak – well I took it home and read it.

So you say why are you telling me all this...? Well a week or so later I'm in this same mall and here I am positioned in front of this same bookseller and he says to me "You know that book you bought last week, well I've got 8 more copies – do you want to buy them – ha ha ha." So I did and I think it was his biggest pattern interrupt all day.

When I got home I thought what am I doing with nine (9) copies of the same book and then it came to me. "I'll give them to my friends the next time they ask – hey what's all this NLP stuff about." So I guess you can cook somethin' with NLP... after all.

A very different style of response is appropriate here. The sender is a storyteller and uses a lot of dialogue, some in the form of internal questioning, and auditory-style language as well as metaphor throughout. To respect that style would be to write in a similar way. (And I had a lot of fun thinking about my answer!) If you are curious about what I said, take a look at "Ask Sue Knight" on www.sueknight.com.

The same principles apply on a bigger scale. For example, it is crucial to ensure that new systems match the style and culture of a company. The concept of match, pace, lead works at every level, not only between individuals but when introducing any new element to a system. It is important that any system you introduce fits with what you already have.

Systems need to fit the style of the company

I've sometimes seen small, informal organizations attempt to "bolt on" more formal appraisal systems that belong to a much larger, more bureaucratic organization. One of the simplest and most effective appraisal systems asked only four questions: What are your goals? How well did you do? What skills would help you develop further? What actions shall we commit to? This was successful because the style matched the informality and openness of the company in which it was introduced.

Similarly, it is important to ensure that rapport exists between managers and jobholders. To continue with appraisal, for a jobholder to accept feedback from his or her manager and vice versa there needs to be rapport. With rapport the appraisal will find its own style and form. Appraisal is about learning and development; it is a vehicle that provides the stimulus for continuous improvement.

MATCHING AND PACING VALUES IN NEGOTIATION

Achieving a state of rapport is the most important outcome at the beginning of a negotiation. From then on, it is important to ensure that you maintain that rapport throughout. Without rapport you have no negotiation. If at any time you lose rapport, rebuild it, and only continue on to anything else of import when you have restored it. When you have rapport, the structure of the negotiation suggests itself. The process of what is happening determines the content.

Genuine commitment to a solution will only exist if it is built on the values of each of the parties involved. Values are the principles by which we live and are core to who we are as people. A partnership, a relationship, a team and a company unite typically because they share common values. People are attracted to us because of the values we communicate.

It is not enough just to think about the values of the other party. Respecting and pacing values is a way of building a deep level of rapport. Without this, any other attempts to match and pace are superficial and temporary. Identifying and pacing values are therefore crucial to skilled negotiation. There are different ways to do this. For example, if someone holds the value of security, they will look for a solution to the negotiation that satisfies this value, but they will also want the negotiation to be conducted in a way that respects their need for security. They may, for example, want the points to be presented in a nonthreatening way. If someone's value is fun, it is possible that they will want their representation of fun to be present both in the way the ideas are put to them and in the solution.

Commitment is built on values

Your partner in a negotiation will be evaluating you and the way you present yourself, the venue of the negotiation and the ideas you discuss, among many other things. They evaluate these things against their own values. If they judge a person by their ability to listen, they will be judging you by the way they recognize this. And even more significantly, they will have a unique way of knowing how each of their values has been met. They know this by a set of rules and standards that constitute their evidence of fulfillment.

Communicators who are considered to be excellent in their ability to achieve understanding and influence are people who can match, pace and lead the other person's values. They identify what conditions have to be true for those values to be satisfied. They operate from the belief that each person is unique.

Each person is unique

Learning the unique indications that have to be present for someone to feel that their values are respected and fulfilled is one of the most sophisticated skills you can develop to negotiate your way through life. The evidence of fulfillment for each of the following values could be (they will be different and unique for everyone):

Value	Evidence of fulfillment
Openness	A willingness to express feelings. Someone who is prepared to state their views before others state theirs. Someone who talks about what is happening in their personal life as well as in their business life.
Security	An acceptance of solutions to problems that have been tried and tested and shown to work in other situations. The ability to express ideas without having them ignored or dismissed.
Creativity	Agreements and ideas that haven't been applied before. People who can think laterally and who can provide a new way of thinking about existing situations.

Value	Evidence of fulfillment
Listening	Someone who doesn't interrupt, who is curious about what is being said and who asks clarification questions. Someone who leans forward and maintains eye contact for the majority of the time someone else is speaking.

To find out someone's values, watch and listen. Pay attention to what excites them and what changes their state to one of interest and curiosity. To what do they pay attention? If they are constantly looking at their watch and want to get on with discussions straight away, you may find that attention to time and to the way time is used is important to them. The more you develop your sensory acuity, your awareness to notice even the smallest of changes in the person with whom you are dealing, the more you will begin to be able to determine when their state changes. Eventually you will be able to "calibrate" these different patterns of behavior to the different states so that you know what outward signs symbolize the different states for your partner.

One of the surest ways of knowing that you have touched on someone's values will be a skin color change. If you make a proposal that meets the values and evidence of fulfillment for the other person, they are very likely to blush. By matching and pacing your partner's values and their evidence of fulfillment, you are building a deep level of rapport. Understanding your own values is a way of beginning to understand those of others.

To find out values, watch and listen

You can learn to calibrate changes in behavior

WHOLE BODY LISTENING

Businesspeople who listen with care and skill are still in the minority. The people who have this ability are usually those who generate immense respect and influence. And we usually find that rapport is a major component of their ability to listen.

When you listen with rapport you are listening with your whole body. Not only do you hear what the other person is saying, you also gain insights as to what they are thinking and feeling. You are influencing the interaction with your nonverbal behavior more often than anything you do. Tom Peters in *A Passion for Excellence* says, "Listening is the highest form of courtesy." Whole body listening can be the trigger that influences someone to gain insight, to find their own solutions and to generate commitment to those solutions.

Contrast someone whose attention is internal, on themselves, and someone who is listening with their whole body:

People whose attention is internal	People who are listening with their whole body
They think about themselves, make evaluations and judgments. They worry about and concentrate on what just happened, what was just said, or even what might happen next. They get distracted.	They are in a state of curiosity. Their attention is entirely on the other person.
Their intention is self-oriented.	Their intention is toward the other person.
Their gaze is defocused or distracted.	Their gaze is on the other person, looking away occasionally to process what the other person is saying.
Their body posture is independent of what the other person is doing or saying.	They match the other person's posture.
Their language is "I" and "me" centered. They make statements and often express beliefs as facts.	Their language is "you" centered and they use key words and language patterns that match the person they are speaking to. They predominantly ask open questions.

Whole body listening means being able to give all of your attention to someone else. Some textbooks on listening advise you to make eye contact. You can probably remember those situations when, although someone was looking at you, you knew that their mind and spirit were somewhere else entirely! Eye contact alone is no proof of listening. NLP provides the techniques to enable you to listen with your whole body. Rapport is a demonstration of whole body listening.

Everything someone says and does will give you some information about their values. They will tell you some explicitly and some may be unknown to them, but they are there. You only have to look and listen.

"I want to talk to you about doing some design work for us. We've worked with one company for a long time now, but they seem to be getting behind the times with their ideas. We've got less time to spend on this than we had in the past, so we want a company who is going to take the initiative to find out what they need to give us what we want. We don't have a lot of time and I'd appreciate you telling me whether you genuinely can work in this way with us."

Let's say that the values of the speaker in the passage above are:

+ Effective use of time.
+ Openness and honesty.
+ Up-to-date ideas.
+ Initiative.

The depth of the rapport you build will depend on your ability to match these values in what you say and what you do. If you start to ramble in the way you respond and if you wait to be asked the next question, you probably won't be very successful.

If, on the other hand, you answer concisely and openly, telling the other person frankly what you can and cannot do, and if you take the lead in asking questions, then you will probably make good progress. This will only ring true, however, if they are values that you also hold.

At one of our open evenings I was talking to a manager of a computer call center. He was explaining the problems they had been having with their computer system. He also explained that when he raised these problems with the software suppliers they poured people onto the site. I also happen to know the software suppliers and I know that when they did that they believed they were satisfying the customer's needs. They didn't have a surplus of staff, so it was a big decision to put so much resource into one place. How sad, then, that it wasn't what the customer wanted! They had made a judgment about what to do based on their own values and evidence of fulfillment for customer satisfaction, not those of the client.

What was in fact important to the customer was personal one-to-one reassurance, not only that the current bugs in the system would be fixed but explanations of what the supplier was doing to prevent any similar bugs appearing in the system in the future.

Everyone has their own way of satisfying their needs, their evidence of fulfillment. It is crucial to know your customers' evidence of fulfillment and to find ways of meeting this if you want to succeed in business.

What would have to be true for you?

Ask your customers the most important question of all: "What would have to be true for you to want me to be your main supplier for the future?" Then sit back and listen. You will learn some of the most valuable information for meeting your customers' needs that you will ever need to know.

THAT EMAIL

Have you come to any conclusions about what didn't work and what might work better with the email at the beginning of this chapter?

My client realized that her response to the original email had been predominantly auditory when her client's email was visual and feelings based. In particular, the client was saying (covertly) that her feelings were not being acknowledged and that was true – in the communication they weren't.

The consequence of this was that Jane replied matching not only the sensory preferences but also the sequence in which she used them, so that they matched the sequence her client had used in her email. They did subsequently have a meeting in which Jane addressed and explored Wendy's feelings. Previously she had assumed that because Wendy was in the purchasing department it would be inappropriate to bring feelings into their communication (despite all the clues in the emails). The consequence was that both parties said they had the most productive meeting they had ever had and they reached full agreement on fees and a way forward.

SHORTCUT TO BUILDING RAPPORT

Before any contact with the other person:

1 Choose the person with whom you would like to enhance the rapport you have or expect to have.

2 Imagine yourself having the kind of rapport with them that you would really like to have.
3 Imagine yourself being connected to them in a way that fully respects who they are.

During contact with them (whether that is face to face or remotely):

4 Pay attention to *how* they communicate as much as if not more than to *what* they communicate.
5 What is significant about their:
   • Behavior?
   • Language?
   • Body language?
   Pick one of the above to concentrate on.
6 Match the element you have chosen.
7 By being similar to this person, what do you detect as being important to them? For example time, silence, integrity, immediacy, innovation, decisiveness, action, strategic thinking, acknowledgment of feelings, sense preference (visual/auditory/feelings) etc.
8 How do you/can you respect this aspect that is important to them?
9 Monitor how the connection between you strengthens.
10 What else can you do to build the rapport even further?

After the interaction:

11 How would you evaluate the strength of the connection between you?
12 What made a difference?
13 What else could you have done/could you do in future interactions?

SUMMARY

Rapport has become a vital skill on which to pin the success of your business. Through your ability to build rapport you can help other people feel at ease in your company – they choose to be with you because you make it easy for them to be so. People relate to you and the services you offer because they feel you are sympathetic to their needs. Even if you are not technically perfect, the rapport you have with the people with whom you live and work determines the lasting nature of the relationship. By building rapport you build trust and understanding.

THOUGHT PROVOKERS

1   The next time you are in the company of others, pay attention to the elements we have covered in this chapter. Notice their posture and their movements. Listen to their voices and the words they use. Identify which people seem to be most in rapport with each other. What similarities are there in these elements?

2   Seek out the company of two people you know who have excellent rapport with each other. What do you see and hear them doing and saying that is similar?

3   Choose one element per day, e.g. head movement, voice tone, body position. Pay attention to that element for each person you meet.

4   Ask a friend to engage in conversation with you. Notice each time your attention changes from external to internal.

5   Choose two pieces of written or typed communication that you have sent recently. To what extent did you consider what was important to the other person when you sent them? If you had paid more attention to their values and their style of communicating, how might you now change this communication?

6   How would you rate the attention you pay to the rapport you have with:
    ◆ Your boss?
    ◆ Your key client?
    ◆ A significant member of your team?
    ◆ Each of your children (if you have any)? If it differs, what is that you do differently with each?
    ◆ Your life partner?
    ◆ Your parents?
    ◆ Your suppliers?
    ◆ Three people you came into contact with when you last left your home?
    ◆ Three people you expect to meet up with when you next leave your place of work?

REFERENCES

Kevin Kelly (1999) *New Rules for the New Economy: 10 Ways the Network Economy Is Changing Everything*, Fourth Estate.

Tom Peters & Nancy Austin (1986) *A Passion for Excellence: The Leadership Difference*, HarperCollins.

Many years ago in the hills of Patagonia there was a village. Its inhabitants were starving. They lived in fear of a dragon that they had seen in their fields and they would not go to harvest their crops.

One day a traveler came to the village and asked for food. They explained that there was none because they were afraid of the dragon. The traveler was brave and offered to slay the dragon. When he arrived at the fields he couldn't see a dragon, only a large watermelon. So he returned to the village and said, "You have nothing to fear; there is no dragon, only a large watermelon." The villagers were angry at his refusal to understand their fear and hacked the traveler to pieces.

Some weeks later another traveler came to the village. Again, when he asked for food he was told about the dragon. He too was brave and offered to kill the dragon. The villagers were relieved and delighted. When he arrived at the fields he also saw the giant watermelon and returned to the village to tell the villagers that they were mistaken about the dragon – they need have no fear of a giant watermelon. They hacked him to pieces.

More time passed and the villagers were becoming desperate. One day a third traveler appeared. He could see how desperate they were and asked what the problem was. They told him and he promised he would slay the dragon so that they could go to the fields to harvest their crops. When he got to the field he too saw the giant watermelon. He reflected for a moment, then he drew his sword, leaped into the field, and hacked the watermelon to pieces. He returned to the villagers and told them he had killed their dragon. They were overjoyed. The traveler stayed in the village for many months, long enough to teach the villagers the difference between dragons and watermelons.

18
Negotiate your way through life: Perceptual positions

If you wish to be fully alive you must develop a sense of perspective. Life is infinitely greater than this trifle your heart is attached to and which you have given the power to so upset you.
—Anthony de Mello

Some people have a magic formula

Have you ever wondered how it is that some people seem to be able to navigate their way through life achieving most of what they want and somehow supporting the people with whom they come into contact to do the same? Maybe you are one of those people. We can all do this to some extent, but there are some people who appear to be able to do it consistently. They seem to have some magic formula that enables them to transform just about every situation into one that has benefits for all involved.

If you are one of these people, then it is unlikely that you know exactly how you do this. You might be interested to compare what you know of your strategy with that of those who show a consistent excellence in their ability both to resolve conflicts and to make progress that is in the interests of all parties involved.

There are those who take a narrow view of the world

Too often today we are experiencing the fallout from those who take a narrow perspective on the world: for example countries who resist commitment to environmental protection treaties with the lame reason that they will be sacrificing jobs and raising unemployment.

It is possible to learn how to:

- Achieve what we really want in ways that enable others to do the same.
- Tap increasingly into what is important to us and express it in ways so that others will listen.
- Learn and grow with every interaction we have, including those we might otherwise have classed as "difficult."

- Deal with people who we feel are regularly trying to block our path.
- Negotiate a win/win in situations that might otherwise be compromised.
- Empathize with others and yet not take on the burden of all their emotions.
- Learn from all experiences in ways that benefit us in all contexts of our life.
- Deal with situations as they arise, managing them in a way that is in everyone's best interests, and move on.
- Let go of resentment, anger, frustration and guilt.
- Increasingly move through work and life as a learning journey that becomes increasingly enriching with every step we take.

It really is quite simple and of course common sense – once we know how. This chapter presents some of the work done by John Grinder and Judith DeLozier to provide shortcuts to powerful techniques such as these. This is an example of what is sometimes referred to as New Code NLP. The strategy that John and Judith developed is a way of learning to take different perspectives on a situation in order to find balance in how we go forward to a solution. Because of this, the strategy for negotiation is often called perceptual positions. After all, the perceptual positions we take in our heads and in our physiology are what makes our life what it is.

Perceptual positions make our life what it is

TAKING A BALANCED APPROACH

John Grinder and Judith Delozier modeled people who were skilled at negotiating a way forward that was a win for themselves and also a win for the person or people with whom they were negotiating. They found that these people were able to experience a situation from many different perspectives and that it was this mental agility that enabled them to gain the insights that provided the breakthrough. Not only did these people find ways to achieve a win/win, they also grew in their learning in life along the way.

We can benefit from the model that they derived from their exemplars.

The principle is that the more perspectives we can take on a situation, the more we have choice and understanding. And therefore the more likely we are to find a way to proceed and learn that is in everyone's interest.

Some other principles apply here as well:

- **Every relationship is a perfect system.** What we get is what we allow, encourage and create. We might not like the system even though it is perfect in the way we maintain it. And we can change it by changing ourselves. We are the only person in any system that we can change, but in doing so we influence everyone else. It is just a matter of time to find the change that we can make in ourselves that influences the other person in a direction that is mutually rewarding.

Generic learning is available to us in all situations

- **Generic learning is available to us in all the situations we experience in life.** So we can take learning that not only benefits the immediate situation but all other contexts in our life too.

There are three primary positions (you can take many more if you choose, but we will concentrate on three). I include below the description of what it means to take this position in your thinking and also some of the questions you can use if you are coaching someone else through the process.

OWN SHOES (1ST POSITION)

By putting ourselves in 1st position, we are able to connect with what is important to us personally. To do this we need to be able to see, hear and feel the situation from our own perspective (in our own shoes). In this position we think in terms of what it is like for me in this scenario. We speak using language such as "I feel," "I want," "I hear," "I see." We tap into the truth of our own perspective on the situation. This is a way of thinking that allows us to know what we really want. We can see and hear the other person (or people) and we experience them from our "map of the world."

THEIR SHOES (2ND POSITION)

By putting ourselves in 2nd position we are able to understand where the other person is coming from and what has to be true for them to be doing or saying what they are. It is quite different to "put yourself" in the other person's shoes as opposed to "thinking" about what it must be like to be in their shoes. By putting ourselves in the other person's shoes, we experience the situation *as if* we are them. We are able to imagine how it is to look out of their eyes and hear out of their ears and be in their body, such that we see, hear and feel the situation as if we *are* them. Of course we can never absolutely do this, but it is amazing just how uncannily close we can get when we are skilled in this way of thinking.

When you are fully in the other person's shoes and have their perspective on the situation, you are able to understand their map of the world. No matter how bizarre someone's behavior might have seemed from your own perspective, in their shoes it is normal and perfectly understandable. To put ourselves fully into the shoes of another person allows us to tap into the emotions behind what they are doing and saying. This is often a position of amazing insight about what is really going on for the other person in a situation.

In 3rd position you have the ability to stand back from a situation and experience it as if you are a detached observer. In your mind you are able to see and hear yourself and the other person as if you are a fly on the wall. You are unlikely to have emotions in this situation as you dissociate from what is going on. You may have concern, but not the emotions that you would have in either 1st or 2nd position.

This is a position of analysis and learning; in fact, it is the only place in which it is appropriate to do analysis. It is in this position that you can stand back and be aware of the dynamic that is going on between 1st and 2nd positions. You can be aware of how inextricably linked you and the other person are in the dynamic of what is happening. This is the position in which you can get the bigger picture, the systems view of what is going on. It is here that you can gain insights about what learning the other person is unconsciously offering you; not just learning about this specific scenario but learning at a much more generic level.

So if you have not been listening to someone, the learning is not just about what you can do with this specific person but how you might improve your ability to listen in all scenarios. Here is where you can identify how you can change to make a difference (and it is only *you* who can change!).

You can experience the situation as if you are in the other person's shoes

OBSERVER
(3RD POSITION)

3rd position is one of analysis and learning

"A story's value lies in the space created by the relationship between the teller and the listener."   *– Anon*

WHERE AND WHEN CAN WE USE THIS APPROACH?

To fully experience what it is like to be in each of these positions, work through the shortcuts at the end of the chapter. The glib answer is to say everywhere and at all times. However, there is often a belief that these approaches work in face-to-face situations and nowhere else. This is far from the truth. This way of thinking can certainly benefit us face to face (and we can learn to do this in real time while we are in conversation, in advance as a form of preparation, or afterwards to review what has happened), but it is just as relevant for remote communication. For example, we can apply this kind of thinking to ensure that we phrase our emails in a way that creates the effect that we really want.

I received an email recently that just said:

Jones
See you on Monday.
Brian

At first I thought it was for someone else. Then I thought my colleague had dreamt up a nickname for me, Jones. Eventually I realised he was answering a question I had asked him in an email several days earlier (for the surname of a mutual contact). In Brian's shoes he read my question and, treating it like a regular conversation, answered the question and closed the message. However, if he had put himself in my shoes, he might have realized that a lot of emails had flowed through the ether between the time I had sent him this question and getting his answer, and the original question was not at the forefront of my thinking.

I cannot make him put himself in my shoes, but I can learn to put myself in his shoes in order to think about how I can learn from this and save myself time in the future.

Perceptual positions thinking works in the design of anything that involves other people. It is interesting how computer games have developed in their use of these different positions. And what is also interesting is the preference people have for the

We can apply this thinking at all times and in all situations

Computer games draw on the various perceptual positions

different positions in their choice of game. For example, there are first-person games (usually first-person shootouts) in which you are associated into the shoes of the key player. Consequently, you are likely to experience the emotions of being that player. And there are "command-and-conquer" games where you take a third position and manage many players or situations as an overseer.

The closest to second position would be RPG (role-playing games) in which you advise and instruct one of the players in the game but from an overseeing position, so it is a mix of second- and third-position thinking. If you play or know people who play computer games, they probably have a preference for which kind of game (depending on the position they adopt) is their favorite.

We can help others to appreciate situations and services by taking them through any one or all of the perceptual positions. For example, the author of the following article from the @demon newsletter is helping us appreciate some of the design features of a website by putting us in the shoes of the web page user.

Browsing the shops one day, imagine you walk into a department store called, say, Inter-Net Universal Superstores. There's no proper signposting and you can't find an information desk or any staff. You look for your favourite magazine but can only find hundreds of magazines, newspapers and paperback books, all mixed up. You try to find a loaf of bread but again, there are no signs. And when you do eventually stumble across the bread shelves, most of them are empty.

You think you'll try the clothing department – but where is it? You turn the corner and trip over a trolley dumped in a darkened corner. You come across a big sign, "Grand Sale Next Week = 50% off," but then you check the dates and realise "next week" has long passed. By now you've had enough. You want to tell the manager how annoyed you are – but no one knows where he is…

It's hard to imagine any shop quite that bad, yet cyberspace is littered with sites that are the Internet equivalent of our fictitious Store From Hell, many of them put there by people who ought to know better.

This insight into how we present ourselves to our audience comes from the ability of the author to put him- or herself into the shoes of the people on the receiving end of what we do. This skill is essential in developing our ability to judge how what we are doing and saying is being received. Skillful negotiators in all

Skillful negotiators use all three positions

contexts and all media instinctively use all three positions as a way of taking a balanced approach to a situation.

IMBALANCED POSITIONS

An imbalanced use of any of the positions has implications for your ability to make progress.

James often had to attend meetings as part of his work. He usually prepared for these meetings by carefully thinking through his proposals. He often had ideas for ways the department could handle new projects. He couldn't normally see why he wouldn't get the go-ahead from his manager. He felt that his manager's style was to stall and throw out objections. James usually felt extremely frustrated by the response he received. As far as he was concerned, his manager was being stubborn. Sometimes his frustration reached such a level that he wondered if it was worth staying with the department.

Excessive use of 1st position leads to lack of understanding of others

Excessive use of 1st position can lead to a lack of understanding and subsequent dismissal of other people's feelings and ideas. You might push for the achievement of your outcomes, but at the expense of others. So, although you may achieve what you want, your achievement is likely to be short lived and may backfire in some way. You may feel overcome by your emotions.

Diane was considered by her team to be caring and compassionate. She became concerned if any of her team experienced problems and would endeavor to help them solve those problems through discussion. However, whenever she did this she found herself experiencing the feelings of the person she was counseling. Not only did she experience these feelings during the discussion, she found they stayed with her, often for the rest of the day and sometimes longer. She began to avoid getting into such discussions for fear of the burden of emotions she might subsequently carry.

Excessive use of 2nd position leads to loss of self-esteem

Excessive use of 2nd position can lead to a loss of self-esteem if you identify with other people's needs and feelings at the expense of your own. Essentially, you would be giving others priority over yourself.

It is possible that by overly identifying with the other person you stop yourself achieving and even thinking about what you really want. You may find yourself taking on other people's feelings and being unable to shake them off. Over time the weight of others' emotions can be mentally and emotionally fatiguing if carried in this way.

David was a member of a project team engaged on a high-profile task for the company. The project team was working to a tight schedule and sometimes tempers flared and discussions would become heated. David, however, appeared untouched by this emotion. Physically and emotionally, he seemed to distance himself. This often irritated the other team members, who felt that he didn't care about the success of the project.

Excessive use of 3rd position can give an image of being detached and unemotional. You would be likely to be objective and analytical without the capacity to experience the emotion of the situation.

Excessive use of 3rd position can give an image of being detached and unemotional

The ability to use all three positions in a balanced way leads to cooperative, assertive behavior and increased choice and understanding.

WHEN TO USE EACH POSITION

1st position is a good one to adopt when you want to stand up for yourself, see things from your perspective, hear things for yourself, get in touch with your own feelings, or when initially setting outcomes for yourself. It is a position from which to ask yourself the question, "What do I really want?" It is also an appropriate position in which to do an ecology check for any outcomes you set yourself; that is, does this outcome fit with who I am/want to be? Developing your ability to experience 1st position can be a way of moving from nonassertive to assertive behavior.

1ST POSITION

When you can't understand another person's behavior, 2nd position is a way of getting behind that behavior and into their experience and feelings. Once you understand or seek to understand (because there will be times when you cannot absolutely check out that you are right), this will communicate itself to the other person and will often give them a feeling of

2ND POSITION

reassurance that you do understand their position. More especially, it will give you greater understanding and therefore choice about how to deal with the situation, taking into account how the other person is affected by it.

3RD POSITION

This position can be valuable when you want to stand back, take stock and think objectively about a situation. It can be particularly valuable when you don't want the emotions attached to either being in or thinking about a situation. People who are able to handle aggression from others in a controlled and unemotional way often do this from 3rd position so that they are not, for example, experiencing the feelings of anger, frustration or hurt that they might be feeling if they were in 1st position.

Andy Wilman was making a documentary about the skills of the fastest people on the planet. He interviewed racing driver Michael Schumacher and the then Ferrari Technical Director Ross Brawn. In an article in the *Daily Telegraph*, he analyzed Schumacher's ability to detach in a way that gave him an edge on all other drivers racing at the time.

"Calmness was another Schumacher asset. Pure wind in the hair speed doesn't blow his frock up. 'When I'm racing my heart rate is very low,' he says. 'Probably lower than yours is sitting here right now.' Such detachment from speed goes hand in glove with another factor vital to every member of the speed elite: the ability to carry out several functions all at once. He could function as an F1 driver and on top of that he could think about the race that was going on around him. You knew he'd come on the radio and tell us to keep an eye on the weather because there were dark clouds forming on one side of the circuit. 'I have worked with other drivers and they just about cope with the driving [said Ross Brawn]. There's no spare capacity. When Rubens Barrichello first came to us I suppose I was expecting to have the same sort of discussions on the radio that I had with Michael, but for the first few races he struggled. Every time I spoke to him he lost half a second a lap. After that he raised his game.'"

IN BLOCKED
SITUATIONS

If you want still further choices in a situation when there is conflict or a block to making progress, then step into the presupposition "Behind every behavior is a positive intention toward you." This is one of the beliefs of excellence explained in Chapter 14.

As with all the beliefs, this does not have to be true. You only have to think and act *as if* it were true. Some creativity helps here in your thinking about what the positive benefit might be. What is the potential benefit in the situation for you? How can you turn the situation into an opportunity, even though it may not have initially presented itself to you in this way? For example, if you are faced with someone who is asking you awkward questions, they may be doing that to test the validity of your ideas so they can decide whether or not they want to back them. That is a reason for them to ask questions for themselves. However, a benefit for you may be that they are providing you (unconsciously) with the opportunity of learning how to deal with awkward questions and thereby improving your skills as a presenter and negotiator.

You only have to act "as if"

In the scenario involving James earlier in this section, his ability to adopt different perceptual positions and to consider the positive intention behind his manager's behavior will affect his response to the situation.

James was experiencing the situation with his manager from a dominant 1st position. When James did eventually step into 2nd position – that is, he put himself into his manager's shoes – he experienced a strong feeling of insecurity and perceived the ideas being presented to him as a threat to his position. James (in 1st position) had never realized this possibility and was shocked to appreciate how his manager might be feeling. When James considered the situation objectively from 3rd position, he realized that the more the James in 1st position pushed and initiated new ideas, the more his manager resisted and blocked him. By continuing to do more of the same, he was intensifying the response he received.

And the benefit to James of his manager's behavior? (Remember, this does not have to be true. He only has to act as if it were.) It could be that:

- He wants James to learn how to show real empathy toward someone else.
- He is helping James to learn how to approach solutions at a slower pace than previously.
- He wants James to prioritize and think through his ideas so he only puts over the ones of the highest importance to everyone.
- He wants James to develop 2nd position thinking!

When James re-evaluated the situation, having experienced it in 1st, 2nd and 3rd positions, he decided to take a different approach to the next meeting. He took more of a back seat initially and supported the ideas his manager put forward. He waited until his manager asked him for an idea before volunteering any, and explained what support he would need for the idea to work. He invited his manager to develop the idea further. He regularly checked out how he thought his manager might be feeling as he did this.

Over time, he gained more and more of his manager's support. Eventually he was able to put forward his ideas without waiting to be asked and he and his manager worked together more cohesively as a team than they had ever done before. When James's manager was appointed to the position of director of special projects, he invited James to join him in the new department as senior project manager.

ORGANIZATIONAL IMPLICATIONS

IMPLICATIONS OF COMPANIES OPERATING PRIMARILY FROM ONE POSITION

We can also detect preferences in thinking in company cultures.

- **1st position** There may be a fire-fighting, crisis management style. The company may jump to conclusions about what the solutions to problems might be without checking that they are the solutions in, say, their customers' minds. They are more likely to be problem oriented rather than solution oriented because they don't stand back, take stock and consider situations objectively. Many high-tech companies have sometimes operated this way as a result of lacking the softer, people understanding skills.
- **2nd position** The company may "go overboard" to do what the customer wants without seeking to influence the solution or the outcome. They would typically make unrealistic promises just to keep the customer happy in the short term. Even though they may "jump" to the customer's requests, they invariably lose the customer's respect.
- **3rd position** This company stays emotionally detached. This is characteristic of some large, bureaucratic organizations where there is no "personal touch." Correspondence will be

written in the third person, rarely signed by identifiable individuals. It is difficult to attach accountability to anyone in particular. Organizations such as this often handle buyouts ineffectively, with the buyout seen purely as a business acquisition and little or no attention paid to the emotions of the people involved.

The ideal is a company that takes all perceptual positions. This doesn't guarantee success, but it puts it head and shoulders above most other organizations.

The ideal is a company that takes all perceptual positions

- **1st position** It has a clear mission statement expressing the vision and mission of the business in a way that provides direction for all its employees. Shareholders in the business participate in the development of the business mission. It has agreed, published values that are upheld and lived out by everyone in the company. Employees' goals and roles tie in totally with the business strategy and are understood by everyone.
- **2nd position** Employees spend time with their customers (internal and external), finding out their true requirements and collecting regular feedback about how they are doing. They listen to what their customers have to say. The company does whatever it can to ensure the success of its customers no matter what that takes, and does this not only with customers but also with suppliers. The enlightened company takes a systems view of commerce and looks for ways to work with organizations that might once have been its competitors.
- **3rd position** Individuals and teams take time to stand back, take stock and review how they are doing. They pay attention to process as well as content. They learn from experience and in so doing ensure they are on a track of continuous improvement. They see the impact of their behavior on others in the system and, equally, the effect of others' behavior and actions on themselves. They take a strategic overview.

ADOPTING A BALANCED POSITION

Having a balanced perspective gives you the ability to stand up for your needs and desires in a way that takes account of other

This is a way to increase the chances of a win/win

people's needs and desires. This is a process of cooperation that leads to the increased likelihood of a win/win outcome. We know from the principles of outcome thinking, explained in Chapter 15, that dovetailing outcomes in this way increases the chances that you will achieve what you want. So assertion is about balance, balance between yourself and others.

Many books and training on assertiveness teach phrases to use and body language to adopt. They teach behavioral solutions. NLP research has shown that for meaningful and lasting change to occur, it is important to understand the implications for identity, beliefs, values, capabilities and environment as well as behavior. For example, it is pointless teaching someone to behave assertively if they believe that aggression is the way to get on in business. The logical levels of change model, explained in Chapter 13, offers insight about the different levels that need to be addressed.

If we manage our thinking we can achieve balance

Our awareness of the subtleties in our thinking can transform our ability to act in a balanced way. If you are thinking how difficult it will be to negotiate a good deal with your customer, it is unlikely that you will handle the situation confidently.

Your thinking influences the outcome.

Dawn's colleagues considered that she behaved aggressively in many everyday situations. Typically, she would promote her own ideas and plans without consulting others. She felt her own ideas were generally more appropriate and worthwhile compared with the ideas of her colleagues. She often got frustrated with others, but was generally unconcerned.

When Dawn explored the patterns of her thinking about these situations, she realized she was outside herself (dissociated). However, it was as though she was somewhere on the ceiling, looking down on the situation. She also noticed that she was much closer to herself in her imagination than she was to others. Although she could see the others and she could see them moving their lips as if they were speaking, she couldn't hear any words.

Dawn experimented with her thinking. First of all, she changed her position in her thinking so that she was at eye level with the people in her remembered situation. She also made herself equidistant from herself and the other people. She then associated into her picture of herself so that she could see the situation as if from her own eyes, hear it from her own ears, and experience the feelings of being there. Eventually, as Dawn brought this balance into her thinking, she began to notice that she contributed a greater balance to the way she handled situations.

Pauline had felt very stressed for several months. She was concerned about her son, who she believed was being bullied at school. She was also concerned about her mother, who had been ill for some time. She herself had recently taken on a lot more responsibility at work. The result of this was that she was continually feeling tired and depressed.

When Pauline described how she thought about these situations, she invariably saw them either as if she were in the other person's shoes, or sometimes, if she was dissociated, she would be close to the other person. Even in this dissociated state she experienced feelings and discovered that the feelings were not her own but those of the other person. There was no place in her thinking where she was free of emotion and, not surprisingly, she felt unable to think about these situations objectively. She was weighed down with everyone's feelings most of the time.

Pauline discovered that by stepping out of 2nd position and giving back the feelings to the rightful owner, she began to feel more relaxed (more like herself again). She positioned herself so she was equidistant from herself and the other person in her thinking; she effectively started to take a more balanced view of the situation. She began to be able to handle situations more objectively.

Your thinking is the template for your experience. If your thinking about a situation is out of balance, then you will probably find yourself giving one part of the situation or one person a greater priority than others. Typically, overuse of second position results from giving others a higher priority than you give yourself. Aggressive behavior results from giving yourself a higher priority than those around you. Excessive use of 1st position thinking can result in aggressive behavior. Excessive use of 2nd position thinking can lead to nonassertive behavior.

> Your thinking is the template for your experience

Similarly, the balance, or lack of it, in your thinking about the situation will influence your level of assertion. If you imagine other people as larger than life with booming voices and yourself as small with a quiet, squeaky voice, it is not surprising to find yourself responding nonassertively.

However, the difference in using NLP techniques to achieve balance in your life compared with more traditional approaches is that by changing your thinking process you will find your own words and phrases. You will discover your own appropriate nonverbal behavior. NLP gives you the space to discover your own solutions and styles that fit with who you are and who you want to be.

NLP coaches work on the assumption that you already have all the resources you need to achieve what you want. With NLP you can learn to draw on these resources when and where you want them.

SHORTCUT TO PERCEPTUAL POSITIONS

Think of a situation that involves another person with whom you would like greater choice and understanding.

1 Put yourself in your own shoes and identify:
   - What you are seeing.
   - What you are hearing.
   - What you are feeling physically and emotionally.
2 Break state.
3 Put yourself in the shoes of the other person and identify:
   - What they are seeing (as if you are them).
   - What they are hearing.
   - What they are feeling.
4 Break state.
5 Put yourself in the shoes of an outsider so that you can see yourself and the other person from a distance and ask yourself:
   - What are you seeing and hearing?
   - How are these two people (you and the other person) maintaining a perfect system by being the way they are being and doing what they are doing?
   - What is it that the more the "you" out there does, the more the other person out there does?
   - What is the positive intention behind what is happening for you (the you out there)? (You could also ask this question as "What is the learning intended for you in this situation?")
6 Go back into your own shoes with this balanced thinking about the situation. What is that like now? How might you now go forward in this situation?

STEPS FOR COACHING
SOMEONE ELSE THROUGH THE PROCESS

The following questions are just a guideline; you can find out what works for you as you coach someone through this process. Your role is to keep the other person clean in the various perceptual positions. Your role is *not* to offer solutions, *not* to explore why they are in this situation, just to take the subject through the experience in way that makes them consciously aware of what they are doing that has maintained the relationship in the way that it has been. Expect to be alongside them as you take them through this process. Mirror their way of speaking and moving. The more invisible you are the better. This is a nondirective style of coaching.

This is nondirective coaching

1 **Getting started** Ask the person to think of a situation that involves one other person and for which they would like some new understanding and choice.
2 **Spatial positioning** You might use spatial positions to support this process. For example, you might ask them to change physical places as they move from one position to the next. This helps them to learn the process in the muscle/in the whole body rather than just relying on their head to remember. It can also help them to change positions in their thinking by changing in reality.
3 **1st position** Invite them to take a seat or stand in a place that represents them in their own shoes. Let us assume that the subject's name is Pat. "So Pat, what is it like for you in this situation with this other person?" Keep the questions clean. Keep them in the present tense, so that the subject is not surmising about what has happened or what might happen in the future, but what it is like right now as they associate into the scenario. And follow up with clean questions: "and (their words) in what way?" "Hmmmm (their words) is there anything else about that?" Your aim is to get the subject deeply associated into what it is like in their shoes. Finally, summarize what you have heard using only their language so they get to hear the scenario mirrored back to them: "So (summary of their words) is there anything else?" If there is, explore it; if not, get ready to move on to the next stage.

4   **Break state** Invite the person to stand up and shake off all the emotions of that 1st position. Do something that distracts them if they are unable to do this for themselves. To be able to break state is a very valuable skill in its own right.

5   **2nd position** Ask the subject where they would place the other person in the situation/relationship. If they are seated, move a chair so that they can sit in that position. Before they do so, position the change: "I would like to invite you to step into the other person's shoes now. And as you sit in this chair (indicating the position where they have said the other party would be, maybe opposite where they were sat before), I would like you to put yourself into this other person's shoes and I will ask you questions as if you are them."

You might want to establish the name of the other party before you do this. Let's say that the other person's name is Paul. Encourage the subject to adopt the physiology of this other person, Paul, as a means of getting into their shoes. "So Paul, what is it like for you being in this situation with Pat?" Expect to get a perspective on Pat from Paul's eyes and ears and feelings. Keep the questions clean: "and (their words) in what way/like what/whereabouts is that/is there anything else about that?" Finally, summarize (no "why" or "what are you going to do about it?" (only clean questions). "So (summary using their words and the present tense) is there anything else?"

If at any time you are aware that the subject is slipping into any of the other positions, prompt them back to 2nd position with "So *Paul*, in your position, what is happening?"

6   **Break state** The same process as before to break state, moving them out of the spatial position that represented 2nd position as you do so.

7   **3rd position** This is the position in which you invite them to take an overview (a systems view) of what is happening in the relationship. It is also where you expect them to realize the learning that is available to them here. Remember that it is learning they are after, not what they are going to *do*! That is significant learning for many people going through this process, especially those who are used to being in a corporate world that encourages task focus and action planning.

Expect to "chunk up" for learning. Make sure they are standing or sitting in a position that is equidistant from both of the original positions. Standing can give them more of a helicopter perspective of what has been happening and can therefore be useful in supporting this 3rd position. So, standing beside them: "Describe what is happening here between Pat and Paul." Encourage them to use third-party language: "So how might you summarize what Pat is doing and what Paul is doing in relation to her?" "What is it that the *more* she does that, the *more* he does this?" In other words, you are inviting them to discover how the two sets of behaviors are completely related. The *more* is a way of summarizing the total of each person's behavior toward the other. You are inviting them to chunk up now rather than repeat what is happening at the same level as when they were in 1st and 2nd positions. For example, the *more* demanding Pat gets, the *more* withdrawn Paul becomes. The *more* withdrawn Paul becomes, the *more* demanding Pat gets, and so on.

Then highlight that if Pat continues to do what she has done, she will go on getting the same response, and that she is the only one who can change here. (That takes a bit of swallowing for some people who might want the other person to change!) You can apply one of the beliefs of excellence (see Chapter 14): "What might be the unconscious positive intention behind Paul's behavior toward Pat? In other words, what learning is available to Pat in this relationship if she chooses to take it?" Encourage an answer at the level of capabilities and above. You do not want an answer at the level of what Pat can do, that is too low a level to be useful as generic learning.

When you have the answer, you can dry run the learning for Pat: "So this learning (use the learning that Pat has identified for herself), do you think Pat is willing to take it (still considering this from the 3rd position point of view)?" If the answer is yes, add: "And can you imagine Pat with this learning and how that might be?" When you get the answer yes to that: "OK, I invite you now to go back into your own shoes with this learning on board and experience what it is like now with this learning."

If the person says no, they are not willing to take the learning, you might leave it at that. But it's unusual for them to do that. You might say: "Is there anything that might make a

Standing can provide a "helicopter" perspective

The more/more way of analyzing highlights how our behaviors are revealed difference so that Pat could take that learning on board?" Remember, it is not for you to decide if they accept the learning or not. Usually people do, but it is their choice.

8   **Back in 1st position with the learning on board**. "So here you are with this learning in place, what is it like for you now?" You are expecting to see and hear a change in state. That is the greatest indication that learning has taken place. Give the subject some time to appreciate this new perspective with this learning. Expect them to be in a new, resourceful state. The learning is the change in state and with this they will discover what they can do differently with the other person when they are next with them. You do not need to know this now. That is how NLP works in real time, not by action planning but by creating learning at a higher level that influences behavior at the time in a way that is appropriate.

SUMMARY

By developing your ability to experience situations from different perceptual positions, you gain a balanced approach in thinking, not only about outcomes but also about any other situation. In situations where you feel there is little or no understanding or progress, perceptual positions can provide a way of developing understanding and creating new choices. This is a very powerful technique for finding congruent solutions that are likely to transform your experience of the whole situation. Putting yourself in your client's shoes transforms your ability to present yourself and your business in a way that fits for them. It doesn't matter whether that client is someone you know well or someone you have never met, and may never meet, even someone who lives on the other side of the world.

Perceptual positions are an elegant and powerful way of creating choice and understanding in situations that might otherwise be blocked. The ability to take on different positions is a way of stepping beyond the limitations of everyday behavior and appreciating the different maps of the world from which we all operate. It is a way of understanding situations from others' perspectives. It is also a way of removing yourself from the emotions of a situation when you need to be able to think in a more detached and objective way about what is going on. Furthermore, it is a way of getting in touch with your own feelings and desires.

The balanced use of these positions, either as an individual or as a company, gives you flexibility and an increased chance of achieving a win/win outcome to which all parties are committed. It also supports you so that you can learn from all the situations you experience in life, in a way that is far more generic than merely an application to the immediate scenario.

THOUGHT PROVOKERS

1   What could be the unconscious positive intention toward you of the following behaviors? (Remember that this does not have to be true!)

   a   Your manager refuses to let you take on the extra responsibility you have requested.

   b   A colleague appears not to listen to what you have to say.

   c   The senior management team in your company reorganizes the structure of the company just as you were beginning to feel settled and secure.

   d   The company you have applied to for a job turns you down.

   e   A colleague in another department fails to respond to your requests for the information you need.

2   From which position (1st, 2nd or 3rd) do you think each of these people is operating?

   a   Peter was explaining to his team what he wanted from them. When the team members didn't understand, he became frustrated and started to explain again in more detail. He felt that although he had put forward ideas that would undoubtedly benefit them in the long term, they were being unreasonable by not appreciating what he meant. He found the whole process depressing and decided to continue with it anyway without consultation, as he knew they would appreciate it in the end.

   b   Jenny was a member of a project team. The success of the project was crucial for the company and the team frequently worked late and intensely to achieve the deadlines. Often the discussion in these late-night sessions would become quite heated. Jenny stayed calm and couldn't always understand why the other members of the team got so upset. Sometimes they would get frustrated with her and accuse her of not caring about the project. She knew that she did, however, and was often able to help reconcile different points of view within the team.

c   Diane was considered to be a caring manager. She always took account of the feelings of her team. She was cautious about change, however, particularly changes that would upset anyone. She was always available to counsel friends and colleagues, but found that she would take on their feelings and often ended the day feeling upset and depressed, even though she knew that she had helped her colleagues by listening to them.

3   From what perspective do you operate primarily with...
  ◆ The person closest to you?
  ◆ Your colleagues?
  ◆ Your boss?
  ◆ The different members of your family?

4   If you have a website, imagine yourself in the shoes of someone viewing it for the first time. What is that like? How does your experience compare with the Store from Hell described in this chapter? (Hopefully not at all!)

5   Read through the three most recent emails you sent. From which position did you write them? How might you write them differently now?

6   Read *English Passengers* by Matthew Kneale.

REFERENCES

Robert Dilts, *Encyclopaedia of Systemic NLP and NLP New Coding*, www.nlpuniversitypress.com.

John Grinder & Judith DeLozier (1996) *Turtles All the Way Down: Prerequisites to Personal Genius*, Metamorphous Press.

Matthew Kneale (2001) *English Passengers*, Penguin.

A father and his son owned a farm. They did not have many animals, but they did own a horse. One day the horse ran away.

"How terrible, what bad luck," said the neighbors.

"Good luck, bad luck, who knows?" replied the farmer.

Several weeks later the horse returned, bringing with him four wild mares.

"What marvelous luck," said the neighbors.

"Good luck, bad luck, who knows?" said the farmer.

The son began to learn to ride the wild horses, but one day he was thrown and broke his leg.

"What bad luck," said the neighbors.

"Good luck, bad luck, who knows?" replied the farmer.

The next week the army came to the village to take all the young men to war. The farmer's son was still disabled with his broken leg, so he was spared. Good luck, bad luck, who knows?

19
Resolving conflict: Parts integration

The point of our crises and calamities is not to frighten us or beat us into submission but to encourage us to change, to allow us to heal and grow.

—Kathleen Norris

Being united enables us to work together toward a common goal

Nicolas Sarkozy, the president of France, has urged Europe and the world to take a united approach to the financial crisis and believes that is the only way to build a future economy that will provide a sound basis for a new way of working together. And together is the key word. We have the United Kingdom, the United Arab Emirates, the United States of America and the European Union. Those who are united work toward a common goal and the support of each other. We do have the United Nations, but it takes more than a name for us to feel connected. I suspect that a common language, and a common culture and tradition, do far more to create a bond than the mere term united. When we truly experience being united we pull together.

What part of the world is not in conflict of some sort? Each time I write some new conflict has broken out somewhere. At least there is some hope: since the last edition of this book a peace agreement has been reached between the UK and Northern Ireland. The question is, how can we achieve this peace in other countries and in other contexts?

Conflict exists at every level

In the work I do in many commercial organizations, the issues are not so much to do with the changing environment but with the battles that smoulder between departments. On the home front, who has not experienced personal relations going through a difficult patch? Conflict exists at every level; it seems to be a symptom of our times. How can we personally influence the strife-torn world we live in and make a positive difference?

Some of the most innovative business thinkers advocate personal coherence as the only way to navigate the choppy waters of global enterprise. It does indeed make common sense to seek to achieve personal harmony in order to deal with the external world. However much we might want to do this, we nevertheless need to know how to achieve this state.

One of the principles I have emphasized throughout this book is that we can only influence by our example. We need to look for a way forward within; by changing ourselves we influence the systems of which we are a part. This is so easy to say and yet I know of no one who fully achieves this in practice. I do know of many who would subscribe to the principle of what I am saying, and still continue doing what they are doing in exactly the same way as before. It takes discipline and skill to resolve the conflict within. The question is: How can we find inner peace?

How can we find inner peace?

"Stress is two forces moving in opposite directions. Be still."   — Anon

ON THE ONE HAND... ON THE OTHER HAND

More often than not it is the symptoms of inner conflict that grab our attention and energy. Rightly so, as the symptoms are one of the ways our body has of telling us that something is amiss and we need to stop and take stock of how we are. Our body has a wisdom beyond the capacity of our conscious mind and we can learn how to listen to what it is seeking to tell us. The chances are that the physical symptoms will increase in volume and intensity until we do.

We have a bodily wisdom that is often ignored

Which of the following have you experienced?

* Moments when you know you are acting in a way that is not being true to what you say is important in life.
* Panic and a pull to react to the worst of what you experience in your environment.
* Times when what you are doing is at odds with what you are saying.
* Decisions when a part of you wants to act and move forward and a part of you – say, a concern or a fear – is holding you back.

- A feeling of going round in circles when what you want to do is move ahead in a straight line toward your goals.
- A sense of being under pressure.
- An ill-at-ease feeling with a goal you have set yourself or one you have accepted from someone else.
- Times when the right hand just does not seem to know what the left hand is doing.
- Phases of life when you feel that how you are living and working is not being true to the way you really want to be.

The following were incidents when either I or one of my colleagues was being given signals by our body to which we needed to pay attention:

- A headache when faced with someone who seemed determined to oppose everything that was suggested.
- A recurrent illness that seems to be triggered by stress.
- An earache when someone close was constantly complaining about the relationship with them.
- A frozen shoulder at a time when others' needs were taking precedence over their own.
- Sickness when faced with unwelcome change.
- A close friend who frequently described herself as being under pressure and then had a severe stroke.

And our neighbor, whose face broke out with a shingles rash every time his mother-in-law came to stay!

There are subtler bodily signals that indicate a lack of coherence:

- An asymmetrical posture.
- Indicating an issue on one hand in conflict with an issue on the other hand (the hands used literally to illustrate this).
- A stammer when talking about a particular issue.
- A difficulty with vision when unable to focus on a future goal.

I am sure you can add many other examples of conflict within yourself that you may be experiencing or have experienced in the past. The pace of change and the pressures to which we can succumb can lead easily to stress and frustration.

WHY BOTHER?

Why is it important to find a way to resolve these forms of stress? Most of us want some form of peace in our lives. However, there are many other reasons for wanting to resolve our inner conflicts. When we have any form of inner conflict the results include:

- We operate at less than our true potential so we reduce our effectiveness in whatever work or play we are engaged in.
- We use energy to manage the conflict within and so we have less energy and ability to concentrate on what is happening around us; we are less able to listen fully to others.
- If we have a goal then we shut down the filters with which we are able to recognize the opportunities in line with that goal, and so hamper our progress toward it.
- The stress becomes a habit.
- Other people start to shut us out: we get excluded from work opportunities, we are avoided, and we are not consulted on issues that matter.

In contrast:

- People at one with themselves are usually leaders; they attract followers. And we are at a time when we need leaders.
- The state of alignment or coherence is the only state in which we can manage ourselves through the complexities and ever-changing circumstances of life.

We need leaders

LISTENING TO THE WISDOM OF OUR BODY

By resolving conflict within, we influence the conflict we experience around us. There were several clues in the list of types of conflict you may have experienced. For example, "Decisions when a part of you wants to act and move forward and a part of you – say, a concern or a fear – is holding you back." I refer to "parts" of us and this is a useful and powerful way of thinking about this. We are not literally in parts, but by considering the differing desires in this way we can act as an arbitrator to our own emotions.

One way to think about this conflict is to imagine that we do have parts, each one with its own identity and characteristics. Imagine that you have an inner team and each part is a player in that team. If the parts are communicating with each other and in harmony, then you have a state of coherence; the chances are you will be more likely to achieve coherent outcomes. If, however, parts of you are in conflict with each other, it is unlikely you are operating at your best – quite the opposite!

For example, have you ever been in a situation where a part of you felt obliged to do what you had been asked to do, but another part felt that you were violating what is important to you? Then again, have you ever felt that everything about you was saying "yes" to a conclusion you had reached and a plan you had set yourself and that the motivation to carry out that plan was unstoppable? These are examples of what it is like to be without coherence and what it can be like to have it.

Parts of ourselves often communicate with us through physical symptoms. For instance, you might get a sharp pain above your eyes whenever you think about a particular decision. The part that is giving you the pain might be the part that lacks the courage to say "yes" to the decision you are considering.

We can learn to listen to the wisdom of our body

By learning to communicate with these inner parts, we learn what they want to tell us; we learn to listen to the wisdom of our own body. By listening to these parts we are learning to listen to our unconscious mind. And by learning how to coach these parts to communicate and work together in harmony, we increasingly create a state of coherence within.

SHORTCUT TO "PULLING YOURSELF TOGETHER"

You may have heard the advice (often given somewhat aggressively) to "pull yourself together." The outcome of the advice, if not the style with which it is given, is sound. To resolve conflict we do need to pull ourselves together, as we do to achieve a state of rapport and resourcefulness. The question is how. By modeling people who are skilled at resolving their inner and consequently their outer conflict, we find that they have a structure for pulling themselves together.

These are the steps to follow:

1 Identify the parts that are in conflict with each other. For example, the part that wants to say yes to an offer you have been made and the part that wants to wait, the "yes" part and the "waiting" part.

2 Take some time to acknowledge these parts in turn. This is the opposite of what many people feel like doing with parts that have been causing conflict. The temptation can be to ignore or delete or get angry with them. The key here is to realize that all parts are working on our behalf and that they do it in their own way, even though we might not at first appreciate that. So thank each part in turn for communicating with you. Listen and sense how each part communicates with you. Some parts might give you an image or a sound, or they might cause a particular sensation. You may notice nothing at first, but thank the parts nevertheless. It is amazing what cooperation you can get from something or someone to whom you show genuine appreciation.

3 Now detach yourself (dissociate) from the emotions of the parts to consider how they can cooperate with each other. Hold your hands out in front of you and use your instinct to decide which part you want to put on your right hand and which part you want to put on your left hand. Imagine that those parts of you are actually in your outspread hands. Hold them out and take a look at both.

4 Decide which part you wish to communicate with first. Now consider that part and describe its characteristics and qualities. For example, it might be a part of you that is aggressive and talks to you in terms of what you must do, using language like "Get on with it" and "What are you waiting for?" Each part symbolizes some aspect of your life. Explore what each represents for you.

Learn to manage the inner team

5 Every part is working on your behalf, even if you have not known consciously how it is doing this. Ask this part what it wants for you: what outcome is it seeking to achieve that is positive for you? Be aware of whatever comes to mind – that is how your unconscious mind communicates with you. Appreciate the answer you get in whatever way you get it.

6 Now repeat steps 4 and 5 with the part that you have on the other hand.

7 Considering each part in turn, ask yourself what quality or attribute this part has to give the other. For example, identify

what gift the first part has that would enhance the other part if it were to accept it. You can explore with the receiving part in what way it would like this gift in order for it to accept it.

8 Imagine this exchange of gifts. If at first this does not happen, ask each part in what way or what form the other part could give this gift in a way that the receiving part can accept. Now imagine the exchange of gifts.

9 Typically at this point, if the previous two steps have been successful there will be an automatic drawing together of hands. This physical bringing together is an indication that you are integrating the two parts in your thinking. If this does not happen automatically, you can suggest it by considering how these two parts might integrate with each other and exist together in cooperation and bring your hands together as you do so. If necessary, go back and repeat steps 7 and 8 until this step is successful.

10 Now imagine how these parts together are a part of who you are, and in so doing bring both hands together to the heart of your chest. How has this enhanced who you are and how you can go forward into your future?

In effect, what you are doing is encouraging different parts of yourself to work in harmony. So often when parts are in conflict, our tendency can be to think that we have to go one way or the other, when in fact it is by exploring how we can have both together that we get the breakthrough in our thinking. The effect of this integration is to create a state of rapport with yourself so that you are being fully who you are and who you can be.

If you are witnessing conflict in other people, first go through the process above so that you have resolved the conflict you experience within yourself. If, for example, I see two friends in conflict with each other, there is nothing I can do to resolve their conflict. However, I can resolve the conflict between the parts of myself that are symbolized by those friends. Interestingly, when I have found the resolution within me, my external experience will change too, as will my way of dealing with that external experience. Our experience of people around is reflected by our perceptions of them. To change what we experience externally, we can change our attitudes and perceptions within. To achieve a change in my circumstances, it helps if I can first of all imagine that change in the way that I truly want things to be.

For the process outlined above to become second nature (so that you are using it unconsciously and in real time, for example while you are in a conversation with someone), it helps to work through it "offline" first of all. Do this with a situation that you have experienced in the past or one that you anticipate may happen in the future. It is rehearsal and practice that make this an unconscious skill.

SUMMARY

We are all connected. We exist in the world and in the universe together. It is futile to choose to believe that we are separate. What we think is what we experience. If we think that there are aliens, terrorists, enemies and conflict, that is what we experience! If, however, we choose to think of ourselves as one, then maybe, just maybe, we will start to experience and influence universal harmony and peace. How about starting now?

THOUGHT PROVOKERS

1   What parts of yourself do you recognize might be in conflict with each other today?
2   What conflict do you experience between people outside of you? How do the people outside of you symbolize parts of you?
3   Remember a time when you experienced conflict and you found a way to resolve it within yourself. How did you do that?
4   What physical symptoms do you recognize as signals from your unconscious to you? How well do you listen and act on what your unconscious is telling you?

A mother, annoyed by her son's constant pestering, invented a game for him to play.

She cut up a map of the world and gave him the pieces to put back together again, thinking that it would take him hours, if he ever managed it.

Ten minutes later he returned with the completed map. When she asked him how he had done it so quickly, he said, "There is a picture of a woman on the back, and when I put her together, the world came together."

20

Giving and receiving feedback

We pardon as long as we love. -Duc de la Rochefoucauld

Today I am working in a remote part of France. All of my work contacts are at least 500 miles away and yet I can interact with each of them in seconds. The systems we use are designed increasingly to give us instant feedback on how we are doing. As I type this page, any spelling mistake is immediately underlined and any grammatical error highlighted. Yesterday afternoon I entered the chatroom on my website and was able to share and receive thoughts instantaneously with delegates on my programs. On my bike I have a "flight deck" computer that gives me immediate feedback on my cadence, my current speed, my average speed and much more. The feedback systems to which we have access grow in number and sophistication every day.

We live in a world of feedback

Gone are the days when we were given a month to prepare for our appraisal system so we could hear how we are doing. Although this fast-becoming archaic management system still exists, we are nevertheless bombarded with instantaneous feedback on our performance in every sphere of our lives. It is by learning to love and thrive on feedback that we can excel in the spontaneity of today's business climate. And by thriving on it we are in the best position to respond with flexibility to whatever arises.

Yet in my experience of working with many different people and organizations, there are very few who have this ability. Most of us have well-developed mechanisms for doing just the opposite, for keeping feedback at bay. If I were to choose one skill in this book that would put you head and shoulders above most

Receiving feedback is a precursor to giving it

people (not just in business but in life), it is the ability to receive feedback. Receiving feedback is a fundamental precursor to being able (and having the right) to give it.

The head of the creative department in a marketing organization wanted to develop the creative team so that they would be open to giving each other feedback and subsequently be increasingly open to feedback from their clients, both within the business and externally. He called a team meeting and told them beforehand that he wanted feedback from them.

In the team meeting he invited them to prepare individually to offer him feedback and gave them time to do this. He asked them to think of something they would like him to do more of, something they would like him to do less of or differently, and something with which they were happy. He then invited them to give him the feedback and he modeled all the principles of how to accept what they were saying with openness and learning. He demonstrated how to live out the beliefs that underpin effective feedback. He was open, accepting and curious about what they had to say. He was not in any way defensive or attacking.

The team members became more and more open and at the end of the meeting they commented on how valuable they had found that time with him. Each subsequently volunteered that they would like to go through a similar process for themselves. This team has become a model of excellence for the rest of the company.

Learning to give and receive feedback is the core of my work

Learning to receive and give feedback is at the core of the work I do with individuals and teams. No matter whether I am coaching one to one or at an initial meeting with a client, or whether I am working with the board or the key leaders within that company, the ability to immerse oneself in a climate of feedback is what I believe makes the biggest difference to their performance. If they were consistently and skillfully to give each other feedback, my role with them would be redundant; indeed, this is my ultimate aim: for them to do this for themselves without the need for anyone external to the business. I aim to encourage and train people, especially those at the head of the organization, to receive feedback constructively and openly. And then to learn how to give it in a way that strengthens the team and the relationships within it and subsequently encourages improved performance from both the individuals and the business.

There are many books and business models that talk of continuous learning and development, learning organizations, appraisal systems, double-loop learning and much, much more. If we are to be able to achieve any of these, we must first be able to receive and give feedback. Once we can do this we will be contributing to the business in a way that offers learning from all people and all circumstances.

FEEDBACK AND MODELING

Where there is excellence, there is openness to and a willingness to learn continually from feedback. Feedback is essential to the process of modeling. When we model someone (let's say someone other than ourselves for the moment), we are studying the structure both of what they do and how they do it. To do this without "contaminating" that structure, we need to be able to accept what they do in exactly the way they do it right now.

On one of my NLP training sessions we invited someone we considered to be a model of excellence for leadership to be modeled by the delegates on the program. He was someone who had led a program of immense change in a manufacturing company that had to close half its production sites. This meant he had to find a way to cut the workforce at one plant by 2,000 people. What was special about this man was that he had done this in a means that gained the support and respect of the employees involved. He had managed an immense cutback and had done so with compassion and support for everyone involved. However, he also realized that there were aspects of this whole process that he could have handled differently if he had to do it again (which he sincerely prayed would never have to happen).

During the modeling process one of the delegates started to offer some thoughts along the lines of "What if you had done it this way?" and "Had you thought that maybe you might have or still could...?"

This totally defeats the objective of modeling, which, in the first instance, is to elicit the structure of the subject's experience. It is not to change that structure or to advise or coach the subject to change, just to unpack the structure of how they do what they do. But to do this we have to be able to accept (receive)

It is of value to give feedback nonjudgmentally

unconditionally what the other person does. And to determine if what we have elicited fits with the subject's experience of how they do what they do, we need to be able to give feedback completely nonjudgmentally.

That might sound straightforward, but doing it requires immense skill. It requires us to be totally objective in how we do this: to accept what others do without influencing it with our own thoughts about what is right and wrong. We need to be an "empty vessel" that is able to learn what is new to us. We need to be able to recognize and, more than that, accept difference.

What happens all too often is that we experience something and within fractions of a second we have made a judgment about it. We hear someone speaking quickly and assume instantly that they are intelligent. We see someone frowning and infer that they are confused. We see someone smiling and decide that they must be a good person. This deductive analysis gets us through life, but it can also get us into trouble and into faulty conclusions.

Carl Sagan once told the story of early astronomers who looked up into the sky with their primitive telescopes and observed the planet Venus. It puzzled them greatly, because Venus had no observable surface. Not at all like the Moon or Mars, it appeared just like a featureless, flat disc in the night sky.

"What on earth could possibly explain that?" they asked.

"Well, suppose it was covered in clouds."

"Yes that would explain it, since clouds obscure everything beneath them."

So they continued, "What surface conditions are needed to make clouds?"

"Well, heat, which we know Venus has because it's closer to the sun, and water."

That made sense, so they continued, "What kind of surface do you get when you have heat, light and water?"

"Well, tropical rainforests, for one thing."

That made perfect sense, so they concluded that the surface of Venus was covered with tropical rainforests. As it turns out, the temperature on the surface of Venus is 900 degrees Fahrenheit and the clouds are made of sulphuric acid!

Quoted by John David Hoag on www.nlpls.com

We need to be an "empty vessel"

BELIEFS THAT SUPPORT FEEDBACK

Our beliefs influence our capacity for feedback. A belief that is fundamental to our ability to give and receive feedback constructively is that there is no failure, only feedback; or, to put it in other words, there is only learning. If we truly believe this, the ability to learn from feedback will be second nature to us. It will be fundamental to our existence as a learner in this world.

There is only learning

There are other beliefs that support our ability to give and receive feedback. The first is that everyone's perception is their truth. We only have perception and each person's perception is unique to them. It may be similar to that of other people; it may be significantly different. That does not make it right or wrong, it just makes it true for them. By accepting a perception from someone else, we are accepting that part of ourselves as they experience it. We are also contributing to the self-esteem of the giver of the feedback in acknowledging their map of the world. If we do not accept their feedback, we do not accept that part of who they are and therefore we do not fully accept them as a person.

Everyone's perception is their truth

I was listening to a manager receiving feedback from one of his team. Each time he heard a piece of feedback, he either said "That's right" if it aligned with what he believed about himself, or he said nothing if it did not. His response indicated that he did not accept that everyone's perception is their truth and he was not at that time open to learning from other people's perceptions. Gradually, his team stopped giving him feedback. He became distanced from what he needed to know in order to run the business.

The second belief is that what we recognize in others is true for ourselves. An extension of this is that the characteristics in others that touch us emotionally are a pointer toward those things being characteristics that we don't want or like to accept in ourselves.

What we recognize in others is true for ourselves

My husband gets frustrated when he is behind a driver that he considers to be dawdling on the road. Just this week he found himself behind several drivers who were proceeding very slowly and holding him up. He commented in exasperation that he would never do that.

Later that day, he was getting some money from a cash machine and as I approached I noticed there was a lady behind him, also waiting to use the machine. He had been totally unaware of this person and had been dawdling in using the machine and getting information about his account. When I pointed out that someone had been waiting for some time, he was horrified to feel he had been holding them up in a similar way to how he had been held up by other drivers.

I certainly don't always want to own the traits I see in other people. I am like my husband in the above example, in that I prefer to dissociate myself from the characteristics I don't like in others. Yet I do know that it is typically those traits that are my "blind spots" and this is where some of the most powerful learning lies for me. If we can recognize a trait in others, then we have that structure in our thinking. This does not mean that we would behave in exactly the same way (my husband was dawdling by the cash machine rather than dawdling in the car), but whatever structure we have in our thinking we have the capability of enacting in some way. How many of us, although condemning of violence in the world around us, are capable of the same or worse in our thinking? It is a small step between thinking something and doing it.

The structure within influences our perception of the external world

This is an essential foundation of NLP: it is the structure we hold within that influences our perception and our feelings toward what we experience outside of ourselves.

I am rarely annoyed by delegates on my programs. One of the things I believe I have learnt with NLP is that difference is valuable and a source of learning. However, I did have one delegate who was the exception for me. I began to notice how distracting she could be by dropping her papers, coughing, sneezing, or in some way making a noise that disrupted the session. What was interesting was that she seemed to do this at the same point in every session: about five minutes after the start. I found I started to expect this disruption and became tense as the first few minutes elapsed.

Then on one occasion, at the same point in the session, she got up and walked across the room in front of me to get herself a cup of coffee. In doing so she rattled the cups, seeming to have no awareness of the effect of what she was doing on the rest of the room and on me. She walked back across the room with her cup of coffee and sat down. I said nothing, but I felt frustrated and annoyed that she had done this.

At the end of the session I told one of my colleagues how I felt. He asked me what it was about her behavior that had bothered me so much

(he had been more or less unaware of what had happened). I replied that it was her focus on what she wanted for herself and her insensitivity to the effect of that on others around her that bothered me so much. My colleague then said, "And how is that true about you, Sue?"

I was quite shocked at first to think that I was like the delegate. Then I realized that I did have similar attributes: a tendency to go for what I wanted and to do so without sensitivity to those around me. I was really amazed how what I saw in her was what I didn't like in myself. Eventually I became quite amused, wondering what aspect of myself she might mirror back to me at the beginning of the next session. And she didn't do anything distracting ever again!

What is important in the context of giving feedback is that if that delegate had been disruptive again and I had chosen to give her feedback, I would have been doing so from a position of identification with her. If I had given feedback to her prior to recognizing how we were alike, I would have done so in a "holier than thou" way, which would most certainly have sounded patronizing and not been accepted by her. By identifying with the person to whom we choose to give feedback, we create a connection that increases the likelihood that we will give the feedback in a way that will be accepted.

The attributes we recognize in others mirror the same within ourselves

We recognize attributes in others because we have the structure of those attributes within ourselves. Those traits in others (good and bad) that affect us emotionally are those very same traits in which we have an imbalance in some way. For example, we might be frustrated by what we see as aggression in someone else because we need more of that within ourselves (not to be aggressive, but to be more assertive). And it is our frustration with our previous inability to develop this aspect of ourselves that we project on to this other person who is mirroring our imbalance back to us. It may equally be that we have too much of what we see in the other. This was the case with the delegate in my example. I had too much focus and too little sensitivity in some contexts of my life, for example when I set myself a business goal.

To hold this belief – that I recognize in others what I am capable of myself – is to have access to one of the best personal development tools available. It means that whenever we experience something in someone else that we either admire or

When we change the world changes

that bothers us in some way, we have the key to releasing the equivalent potential within ourselves. Our acceptance of this feedback enables us to recognize the traits to which we might otherwise have been blind.

To hold this belief fully is to let go of frustration and anger with others and realize that there is only one place to look for the answers to our dissatisfactions: within ourselves. Once we change the perception within ourselves, it is amazing how suddenly the world around us, including those people who may have pushed the most sensitive of buttons, seems to change. Energy directed negatively toward others is wasted, life-draining energy. Energy directed inward to accept our own inadequacies and our strengths is life giving, not only to ourselves but to the people with whom we come into contact.

RECEIVING FEEDBACK

The sense of recognition of what is similar creates an unspoken connection. This allows for an openness of feedback that might not otherwise be possible. From this belief flows the skill of giving and receiving feedback outlined below.

"Feedback isn't absolute truth but it is truth for the person who is delivering it."

Gene Early

I put the skill of receiving feedback first, as I have found that to give it we need first of all to be able to receive it. Your ability to receive feedback is central to continuous learning and growth, as well as being key to healthy, sustainable relationships, both in business and in life.

What can you do to model excellence in the way you receive feedback?

◆ Get yourself into a resourceful state for receiving the feedback. Anchor a state that has worked well for you in this way in the past. The state could be one of learning, for example, or one of openness, self-confidence, humility or curiosity.
◆ Remind yourself of the beliefs above.

- Respond in a way that presupposes acceptance, saying things like "In what ways do I do this?" "What effect does this have on you?" (Use present-tense language.)
- Always anticipate feedback and always invite it when appropriate so that feedback is in constant supply to you.

Every employee in Cisco Systems has an open feedback form online to everyone else in the company. Anyone can add feedback to this form whenever they choose so that each has a continuous supply of current feedback from anyone in the company.

- If the feedback is personally challenging and you find it potentially uncomfortable to take on board, then dissociate for a moment, step back as if you are an observer of yourself. Having dissociated, check out what further personal resources you need to be able to accept the feedback, and then give those resources to yourself before stepping back into your own shoes (associating) in order to accept the feedback for real. If you have not done this before, it helps to do it in your imagination "offline" with feedback that you either anticipate getting and you feel might be challenging, or that was offered to you and you found difficult to accept at the time. The more you do this the more you are able to do it "online," whenever you need more resources to accept what is being offered.
- Take full responsibility for building and maintaining rapport with the giver of the feedback, even (and especially) if the giver is not taking any responsibility for this themselves.
- Seek fully to understand the feedback by questioning (clean questions work wonderfully in this situation). For example, ask, "In what way do I do/am I that?" "What is it that I do that gives you that impression?" "Give me examples of how I do this?" "Is there anything else about that?" These are all questions that demonstrate your willingness to accept the giver's perception and learn from it. (What they don't do is rationalize, explain, defend or attack in any way whatsoever.)

Seek to understand the feedback

- If the feedback indicates that you have upset, annoyed or caused any negative emotions in the giver of the feedback, apologize for that even though you may have been unaware of the effect at that time. In this way you are taking responsibility for the effects you have on others.

- Check out what it is that you can do instead. Ask, "What do I have to do for you to know that I do (whatever the giver is saying you don't do)?"
- Imagine yourself having taken on board the feedback and now behaving in a way that demonstrates you have done so. Do this in a way that fits not only for the giver but also with the other key people in that context.

The effect of accepting feedback in this way is to encourage the giver to want to give more feedback in the future. You are thus making a significant contribution to creating a climate of learning, whether in a business or a personal relationship.

"Man is part of a chain of connecting humanity within a greater universe. Feedback is a behavioural manifestation of beliefs and values about the importance of interconnectedness between people. By practising and developing feedback I nurture and develop the connections between us and release myself to become who I truly am. 'I' becomes 'we/us'. By connecting with you, I release myself from my own internal prison."

Brian Keenan

GIVING FEEDBACK

The bonus of modeling is that as a result of the process, we have feedback to use for our own development and feedback to give to the person or people we have modeled. However, just having the feedback is not a sufficient qualification for giving it. A number of other factors need to be present before and during the process of offering and delivering the feedback. By giving feedback we can also verify that what we believe we have detected is also recognized by our subject.

Below are some steps that help ensure that the feedback we have to give is received in a way that enhances learning for both the giver and the receiver:

- Check that you are in rapport with the person to whom you propose giving the feedback. If you are not, do whatever it takes to get that rapport before you even start the process.

- Ask yourself, "How is this feedback as true about me as it is for the person to whom I am offering it?" In this way you will create a connectedness in your thinking and in the way you offer the feedback.
- Imagine how by accepting the feedback both you and the other person can improve. Create this as a well-formed outcome in your thinking.
- Frame the feedback first to say how it has come about or what area of performance it relates to, so that you warm up the receiver to what you are going to say next.
- If the other person does not immediately accept the feedback, find another way to give it so they can understand what you are offering them. Their ability to receive the feedback is a measure of your ability to give it.
- Maintain direct eye contact and imagine the receiver of the feedback both accepting and using the feedback constructively as you do so.
- Recognize that the response you get from others is coming from the part with which you are choosing to engage. If you do not understand what I am telling you, it is the "nonunderstanding" part with which I am choosing to engage.
- Be an example at all times of the response you want from others.
- Ask the receiver of the feedback to tell you what they are going to do with what you have given them. Sometimes it helps to ask this before you give the feedback, e.g. "If I give you this feedback what will you do with it?" (This is useful if you know that the person has a habit of shrugging off or avoiding feedback.)

The ultimate measure of your skill in giving feedback is that as a result of the process, both you and the person or people to whom you have given the feedback learn from it and deepen your connection with each other.

"Today we give each other feedback and we learn from it. What we used to give each other was abuse!"

Delegate on an in-company course

SHORTCUT TO DEVELOPING
YOUR ABILITY TO GIVE FEEDBACK

1 Choose someone to whom you would like to give feedback.
2 Think of the feedback that you would like to give them and the win/win outcome that you want to achieve by giving them this feedback.
3 Imagine the context in which you would like to give the feedback that will be most conducive to its being accepted.
4 Think about how this feedback is as pertinent to you as it is to them.
5 Think of what resources you need to be able to give this feedback constructively.
6 Imagine how you can ensure that you are in very strong rapport with the other person before you give the feedback.
7 Imagine giving the feedback and imagine the other person receiving it in the way that you would like them to.
8 Step back so that you can see yourself and the other person in this process. Are there any other resources that you need to make the giving of the feedback any more constructive? Imagine yourself in that scenario with those resources, giving the feedback in the way you want to.
9 Imagine both you and the receiver of the feedback learning from the feedback in such a way that you strengthen your relationship in the future.
10 What have you learnt from this whole process?

SUMMARY

The opportunities for feedback surround us in every medium in which we choose to work. We can learn and grow continuously if we choose, provided that we have the beliefs and skills to give and receive feedback. Feedback is how we can know if what we are doing is working. What could be more important than that?

THOUGHT PROVOKERS

1 Identify someone who is significant to you in:
    ◆   Your personal life.
    ◆   Your work.
    ◆   Your community.
    Decide on a time and a way in which you can ask each for feedback on the extent to which you support them in the way they want you to.
2 Identify someone with whom you have some difficulties. Think of a way in which you can ask them for feedback on what you could do that would make a positive difference between you.
3 Identify someone in your work or your life generally that you wish would be different in some way. Ask yourself how you are not being what you want them to be, and how you can be an example of what you do want them to be.
4 Who is your most important customer? When did you last ask for feedback from them? How might you ask for feedback now? How might you set up a feedback system for your most important customers if you don't have one in place right now?
5 How could you reproduce a similar system to the one in Cisco Systems whereby you are getting continuous, real-time feedback?

REFERENCES

Brian Keenan (1993) *An Evil Cradling*, Vintage.
Peter M. Senge (1993) *The Fifth Discipline: The Art and Practice of the Learning Organization*, Random House.

At the age of fifteen, in the middle of my junior year, I quit Exeter, one of the most highly regarded preparatory schools in the nation.

As I look back on that turning point in my life, I am amazed at the grace that gave me the courage to do it. Not only was I dropping out of a prestigious prep school against my parents' wishes, but I was walking away from a golden WASP track that had all been laid out for me. Hardly aware that it was what I was doing, I was taking my first giant step out of my entire culture. That culture of "the establishment" was what one was supposed to aspire to, and I was throwing it away. And where was I to go? I was forging into the total unknown. I was so terrified I thought I should seek the advice of some of Exeter's faculty before finalizing such a dreadful decision. But which of the faculty?

The first candidate who came to mind was my advisor. He had barely spoken to me for two and a half years, but he was reputedly kindly. A second obvious candidate was the crusty old dean of the school, known to be beloved to tens of thousands of alumni. But I thought that three was a good round number, and the third choice was more difficult. I finally hit upon Mr. Lynch, my Maths teacher, a somewhat younger man. I chose him not because we had any relationship or because he seemed to be a particularly warm sort of person – indeed, I found him a rather cold, mathematical kind of fish – but because he had a reputation for being the faculty genius. He'd been involved with some kind of high-level mathematics with the Manhattan Project, and I thought I should check out what I was considering with a "genius."

I went first to my kindly advisor. He let me talk for about two minutes and then gently broke in. "It's true that you're underachieving here at Exeter, Scotty, but not so seriously that you won't be able to graduate. It would be preferable for you to graduate from a superior school like Exeter with lesser grades than from a lesser school with better grades. It would also look bad on your record for you to switch horses in midstream. Besides, I'm sure your parents would be quite upset, so why don't you just go along and do the best you can?"

Next I went to the crusty old dean. He let me speak for thirty seconds. "Exeter is the best school in the world," he harrumphed. "Damn fool thing that you're thinking of doing. Now you just pull yourself up by the bootstraps, young man!"

Feeling worse and worse, I went to see Mr. Lynch. He let me talk myself out. It took about five minutes. Then he said he didn't yet understand, and asked if I would just talk some more about Exeter, about my family, about God (he actually gave me permission to talk about God!) – about anything that came into my head. So I rambled on for another ten minutes in all, which was pretty good for a depressed, inarticulate fifteen-year-old. When I was done, he inquired whether I would mind if he asked me some questions. Thriving on this adult attention, I replied, "Of course not," and he queried me about many different things for the next half-hour.

Finally, after forty-five minutes in all, this supposedly cold fish sat back in his chair with a pained expression on his face and said, "I'm sorry. I can't help you. I don't have any advice to give you. You know," he continued, "it's impossible for one person to ever completely put himself in another person's shoes. But insofar as I can put myself in your shoes – and I'm glad I'm not there – I don't know what I would do if I were you. So, you see, I don't know how to advise you. I'm sorry that I've been unable to help."

It is just possible that that man saved my life, and that I'm able to be sitting here writing this today because of Mr Lynch. For when I entered his office that morning over forty years ago, I was close to suicidal, and when I left I felt as if a thousand pounds had been taken off my back. Because if a "genius" didn't know what to do, then it was all right for me not to know what to do. And if I was considering a move that seemed so insane in the world's terms and a genius couldn't tell me that it was clearly, obviously demented, well then maybe, just maybe, it was something God was calling me to.

So it was that man, who didn't have any answers or quick formulas, who didn't know what I should do and was willing to be empty, who was the one who provided the help I needed. It was that man who listened to me, who gave me his time, who tried to put himself in my shoes, who extended himself and sacrificed himself for me, who loved me. And it was that man who healed me. It was an extraordinary act of civility.

Reproduced with permission from M Scott Peck (1997) *The Road Less Traveled: A New Psychology of Love, Traditional Values and Spiritual Growth*, Simon & Schuster.

21
High-performance coaching

Every time our world seems to be cracking like a piece of glass we start putting it back together when in fact our glasshouse has to shatter. —Genpo Roshi

There is an awakening to self-development

Most people are familiar with coaching in a sporting context. There are football coaches, tennis coaches, skiing coaches – there aren't too many sports that don't have some aspect of coaching associated with them. And what about personal fitness coaches or trainers? It seems that more and more people have someone to support or push them to a state of fitness. Only recently one of my colleagues, with the support of a personal coach, trained to run the London Marathon and went from never having run before to completing the marathon in five hours after just eight weeks of training. And more recently you may have seen the term "life coaching." It is as if there is an awakening to the value of developing oneself to achieve a state of physical and mental fitness.

In my work I have experienced a boom in the demand for personal coaching. Leaders in business are not content to rest on their laurels but want to concentrate on how they can achieve greater personal effectiveness. And those leaders also want to learn how to coach their staff to do the same. It is as if we have explored all the external possibilities for gaining a competitive edge, which are becoming more and more unreliable, and people are now beginning to look within themselves for fresh answers.

David had changed companies three times in the past two years. In each company where he was employed, he was always one of the top salespeople. However, he felt frustrated, as his goal was to lead a team rather than to work as an independent salesperson for the rest of his career. He had been given a few opportunities to prove himself and most recently had been put in charge of a team in his company. Nevertheless, each time he assumed such a role he started having problems in his relationships with some of the key people. The result was usually that he got so frustrated that people didn't cooperate in the way he expected them to that he eventually left and found another sales position. He did this until he worked his way once more to a leadership role. We repeat our patterns unless we learn how to interrupt them.

We repeat our patterns

This is a familiar trend in many companies and there are many similar examples of people who have ambitions they seem destined not to realize. What is the typical solution? Usually it is to let the person go. Some companies might invest first in some training, believing that there are techniques of people management that can be learnt to resolve the issue. Some companies might invest time in personal appraisal, where David would be given advice as to how best to deal with the person with whom he was having problems. Some companies might just shake their heads and say, "You always lose a good salesperson when you try to make a manager out of him." So where does NLP coaching come in?

THE AIM OF NLP-BASED COACHING

The aim of NLP-based coaching is to support people in realizing their true potential. It is based on the premise that most of the limitations to our true potential are not represented by other people, but by unhealthy strategies that we have learnt and that are entirely within us.

NLP is "the study of the structure of subjective experience." In David's case this means that there is a structure to how David is creating this repeated experience. The fact that it is repeated is a clue. His problems lie not in the other people (he re-experiences the same problems no matter who the people are) but in himself.

NLP is the study of the structure of subjective experience

What patterns do you repeat? Do you for example:

- Find that you frequently lose key people in your team?
- Invariably end up in conflict with your management and finish up leaving the company?

+ Often find yourself disagreeing and frustrated with people in authority?
+ Find it hard to stay in long-term relationships?
+ Find that you prefer to distance yourself from anyone who gets too close?
+ Somehow seem to miss achieving your important goals just as you are on the brink of success?
+ Find that most work is difficult and hard?
+ Feel that you are often hard done by?
+ Experience life as being not fair?
+ Find that the people in whom you pin your hopes always seem to let you down?
+ Feel that success is always just round the corner?

On the other hand, are you one of those people who:

+ Appear easily and almost effortlessly to achieve what you want consistently?
+ Are frequently surprised by just what a good hand life has dealt you?
+ Find that you seem to attract good people to support and work with you?
+ Are surprised by the opportunities that come your way and feel you have been very lucky?
+ Feel passionate about your work and what you do?
+ Recognize that you are being the best you can be and that you have worked hard to achieve that?

The significance of all of these, good or bad, is that they are learned patterns that we act out in the world, no matter what the quality of the external circumstances. NLP-based coaching is about discovering those patterns, and either coaching ourselves or others to make choices that do lead us to achieve what we really want and realize that true potential. In essence, the purpose of NLP-based coaching is as follows:

+ To discover our own and/or others' patterns (strategies), especially those of our outstanding talents, so that we can reproduce them or transfer them to other contexts. For example, if you have an outstanding strategy for connecting with people socially but find it challenging to do the same when you are in a business meeting with new contacts, you can learn how to transfer the strategy that works socially into the business context by using NLP.

* To discover the strategies that are leading us to get results we no longer want in our lives. By finding out how we are doing what we are doing, we can reprogram ourselves or coach others to reprogram themselves to make new choices. For example, if you lack sensitivity in a sales situation to the signals the other person is giving you and inadvertently sabotage good sales opportunities, you can discover what you are doing and learn a new strategy that works for you in getting you the results you do want.
* To learn how to self-coach yourself through problem issues in your work and life and support others to do the same.
* To support yourself and others to develop the self-confidence and self-esteem to recognize that you already have all the strategies you could ever want in your life. With NLP coaching, you can learn how to build this confidence and tap into these strategies when you choose.
* To enable you to find your own unique brand of excellence so you achieve the success that only you can. In other words, with NLP you can learn how to differentiate yourself with the natural talents you have already.
* To learn how to manage yourself to achieve what you want by influencing yourself from within or coaching others to do the same.
* To develop the ability to learn from every circumstance in your life and coach others to achieve the same level of empowerment.

THE PRINCIPLES OF NLP-BASED COACHING

NLP coaching is generic. One of its aims is to find the point of greatest leverage for learning. This is true for one-to-one coaching, just as it is for group training.

NLP coaching is generic

A theoretical structure for understanding the kinds of learning available to human beings evolved from Bertrand Russell's theory of Logical Types and was subsequently described by

A name is not the thing
named –Bertrand Russell

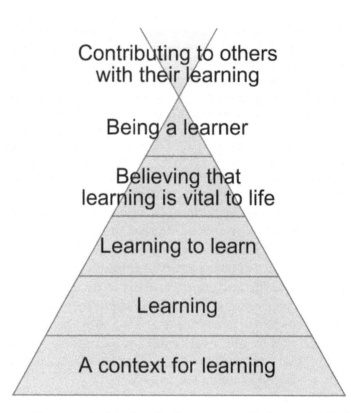

Contributing to others
with their learning

Being a learner

Believing that
learning is vital to life

Learning to learn

Learning

A context for learning

Learning takes place at
different levels

Gregory Bateson in his book *Steps to an Ecology of Mind*. The principle is that learning takes place on different levels.

At one level we do things. For example, I did maths at school but didn't understand what that mathematics was really about. I just did it. My husband, however, is doing a maths degree and now understands the significance of the maths that he learnt previously at school and in his engineering degree, so that he can proceed independently of his tutors to learn more about the subject.

Moving up from one learning level to the next allows us to have more choice. In that choice (which is referred to as "requisite variety") we have more survival strength through our greater flexibility to cope with change. Being able to change levels in conversation significantly influences the nature of the conversation and can provide the leverage for progress in negotiations and conflict resolution.

Greater flexibility = greater
survival strength

Friends may do things for us. Coaches support us to do things for ourselves. True friends do both.

We can use this model to learn how to switch levels and how to facilitate others in doing so. Our skill in this affects our ability to set outcomes for ourselves, to handle resistance and objections both externally and internally, and to reframe our experiences so that we can perceive situations differently and thereby manage our emotional state. This model is a powerful tool for managing change, both for us and for others. It is most certainly something we need to be aware of if we are engaged in giving feedback or coaching. The level(s) at which we intervene will be instrumental in the way in which our clients learn.

The principle is that by influencing at a higher level we affect all the levels below. For example, if we simply tell someone what to do we are intervening at a low level. If, however, we challenge the way in which they learn or how they identify themselves as a learner, we will have a more far-reaching impact on their development.

By intervening at a high level we affect all the levels below

If David were to come to me for coaching, I could concentrate on what is happening in the current situation between him and one of the key people in his team. I could explore with him what he is doing wrong as a leader and what he could do instead. However, if I were to do this, it might help him fix the problem for a while, but it would not resolve the underlying pattern. That would be an example of a low-level intervention and not particularly effective or sustainable over time.

Alternatively, I could go back to the source of the pattern. It is possible that David experienced difficulties as a child with his father or equivalent and that he was unable to cope emotionally. When children experience overwhelming emotional situations that they cannot deal with in a productive way, they shut them out. Either that or they dissociate from the experience or distort it in some way so that they are able to make sense of something that is beyond their comprehension.

I could adopt any of these approaches, but with NLP what we are interested in is how we make sense of our experience in the present.

We are interested in how we make sense of our experience in the present

David has a structure that he brings to each of the situations he experiences. Changing his place of work or the people with whom he works will not ultimately make a difference. What is important is that he learns how to change the structure of his thinking and behavior so that it is increasingly in line with the outcomes he really wants.

NLP-based coaching is about the process and not about the content. When we find a way to develop the process of what we are doing, we influence all situations of the same kind.

Give a man a fish you feed him for a day – teach a man how to fish and you feed him for life.

In essence, what we are doing when we coach using NLP is making the person being coached aware of their patterns at many levels. Simply becoming aware of this process creates choice. And standing back and reviewing the structure of that experience and deciding which bits we want to keep and which to develop is life changing. This is how with NLP we can learn to remove the self-learnt barriers and the obstacles to being the best we can be.

At the age of 90, my mother had an intruder break into her home in Liverpool and steal jewelry and money. As you might imagine, the shock of the experience was more potent than the loss of her belongings. The police asked her if she would be willing to help in an identification parade. Despite being an invalid, she immediately began to explore how she might do this. She had very strong principles and wanted to help prevent similar crimes being carried out in the future.

She called me to ask my advice. "Do you think I should help with this identity parade?"

A part of me wanted her to say "No" to protect her from the emotions of the experience, but my instinct was to say "Yes, I believe that is the right thing to do." That is what I said and she thanked me for my answer. Her question presupposed the answer.

If any business colleague were to ask me a question with the same format, "Do you think I should...," and if my outcome were to support them in finding their self-esteem and confidence, then my principle is usually to say "Yes." By saying yes I am confirming the perception they have already formed within themselves. I am confirming that their map of the world is valid. By saying yes I am presupposing that they do have all the resources they need within themselves already. And by saying yes I am acting in a way that is more likely to boost their independence, self-esteem and confidence than if I were to offer a solution of my own.

The main role of a coach is to support others in realizing their true potential. I also believe that the fastest and most effective way to do this is to help them to find the resources they already have within themselves. In the context of coaching, it is often more appropriate to find ways to boost self-esteem and confidence than it is to get the "right" solution.

I have certainly had some of my most powerful learning experiences through the mistakes I have made. Coaching requires us to be prepared to give others the space to make their own mistakes and realize their successes. They can only do this if we encourage them to do things their way and to learn from doing so.

Ironically, although my mother was very shaken by her experience with the intruder, it also gave her the motivation to ensure that justice was done. In a way, by supporting the identity parade she felt she was making a more significant contribution to society than she had done for years. Who was I to take that away from her to protect my own fears?

When we coach others, it is important to be able to keep our own emotions out of the way. To develop someone's confidence in themselves and therefore in their ability to draw on their own resources, I want to reward and confirm any opportunity when they are indicating that this is what they are doing. If someone has the structure of the answer in their question, my role as a coach is to reinforce that.

Examples of questions in which the answer presupposed is "Yes" include:

- Do you think I should take the job I have been offered in this new company?
- Do you think I can find the confidence to do this?
- Should I really reconsider that decision?
- Am I being very direct in the way I am saying this?

This last question invites direct feedback: "Yes." And yet I have witnessed many coaches seeking to reassure in response to a question like this, rather than confirming the truth that the questioner already knows within themselves – and of course giving and receiving feedback, which is the subject of Chapter 20.

> The role of a coach is to help others realize their true potential

> The question presupposes the answer

FINDING OUR INNER RESOURCES

Chapter 11 introduced the TOTE (Test→Operate→Test→Exit). This is a flowchart for mapping the strategies we use to get ourselves from our present state to a future desired state.

On my bike I have a mini computer that can track the current speed, the average speed, the distance covered, the top speed and more. One of the measures is cadence – pedaling speed. Learning to manage cadence is one of the ways in which skilled cyclists develop their racing ability. The faster they can turn the pedals, the more efficiently they can use their energy. I aim for a cadence of 90, so as I cycle I watch the feedback on how I am doing. If the cadence drops below that, then I change my pedaling speed. If I am unable to increase my speed, I change down to a lower gear until I reach my target cadence once more. When neither of these strategies works, I explore my inner state to find ways in which I can tolerate a greater level of discomfort to increase my pedaling power.

This process mirrors the elements of the TOTE. My desired state is a cadence of 90. By watching the bike computer I *test* to see that it stays at that rate. If the feedback I am getting indicates that I have dropped cadence speed, then I *operate* by pedaling faster. If that works (the present state matches the desired state) when I *test* by reading the monitor, then I temporarily *exit*. If by *operating* in that way I do not achieve the desired state, then I carry out another *operation* by changing gear and *test* again. The more *operations* I can carry out, the more likely I am to achieve my desired state and therefore *exit* the TOTE.

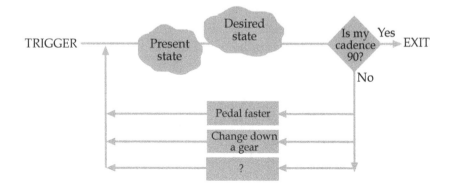

The person with the most flexibility in the way they think and behave is the person most likely to achieve their outcomes. Once we understand how this works for ourselves we can use the same process to coach other people.

The belief that "We have all the resources we ever need" is key to the TOTE process. The question is: How do we find them?

Suppose that you are about to make an important business presentation and you fear you will be unable to handle interaction in the presentation because you are so nervous. Your present state is one of nervousness and your desired state is one of ease, especially ease with your ability to deal with questions.

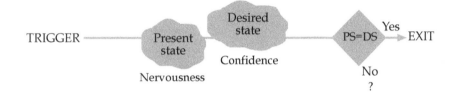

Your present state most certainly does not yet match your desired state. What steps can you take?

1 Identify what you believe you need in order to achieve the desired state. What you identify is an emotional state of confidence. The question is how to obtain it.
2 On the premise that you have this resource already, the question to ask yourself is: Where in my experience (no matter how fleeting) did I have the kind of confidence I want right now? You can find a situation in your experience, even it if is months or years old.
3 Step back into that time (associate) so that you relive it, especially the confidence. To do this it helps to imagine what you were seeing then, what you were hearing and feeling physically, and to do this from your own shoes so that you now re-experience what you were feeling emotionally – that state of confidence.
4 Once you have this, anchor it with a touch, a word or an image and bring the state of confidence back to you in the present as you prepare your thinking for the presentation.
5 Now test again. Does your present state match your desired state? If yes, you have what you want; if no, ask yourself what else you need to realize your desired state.

The person with the most flexibility is the one most likely to achieve their outcome

6 This time you realize that what you need is to build rapport with some of the people who will be at the presentation.

7 Explore and plan ways in which you might do this. You can either imagine yourself doing this to test if that is all you need, or you can do it in reality and go through the TOTE again.

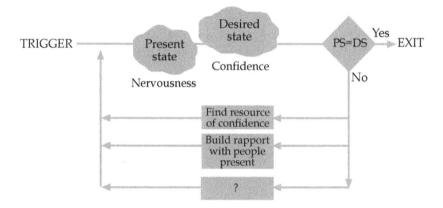

Whatever resource you need, the belief is that somewhere you have it. Examples of emotional resources that we have somewhere in our experience include:

◆ Courage.
◆ Peace of mind.
◆ Enthusiasm.
◆ Motivation.
◆ Determination.
◆ Fun.

We each have our own representation for each of these kinds of big chunk words. What matters is that we know what we need and we know where in our experience we can find it.

RECOGNIZING A STATE OF HIGH POTENTIAL

It is not just knowing what our desired state is, it is important to know how to recognize it when we have it. The value of feedback is that it enables us to regulate what we are doing and how we are doing it. If we know the characteristics of the state we want, we have a means of measuring when we have got there.

Objective, factual feedback is a potent force for change. If we know what characterizes what we want and we know what we have got (and it is not yet the desired state), then we create a tension between the two. This tension is what we might call motivation, and it has a momentum of its own that seeks to close the gap between what we have and what we want.

We can use this knowledge in coaching. For each of us our most influential state is congruence. Congruence is a state of total rapport with ourselves, when all aspects of who we are and what we are doing are in alignment. Sportspeople often call this state the flow zone. It comes as a result of much training and discipline and is the culmination of everything, when the sportsperson can achieve their personal best with effortless ease.

In Chapter 13 I introduced the logical levels of influence model. The same model is a way of thinking about how congruent we are.

1 Think (just briefly) of a time when you felt uncomfortable with what you were doing and how you were doing it. It might have been a time when you felt emotionally uncomfortable and ill at ease with how you were handling a situation. You might have felt that you were violating something you consider to be important or compromising some deeply held beliefs or values. You will have felt in conflict with yourself and possibly you were having an inner dialogue to that effect, to the point where you were unable to give the kind of attention you would truly have liked to the people or the situation.

2 Stand outside of yourself and look and listen to how you were being at that time. What do you notice about your nonverbal behavior? What is characteristic in how you sound? Can you specify your behavior at that time so that you would recognize if you were to be in the same state again?

3 Think of a time (which might be right now) when you felt that what you were doing and how you were doing it were just right for you – a time when your natural abilities just flowed, everything you wanted to achieve seemed to come together, and you felt that your body and mind were saying "Yes" to how you were as a person.

4 Stand outside of yourself and look and listen to how you were being at that time. What is characteristic of you now? If you

Objective feedback is a potent force for change

were to tell someone else, how they could recognize you in this state? What would you tell them?

As a coach you need to be vigilant to spot the difference

One of the roles of a coach is to give this kind of feedback to the person they are coaching. This involves watching and listening to the person you are coaching to such a degree that you can tell when they are in a state of congruence and when they are not. If someone has come to you because they have been in a problem state for some time, you might only get a fleeting glimpse of their congruent state. However, you need to be sufficiently vigilant to catch it when it happens.

Here is an example of what you might see and hear in someone in an incongruent state:

- Tension in the facial muscles.
- Pale complexion.
- Glazed, fixed expression.
- Asymmetrical body posture.
- Reference to problem people by pointing to them in the air outside of themselves.
- Use of the words "must," "try" and "should."
- Emphasis on a problem state characterized by vocabulary such as "don't want," "not" and "never."
- Hesitancy in the voice.
- Lack of resonance in the voice.

And in a congruent state:

- Relaxed facial muscles.
- Flushed complexion.
- Active eye movements.
- Symmetrical body posture.
- Consistent gesturing to within themselves.
- Use of words such as "want to," "can" and "really like."
- Nodding of the head.
- Pauses in the conversation.
- Use of active language.

This will not be the same for everyone. It is your role as a coach to be able to tell the difference and give precise feedback on the characteristics of each state. This is liberating information: once someone has this information they have choice. They can choose whether they stay in a stuck problem state or whether they choose the congruent state (typically a state of self-fulfillment).

THE LADDER TO SUCCESS

What prompts a desire or a need for coaching is usually a state of incongruence. Maybe we feel we are working in a way that contradicts what we think is really important. Or maybe we are contemplating a decision that means sacrificing some of our commitments to people who are important to us. Or perhaps we know that we are just not working to the best of our ability. Whatever the situation, any incongruence will mean that we are limiting or even blocking ourselves from realizing our true potential.

Sometimes this incongruence occurs because we choose to delete what we intuitively know is not right and hope that things will sort themselves out over time. Although this might sometimes happen, it is more likely that things will deteriorate. The longer we ignore the issues, the more of a challenge they become to resolve.

One of the simplest and yet sometimes most powerful ways of using the logical levels of influence model is to coach using questions to chunk up and chunk down the levels to recognize in what ways you are (or are not) making a decision that is congruent. The questions to do this with are shown in the following diagram.

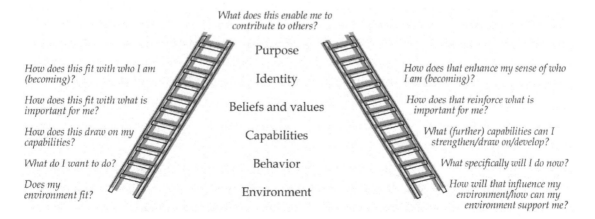

What does this enable me to contribute to others?

Purpose

How does this fit with who I am (becoming)?

Identity

How does that enhance my sense of who I am (becoming)?

How does this fit with what is important for me?

Beliefs and values

How does that reinforce what is important for me?

How does this draw on my capabilities?

Capabilities

What (further) capabilities can I strengthen/draw on/develop?

What do I want to do?

Behavior

What specifically will I do now?

Does my environment fit?

Environment

How will that influence my environment/how can my environment support me?

PRESUPPOSE EXCELLENCE

One of the biggest influences we have as a coach is our belief in the person with whom we are working. If we cannot imagine the person we are coaching achieving the kinds of outcomes they express, or if we cannot imagine them realizing any kind of higher potential, then we should not be coaching them. If, on the other hand, we can imagine this person being the person they want to be or someone realizing a greater potential, then that is what we communicate to them.

If I think of you as stupid, I will engage with the "stupid" part of you. If I think of you as stubborn, that is what I am going to encourage and experience in my dealings with you. If, however, I can see the confident part of you, my interactions with you invite that part of you to emerge. If I can see, hear and feel you letting go of any limiting patterns and being fully and congruently who you are, then that is the "you" that can increasingly emerge.

I see the confident part of you – and that is the part of you with which I engage

Suppose you have a colleague, a member of your family or an associate with whom you feel frustrated. Maybe you feel that they could be achieving more than they currently are. It may be that this person has not excelled in what they have done to date, but coaching is not about facts, it is about processes and beliefs.

Maybe you can recall someone who, irrespective of the facts of the situation, demonstrated a belief in you at a key point in your life to the degree that it inspired you to achieve something beyond anything you had done previously. Perhaps it was a teacher who took a special interest in your emerging talent. Maybe it was a boss who showed a trust in your capabilities. Or maybe it was your parents who stuck by their belief in you no matter what happened. This is the foundation of great coaching.

We influence others by the beliefs we hold in them, irrespective of the facts or the circumstances. Coaching is an emotional process. Think of your children, your family, your colleagues and your associates. Is there any one of them in whom you show this outstanding belief? And is there any one of them about whom you hold any doubt? Your belief can strengthen their belief. Your doubt potentially deepens their doubt. It is your responsibility as a coach to believe in the people you are coaching, whether they are members of your family or people with whom you work.

It is your responsibility to believe in the people you are coaching

How do you strengthen belief? Belief comes from our ability to imagine either ourselves or other people achieving outcomes. If we can see, hear and emotionally experience them realizing their dreams, that translates itself into a belief and we communicate this to them whatever we do and say. Imagine this person realizing a potential beyond the level at which they are currently operating.

One of my colleagues is exceptional in her ability to advise people on issues relating to their image. She sees beauty in everyone she meets.

WHO IS COACHING WHOM?

When someone comes to me for a coaching session for the first time and tells me their issue, one of my first reactions is to ask myself, "Do I want to deal with this issue in my life right now?" Coaching is a mutual process. I can only offer the structure of what I have managed for myself or what I am managing for myself in my life at this time.

Coaching as a mutual process

In essence, when we interact with another person we are one system. We are not "doing coaching" to others, we are part of a coaching system. What we offer is what we receive and what we receive and accept for ourselves is what we can give.

With the people we are coaching, we bring out and engage with those parts of ourselves that we need to resolve or that we have resolved and for which we can now be an example.

We teach what we need the most. I may not behave in exactly the same way as the people I am coaching, but I will have a parallel structure or capability in my experience. For example:

We teach what we need the most

What I experience in the other person	What I am doing
They are dismissive in the way they speak to colleagues.	I am dismissive in the way I speak to my family.
They avoid making a commitment to change.	I avoid commitment to one of my stated outcomes.
They are aggressively focused on what they want and insensitive to the needs of others in the way they behave in a meeting.	I am single-mindedly aggressive in my focus on my work goals and oblivious to the effect on my friends and family.

However, while I am resolving issues for myself, I begin to recognize and consequently reinforce these kinds of issues in others. For example:

Issues you might deal with personally

Your willingness to let go of something of material importance to you.

Your ability to tell someone close to you how much you care for/love them.

A decision to reinvent yourself and move on to new approaches or new business.

Your ability to let go of trying to control others (family members or work colleagues) and let them find their own solutions.

Issues you might support in others

Their ability to let go of behaviors, people or material possessions that are familiar and comfortable yet limiting.

Their ability to forgive and let go of past judgments and be intimate.

Their ability to let go of the must haves or the should haves to have what they really want despite the cost.

Their ability truly to delegate and give people the space to find their own motivation.

SHORTCUT TO COACHING

The best coaching is the simplest coaching. NLP is a state of interest and curiosity. Applying these two principles, here is a shortcut to coaching.

1 Invite someone to tell you an issue for which they would like new choices or increased understanding.
2 Get into a state of curiosity and acceptance.
3 Get yourself into a similar posture and way of moving as the other person. This is approximate – you don't have to mimic. Think of yourself as being connected to them.
4 Listen intently to what they are telling you. Mentally note the words they are using and the gestures they are making.
5 Ask them clean questions (see Chapter 6), using only the words they give you. Don't in any way try to give suggestions or make changes to what they are saying, just be curious to the degree that you understand fully what they are saying, only exploring those aspects of the situation that they are giving you.
6 Summarize back to them from time to time, using their language. Keep to their vocabulary and use their nonverbal style of communicating when you do this summary.
7 While they are talking, identify how you have the structure of this issue within yourself too and how you either have dealt with or are dealing with it in your life.
8 Imagine the other person achieving what they really want. See, hear and feel it until you believe that they are capable of

a greater potential than they have demonstrated to date, either with respect to this issue or in their life as a whole. Think this as you speak to them (keep this vision to yourself).

9   Give them feedback on the distinctions between what you experience as their incongruent and then their congruent state.

10 Recognize that the person is bringing this issue to you so that you can learn too.

11 Reinforce their learning by running it through the levels of influence with them.

12 Summarize what you have heard and what you believe the other person is feeling.

13 Ask them if there is anything else they want to talk about.

SUMMARY

NLP high-performance coaching is founded on the study of our subjective experience. By discovering how we structure our memories, our imagination and our thoughts, we can find out how we are making our work and our life exactly what they are.

THOUGHT PROVOKERS

1   Ask a colleague or friend if they will take part in an exercise with you. Tell them you are going to talk with them about their goals. Ask them to tell you about their progress toward their goals. For the first few minutes (no more than that), think about how *unlikely* it is that they will achieve their goals. Think of the difficulties and the impossibility of what they are saying. You do not have to say what you are thinking, but do engage in some interaction with them as they are speaking.

    After a few minutes, change your thinking so that you are imagining them achieving all they are saying and more. Picture what they are doing and hear how they sound in this future desired state. Notice how you feel toward them as you do this and engage with them as they continue to tell you about these goals. Do this for a few minutes or more.

    At the end of this time, ask your colleague how they felt during the conversation. Did they notice or experience any differences in how you were toward them or even how they felt about themselves? Did you notice any changes in their responses to you as you changed your inner thinking? What were they?

2 Think of someone with whom you find it difficult to work. Ask yourself about the image of this person that you have had prior to and during each interaction you have experienced as difficult.

Now think of someone you find easy and a pleasure to deal with. What is in your mind before and during your interactions with them?

3 Think of an outcome that you want to achieve in your life or your work right now. What is your desired state? What is your present state? What quality do you need to find in yourself to begin to bridge the gap between the two? How might you re-experience that quality so that you can bring it to bear on the outcome that you want to achieve today?

4 Think of someone in your work, your personal life and your community you don't get on with as well as you might. What is it about each of them that you feel is the cause of the difficulty? How is the aspect of each that you have identified true about you?

5 Think of someone in your work, your personal life and your community you do get on well with. What is it about each of them that you admire? How is that aspect of each true about you?

6 Who are people who have believed in you during your life? What effect did they have on you?

REFERENCES

John Whitmore (2009) *Coaching for Performance: GROWing Human Potential and Purpose – The Principles and Practice of Coaching and Leadership*, Nicholas Brealey Publishing.

Robert Dilts already knew this strategy when a young boy who had been categorized as learning disabled was brought to him to see if Robert could help him progress with his learning. The boy was 11 years old and was believed to be unable to spell.

Robert and he got talking and it emerged that the boy loved watching films. Robert asked him what his favorite film was.

"Star Wars," he replied.

He then asked the boy who was his favorite character in the film and he said it was the Wookie (a large, bear-like creature).

Robert asked the boy if he would be willing to play a game and he agreed. He asked the boy if he could see the Wookie now and the boy looked up momentarily and said he could. Robert asked him if he could make the Wookie put his arms out horizontally by his sides (he demonstrated this) and the boy (looking up again) said yes.

"Now," said Robert, "I want you to hang some letters underneath the Wookie's arm – put a P, now an H and then an E underneath his arm side by side." He paused between each one. "Have you done that?"

The boy nodded.

"Can you make the Wookie open his mouth?"

Again, the boy nodded.

"I want you to see the Wookie open his mouth and you will see some letters come out. The first letter is N. Can you do that?"

Once again a nod.

"Now see the Wookie open his mouth again and this time the letter that comes out is an O. And again and this time the letter is M and finally as the Wookie opens his mouth again an M comes out. And now an E. Have you done that?"

"Yes," said the boy, although Robert already knew the answer.

"Finally I want you to hang some more letters under the Wookie's other arm. First an N now an O and now an N."

When the boy indicated that he had done all of that, Robert said to him, "Now tell me what letters are hanging under the Wookie's right arm" (he indicated which arm he meant).

The boy said without hesitation "P, H, E."

"And now the Wookie is opening his mouth and the letters are coming out again – what are they?"

"N, O, M, E" the boy replied.

"And now tell me the letters hanging under the Wookie's left arm."

"N, O, N," said the boy, who had just spelt (without hesitation) PHENOMENON.

22
Heal through humor

Laughter is carbonated holiness -Anne Lamott

Something happens in our brain when we laugh

Provocative = to provoke a healing response

What does laughter have to do with excellence? Surely excellence is a serious affair and no laughing matter? Well, am about to dispel that myth. The ability to stand back and laugh a ourselves has to be one of the surest ways of cutting through the wel of tangled myths we create.

Something happens in our brain when we laugh. Change happens We hotwire the lifeless engine in our mind that has become stuck with too much serious deliberation to the source of energy that can spark us into life again. Being able to laugh at ourselves implies that we car stand back to see and hear ourselves, and that is part of the remedy When we are stuck in only our own perception of a scenario, we have limited choice. Standing back enables us to discover a horizon way beyond the old boundary fence with which we have hemmec ourselves in.

Think of the people you admire, people you hold up as models o excellence. I would be prepared to wager that many of them have the ability to laugh at themselves, to laugh with others and to generate humor. Humor has always been a part of NLP in the way it is taught When Richard Bandler and John Grinder began their research into excellence, one of the first people they modeled was Frank Farrelly already famous for his provocative therapy. Provocative can mear many things and in the context of the way Frank worked it meant to provoke a healing response - part of that healing takes place through laughter.

Research has shown that the ability to laugh at the same things is one of the ingredients for a successful relationship, and tha incompatibility in what we find amusing can be the deciding factor in whether or not two people stay together. It is also now believed that humor has played a key role in the development of human beings as the species that we are today (good and bad!). What we do know is that when we laugh we lower our stress levels and boost our immunity and human growth hormones. Simultaneously, we lower the incidence of those hormones that cause obstructions in our arteries and we decrease our blood pressure.

When we laugh we decrease our blood pressure

Laughter is a mechanism for change and healing and is present in most models of excellence. So it is surprising that so many coaches expect to be serious in their interactions with their clients!

There are many books on NLP, but few that describe the use of humor and its power to heal, to strip away the patterns of sabotage to get to the truth and to build instant and powerful rapport. It is often the way that the piece that makes the difference is omitted. The key to our excellence often lies in the very things that we take for granted and consciously delete.

The key to excellence lies in the things we take for granted

When I first met David Hemery and John Whitmore and experienced their GROW model of coaching, I was overwhelmed by their amazing ability to build rapport with the people they were coaching. And yet at first the concept of rapport was not something they included in their writing. They took for granted one of the things that they did with astounding excellence. They do now include it, and I recommend that not only do you read John's book, you also experience their amazing skills in action.

The whole approach that is provocative coaching or therapy is too big a subject to be covered here, but I will outline some of the key elements and hope that whets your appetite to find out more. See the end of the chapter for further references.

What I do offer in this chapter is how, as a coach or just as someone who wants to connect quickly and powerfully at a deep level with others, you can access this liberating humor. The elements here are based on my years of modeling Frank Farrelly in action and observing humor at work in everyday work and personal contexts. Humor has become increasingly a part of my style of training.

HOW DOES HUMOR WORK?

Laughter affects the way
we think

Humor changes the way we experience our issues. Laughter affects our physiology, our muscle tension, the way we think. When we are immersed in our issues and overwhelmed with the emotions that accompany them, it is just about impossible, to engage objective thought. When we get absorbed into a problem we tend to think about it more and more. And the more we think about it, the more intellectually absorbing it becomes. We cut the grooves deeper that take us down that old familiar path. Thinking about the issue in the way we have always thought about it doesn't get us any nearer to our ideal state. We need to find a way to break out of this self-defeating spiral.

Humor does just that. When we can laugh at ourselves and our situation, we have detached ourselves from the original debilitating emotions. The moment we detach we bring a new, healthier perspective to what we have been experiencing.

WHAT KIND OF HUMOR?

Humor takes many forms: laughing at a joke, for example, or being able to tell a funny story. There are stand-up comedians who can recite strings of jokes; there are those like Billy Connolly, Jack Dee and Eddie Izzard who can talk about everyday life in a way that makes others laugh. Their observation and outrageous translation of events and timing can change everyday situations into entertaining events.

"In this sense, a person with a 'good sense of humour' is one who can see him or herself and others in the world in a somewhat distanced and detached way. They view life from an altered perspective from which they can laugh at, yet remain in contact with and emotionally involved with people and events in a positive way. Such a person has the ability to perceive life comically and maintains love or respect for him/herself and humanity in general."

Raymond Moody

Le rire, comme les essuie-
glaces, permet d'avancer
même s'il n'arrête pas la
pluie. –Gérard Jugnot

The consequence of being able to perceive life in this way is that anyone who can do so not only has the facility to help themselves take a healthy perspective on life and its events, they can also facilitate and coach that in others.

WHOLE BODY WISDOM

Logic and reason may work with scientific and technical problems, but with the challenges life throws at us we need to be able to engage our intuitive, whole body wisdom. In some instances intellectual reasoning can take us deeper into the issue and may even be the source of it. In these instances we need to find a way to experience the issue differently.

An interesting phenomenon is that we cannot think and laugh at the same time. Laughter creates a multitude of changes: our muscles lose their tension ("we go weak with laughter"), our bodies shake, we lose the ability to hold on to things tightly (and that is an interesting metaphor for change), we seem to create the ability to create new connections in our brain so that we perceive situations differently. The submodalities of the way we represent a situation change when we laugh and therefore our experience of the issue changes with that.

We cannot think and laugh at the same time

FIRST AMUSE YOURSELF

The starting place is you. How can we ever hope to trigger humor in others and encourage them to take a humorous stance on life if we are unable to do so ourselves? Each of us has a unique sense of humor; I'm not just talking about laughing at funny incidents but taking a humorous perspective on life.

Begin by asking yourself some questions:

1 When did you last laugh at yourself?
2 When did you laugh at yourself in the most intense way?
3 Whereabouts were you?
4 What was happening?
5 In what way were you laughing? What is it like to laugh like this?
6 What happened just before you started to laugh – what is the trigger?

7 What happens in you as you laugh?

8. What else is there about the way you laugh?

9 Is there anyone who triggers your ability to laugh at yourself? If so, how do they do this?

What have you learnt about your humor by answering these questions? I suppose there is another possibility: you don't laugh! If that is the case, you might just skip the rest of this chapter and concentrate on the other stuff in the book. Not everyone can find insights in life in this way. Or maybe it is time for you to experiment with what might work for you and therefore this chapter really is for you!

How might you now use the learning you have from answering these questions? For example, now you know what triggers your laughter, how might you trigger this for yourself? Do it now.

1 Think of a situation for which you would like a breakthrough or some insight and a way forward.

2 Identify the trigger that precedes moments when you find a way to laugh at yourself.

3 Apply that trigger now.

4 Remember your physiology when you laugh. Adopt that physiology if you have not already done so.

5 Identify that person who triggers laughter for you. Imagine that they are doing that now for you in this situation.

6 What is happening?

7 How are you experiencing the situation?

What have you learnt by applying these questions to yourself?

Linda realized that the occasions when she laughed at herself were when she stood back and saw and heard herself as if she were an outsider. She assumed the style of her mother, who had invariably been able to see the funny side to a situation. She realized that when she did this she often created an absurdly metaphorical way of seeing the situation and when she exaggerated that, her whole perspective on situations changed. When she did this she was also aware that instead of holding her shoulders in a hunched, tense way, she let them drop and relaxed her jaw and face muscles. It was like letting go of a burden she had been carrying.

She had recently been feeling very frustrated by the lack of support from the rest of her family in the care of her elderly parents and she realized that she was getting more and more frustrated as time went on. She remembered her way of breaking out of such negative patterns and she imagined herself standing back and seeing herself, her parents and the rest of the family. She relaxed her shoulders and stretched. She acknowledged that she had put herself into the role of martyr and she imagined herself sitting in this huge chair with "martyr" written on the back of it. She also appreciated that this chair was one of her own choosing and it was getting bigger day by day. It wasn't an interior design that she liked, so she rearranged the furniture and threw out the martyr chair. As she did so in her imagination she found herself amused by the whole situation. Coincidentally, she subsequently talked to her family about the care that was needed and enlisted their help. She lost her feelings of frustration.

We can only facilitate in others what we have the structure for in ourselves. So finding the ability to laugh at ourselves really is the starting point.

HUMOR: THE ANTIDOTE TO RESCUE

"There is little success where there is little laughter."

Andrew Carnegie

As a coach, trainer, manager or friend, we are often faced with people with "issues." It may be that someone is not performing in their job in the way that we would expect. It might be that we have a "tricky" delegate who does not seem to get closure on their issues, or it might be a friend who is airing some of their problems. It may be a genuine request for help, in which case we might coach the person; but it might not, and it is important to recognize this. Humor can be the way to avoid the trap that awaits us.

One of the greatest temptations for a new coach or therapist is to sympathize with and want to help the client. It is a natural reaction and at the same time can be one of the most unhelpful things we can do.

When I first learnt to coach I thought I was God's gift to the coaching world. If someone presented just the hint of a problem I was in there feet first, offering to coach and sometimes not even offering, just getting stuck in. I cringe when I think about it now.

THE DRAMA TRIANGLE

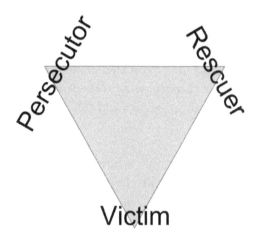

The temptation to help when uninvited drops you straight into the role of rescuer and into the unhealthy dynamic of the Drama Triangle. The Drama Triangle is a game (you can read more about games in Eric Berne's work; see the reference at the end of the chapter). Games are familiar patterns of behavior that we find ourselves repeating out of habit and that result in a lose/lose outcome. There are no winners in these kinds of games. The only win is that we prove to ourselves that we were right all along not to trust, not to believe, not to respect! Not a recipe for excellence.

Once we engage in the game, we are destined not only to fulfill the role of rescuer, but to find ourselves moving to the other roles of victim and persecutor too. I give uninvited help. The person on the receiving end persecutes me for not actually helping and blames me for the outcome. I move to persecute them by criticizing them for not valuing my help and for being so ungrateful. And so it continues.

This game can emerge anywhere in any context, but it finds a fertile feeding ground in training programs and coaching sessions.

THE STRUCTURE OF HUMOR

In studying all forms of humor we discover that there is a structure. We are amused when the brain experiences something that surprises it. This is apparent even in very young children; hence the success of games like peek-a-boo that rely on timing and surprise to trigger laughter.

Ken, who rarely showed public appreciation for his wife, was commenting on her cooking (which was outstanding): "With a wife who cooks like that you would think..." Before he could finish his sentence with "you would be fat!" this was drowned out by an interruption from one of the guests: "you would be on your knees worshipping her!"

The tactic of interrupt and surprise is a hypnotic strategy. When our expected process is interrupted we go into trance. This is an opportunity both to trigger laughter and to change simultaneously. It is a powerful and rapid agent for change.

When I was traveling on an airline recently, the steward made the usual announcement: "Please remember that it is not permitted to smoke until you have left the airport premises. And If I may be allowed to add a bit of personal advice, for your own health I would advise you not to smoke at all!" The passengers laughed and most thanked and joked with this steward as they left the plane.

The ability to recognize patterns, which we do unconsciously, sets us apart from the rest of the animal kingdom. To be called "quick witted" is considered a compliment in most cultures. The necessary element of surprise in humor means that our attention is drawn to the aspects of the exchange that are novel and unexpected.

"After starting a new diet I altered my drive to work to avoid passing my favorite bakery. I accidentally drove by the bakery this morning, and as I approached, there in the windows were a host of goodies. I felt this was no accident, so I prayed, 'Lord, it's up to you, if you want me to have any of those delicious goodies, create a parking place for me directly in front of the bakery.' And sure enough, on the eighth time around the block, there it was! God is so good!"

Wait upon the Lord, courtesy of Frank Farrelly

FACILITATING HUMOR FOR OTHERS

How can we find a way for others to take a humorous perspective on themselves and others? The objective is to get them to laugh at themselves and to see the absurdity in continuing to experience the issue as they have been doing. In other words, the objective is to facilitate a shift in the way they experience a situation so that they free up all the resources they ideally have at their fingertips.

There are many books that explore examples of humor and people who are able to generate laughter, but few that explain how to do it.

Just this morning we were in the café in the local village. The owner of this café, Jean-Christophe, is renowned for keeping all of his customers in a constant state of amusement. There is always laughter and smiles and the café is usually full.

I watched Jean-Christophe as he greeted and served his customers. He always has a twinkle in his eye; he appears to be waiting for the opportunity to laugh and create laughter. There is always the beginning of a smile on his face. Something signals that he expects humor to be present at any time and if he sees an opportunity (which he does most of the time) then he makes it happen. He gives full attention to everyone and is often "playing the audience" so that he has the whole of the café in his sights. He pauses before he responds and in that pause makes an exaggerated gesture of some kind. It might be hand on hips if he is exaggerating surprise, or he might tilt his head back with an astonished look on his face. His movements are marked and his expectation of humor triggers them. His café is a great place to start the day. And many people do just that...

When facilitating humor, some of things it will help you to know or discover about the other person are:

1 What is their kind of humor? What sorts of things amuse them?
2 In what circumstances do they take a humorous perspective on life?
3 In what contexts does this happen?
4 What naturally triggers this state: what happens just before?

5 What anchors work for them most readily, so that you know how to anchor the state and trigger it again?

6 How do you communicate to them in a way that they recognize that you care about them and have their best interests at heart?

7 Where are their areas of vulnerability, where do they defend themselves?

You might have learnt this about the person over time and therefore you know how to trigger humor in them. But let us suppose that you are meeting someone for the first time and you know very little about them. What then?

1 Choose a state of connectedness. First and foremost, check your own state. It is important that you are in a state of care and connectedness with the other person, a state of rapport. You don't have to know someone to have this state; you can assume it. Remind yourself of a time when you have been in this state with others: maybe out socially, at ease with close friends, when you could tease each other and yet be speaking truths and knowing that it was all done in love. This is the state you want. Take yourself back to this time and anchor this state (see Chapter 12 on anchoring). With this state in place, now consider the person you are about to meet or have just met and assume this rapport with them.

2 Be sensitive. Ensure that you are also in a state of high sensitivity to the other person, what they do and how they respond to you. Note especially their nonverbal behavior. Notice muscle tension, skin flushing, repeated mannerisms and if they change, any exclamations, eye movements or internal processing. Calibrate to their different states so that you begin to know when they are in their head answering intellectually and when they are off guard, taken by surprise. Note especially when they have let down every barrier and are just laughing and going with the flow, not seeking to control or defend anything. This latter state is the one you are after. This state presupposes that the other person trusts you and themselves to enjoy and learn in the moment.

CREATE A STATE OF LAUGHTER

The meaning of the communication is the effect. What works? Explore how you create a state of humor in someone else and build on it. Pay attention to what it is that is creating that state and, just as you might build on a "yes" state in hypnosis, build on the state of laughter or humor.

1   Pay attention to *how* the other person behaves and *mirror* that in an exaggerated way. Pay little attention to what they say. Pay most attention to how they behave and how they present themselves. You can encourage the humorous perspective by highlighting how the way they respond to people and situations is crazy or ridiculous. Rather than tell them, show them.

   One way of testing what changes their state is to mirror back to them their behavior in an exaggerated way. If they are tense, you tense up even more, but do so with a mannerism that signals humor. This might be a slight smile. The overemphasis of the behavior itself usually acts as a signal. This mirroring back or caricaturing is one of the most naturally occurring sources of humor that I witness.

   Rather than mirror, you might play the counter hand. So if someone is being firm and aggressive, you might feign fear. Or if they are being aggrieved, you might act even more aggrieved at the situation but in an amateurish, acting way. Remember to keep checking the state of connectedness with the other person. Maintain rapport. If at any time you sense you might be losing that, go back and restore it.

2   Agree with the problem. Agree with whatever they say, especially the problem. If they say there is no hope for them in their work, agree with them, in a "tongue in cheek" way that signals humor. This can provoke a healthy defensive state in which they come back and disagree with you (and of course with the way they originally presented the issue).

In a talk I was giving about the diverse cultural applications of NLP, I was challenged by a member of the audience to prove how NLP could be used in their country (as they didn't believe it could be applied there). I agreed with them and replied that they were probably right, it could be applied in most countries but, now that they mention it, maybe not theirs. I said this with a wry smile. They immediately came back with: "Why not?"

3   Exaggerate the problem state with wild generalizations: "Well, all men are like that!" "No one ever believes a word we say!" "All children are brats!" "What can you expect, you are young and good looking, no one is going to take you seriously!" Always with a twinkle in your eye and a smile.

4   Give outrageous reasons for the person keeping the problem state. In the previous example I suggested it would be good for the world to have an NLP-free zone – a zone that could be free of any awareness of excellence – and that their country could be the prime candidate for that. When you do this, when you don't cooperate with their "victim" role, you signal something very important: that you are not going to collude with the unconscious negative game they are playing with themselves.

5   Make insane suggestions. Give the wildest suggestions for how to overcome the issue. The bizarre often triggers humor. Offering outrageous suggestions is more likely to prompt the other person to start coming up with their own, "more practical" ideas. You playing the fool helps them to realize that they must be able to come up with something better than this!

6   Exaggerate the symptoms and invite the other person to do the same. Ask them just how stressed, frustrated, depressed or angry they can get. If they can exaggerate the symptoms and be amused at their skill, they can also diminish them.

These are all possibilities and you will be able to find your own strategies for taking a humorous perspective on life too. The key is to try different strategies till you find what works and when you have that, play with it. Make it conscious and enjoy the change!

SUMMARY

Humor is a fast track to rapport, to influence and to change. Everyone has a unique sense of humor and we are usually unaware of how significant a role it plays in our everyday life and work. Humor is rarely taught in the halls of persuasion, negotiation, coaching and leadership – it is so vital, yet we often overlook it as something worthy of study and attention.

"If God is watching the least we can do is be entertaining!"   *– Anon*

THOUGHT PROVOKERS

1   Think of a time when you had this kind of rapport with someone who brought a personal problem to you, a time when you both found a way to laugh at what had been happening. What was that like as you remember it? How might you access that state again when you choose?
2   Identify someone you know either personally or remotely who uses an approach like this successfully. What characteristics do you think make the difference? Which of those characteristics might you adopt in order to experiment?
3   Choose one or two of the tactics and plan how you might experiment with them in a safe environment – perhaps asking a friend if they would cooperate with you as you learn.
4   Attend a training program for Provocative Coaching.

REFERENCES

Eric Berne (1973) *Games People Play*, Penguin.
Alastair Clarke (2008) *The Pattern Recognition Theory of Humour*, Pyrrhic House.
Frank Farrelly (1989) *Provocative Therapy*, Meta Publications.
Thomas Harris (1005) *I'm OK, You're OK*, Arrow Books.
Raymond A Moody (1978) *Laugh after Laugh*, Headwaters Press.

For videos of Frank Farrelly at work, visit www.youtube.com, www.nlp3.com and www.provocativetherapy.com.

A store that sells husbands has just opened in New York City, where a woman may go to choose a husband. Among the instructions at the entrance is a description of how the store operates: You may visit the store ONLY ONCE!

There are six floors and the attributes of the men increase as the shopper ascends the flights. There is, however, a catch. You may choose any man from a particular floor, or you may choose to go up a floor, but you cannot go back down except to exit the building!

So, a woman goes to the Husband Store to find a husband. On the first floor the sign on the door reads: Floor 1 – These men have jobs and love the Lord.

The second floor sign reads: Floor 2 – These men have jobs, love the Lord, and love kids.

The third floor sign reads: Floor 3 – These men have jobs, love the Lord, love kids, and are extremely good looking.

"Wow," she thinks, but feels compelled to keep going.

She goes to the fourth floor and the sign reads: Floor 4 – These men have jobs, love the Lord, love kids, are drop-dead good looking and help with the housework.

"Oh, mercy me!" she exclaims, "I can hardly stand it!" Still, she goes to the fifth floor and the sign reads: Floor 5 – These men have jobs, love the Lord, love kids, are drop-dead gorgeous, help with the housework, and have a strong romantic streak.

She is so tempted to stay, but she goes to the sixth floor and the sign reads: Floor 6 – You are visitor 4,363,012 to this floor. There are no men on this floor. This floor exists solely as proof that women are impossible to please. Thank you for shopping at the Husband Store. Watch your step as you exit the building, and have a nice day!

This is for all men for a good laugh and to all the women who can handle the truth!

Husband Store, one of Frank Farrelly's large collection of stories.

Glossary

Anchoring The process of making associations that work through conscious choice so that you can reaccess your own or trigger others' chosen state when appropriate.

Association The state of being inside your skin, seeing the world from your own eyes, hearing the world from your own ears, and feeling the emotions of the situation, whether current, remembered or imagined.

Beliefs Emotionally held opinions treated as facts and the basis of our everyday decisions, skills and behaviors.

Clean questions A nondirective tool for facilitating people to explore their experience and how it is structured in their own way. In particular, a means for exploring the metaphors by which people live their lives.

Congruence Having all parts of yourself working in harmony, without conflict.

Criteria The values and standards used as the basis for decisions.

Dissociation The state of observing yourself as if you were an outsider. Seeing and hearing yourself from the outside, i.e. you can see you in your entirety, not the way you see yourself from within your own body. The effect of dissociation is to disconnect from emotion.

Eye accessing cues Movements of a person's eyes that indicate visual, auditory or feelings thinking.

Filters Levels of thinking that determine where you put your attention, how you make your perception what it is, and what defines how you respond to situations and people.

Linguistic The study of language and, in the context of NLP, the patterns in language that communicate your thinking strategies.

Logical levels of change A form of personal and organizational hierarchy that affects change and how effectively you bring about change for yourself or for others, consisting of environment, behavior, capabilities, values, beliefs, identity and spirituality or systems.

Metaphor A parallel means of describing or observing. Metaphors can be parables, stories, analogies, pictures and actions.

Modeling The process of unpacking your own and others' conscious and especially unconscious strategies in order to duplicate the results.

Neuro The way you use your brain.

Neuro linguistic programming Defined as the study of the structure of subjective experience. The name was developed by John Grinder and Richard Bandler in 1975. It is a process of modeling and increasingly the term is used to encompass the techniques and skills uncovered as a result of this process.

Outcome (well-formed) A goal that is characteristic of someone who consistently achieves what they want in ways that are a win for others as well as themselves. Different from traditional methods of goal setting in that it involves the use of all senses, including emotion.

Pacing Respecting the values, needs and style of another person in a way that leads to rapport. Going along with aspects of what is important to another person and yourself.

Perceptual positions The mental strategy used by skillful negotiators, involving moving mentally between being in your own shoes, the shoes of the other person and an outside detached position. There is an old Indian saying, "You must first walk two moons in a man's moccasins before you can understand him."

Programming Not the computer kind, but similar in that it is to do with the sequences of thinking and behavior patterns that constitute your strategies for achieving the results you do.

Provocative coaching (therapy) A system of psychotherapy/coaching in which the therapist plays devil's advocate, siding with the negative half of the client's ambivalence toward their life's goals, their relationships, their work and the structures within which they live. The approach, based on Frank Farrelly's life's work, is designed to provoke a healing response through humor and love.

Rapport The ability to relate to yourself and others in ways that create a climate of respect, trust and cooperation.

Reframing The ability to make meanings for events in ways that work for you and create desirable emotional states.

State The mental, physical and emotional condition of a person.

Strategies A set of thinking and behavioral steps to achieve a result.

TOTE Test→operate→test→exit, the feedback loop used to guide behavior.

Well-formed outcomes *See* Outcomes.

Acknowledgments

Spence, my husband. We are a team. What I do I do because of you and with you and for you. You are my critic, companion, bag carrier, chef, web-boy, gardener, lover, friend, pool maintenance man, geek extraordinaire, problem solver, Quantum, Maths and Metaphor presenter, course assistant, coach, joker and so much more. Thank you.

Nicholas Brealey, my publisher who sticks with me through new ideas, draft and sometimes daft proposals, outrageous suggestions, but finally helps me through to the books that make the difference for me and my life.

All my Indian friends. India has become our second love (after France) and it is because of you: Ashok, Arul and Anand and the home you have created for us there. What we do in India is only possible because of you.

Mitt, our architect in France, who created a space that is the perfect metaphor for our ideal selves. We still have to pinch ourselves to believe that dreams can come true in the way that they have here.

David Grove, originator of clean language and symbolic modeling, who so very sadly died early in 2008. And to Penny Tompkins and James Lawley who had the foresight to model David so that we have access to some of his groundbreaking work with metaphor.

My Mum, who died four years ago now. She would still have been asking: "Susan, another book! Where does it all come from?" I wonder!

Gene Early and Frank Farrelly who, in very different ways, have both been powerful and ever-present influences on the success I have in the way I work. Your legacy to me is the way I work and influence others. Your lessons ripple out to thousands.

Everyone who has been a delegate on my courses. You are my inspiration and my source of thoughts and ideas. I love every moment with you all. You are all my favorites!

And my supporting team in the office and on the courses. Thank you for your generosity in the way that you dedicate yourselves to the learning.

And of course, last but most certainly first and foremost, my sons, James and Alex. You are my *raison d'être*. I love you in a way that is beyond all words.

And I owe everything to the grace that I have been given in doing what I do and the way in which I do it. The blessings I have been given in my life are indeed beyond understanding.

Taking your learning further

Sue Knight provides in-house training and open programmes leading to recognized certification in NLP. For examples of in-house training programmes, take a look at www.sueknight.co.uk. These include teambuilding, leadership, influencing skills and many more, all tailored to clients' needs.

Open programmes leading to certification in NLP follow these stages:

* **Stage 1 – Introduction to NLP**, a practical and comprehensive introduction to the foundations of NLP.
* **Stage 2 – Business Practitioner training**, leading to certification in NLP. This programme covers the material that is included in this book.
* **Stage 3 – Master Practitioner training**, advanced programme leading to certification, concentrating on the skills of modelling and centred around delegates' modelling projects.
* **Stage 4 – Trainer training**, not only for trainers but for anyone who wishes to learn how to communicate and train or coach others in the principles of NLP. Successful completion of this programme gives you the authority to issue NLP certification to others on acceptance by the Association for NLP.
* **Stage 5 – Masterclasses**.

At the time of writing, Sue is running these programmes in the UK, France, Denmark, Portugal, Ecuador and India and more countries are coming on line with her work every year.

Sue Knight can be contacted at:

PO Box 1008, Slough, Berkshire SL1 8DB, UK

Telephone: +44 (0)1628 604438, Email: sue@sueknight.co.uk Website: www.sueknight.com

Sue Knight works both in the UK and internationally. She collaborates with consultancies and training centres throughout the world who work to similar values. These are listed below with contact numbers for each. If any company would like to discuss future collaboration and inclusion in this list, please contact Sue Knight on sue@sueknight.co.uk.

AUSTRALIA

Universal Events, Australia's largest NLP training company, was established by Karen Corban in 1993 to provide people with the world's leading NLP training and resources. Our mission is to provide information to support individuals and companies to fast track their success and achieve their greatest potential.

We are committed to learning and sharing knowledge with people to help enhance their lives. The values that we aspire to are integrity, passion, growth, service, support, love, continuous learning, commitment, excellence and fun.

We believe that NLP changes people's lives in the shortest amount of time and offers people the opportunity for fast and lasting change. We hold the belief that anything is possible and that it is easy to transform and live the life of your dreams.

Universal Events, Suite 513, 15 Lime St, Sydney NSW 2000, Australia

Telephone: +61 2 9925 8000, Fax: +61 29925 8099

Email: info@universalevents.com.au, Website: www.universalevents.com.au

CANADA

Success Strategies/Stratégies de réussite is an international training and consulting company specializing in communication and influencing. We help solve impossible communication problems.

Success Strategies' president, Shelle Rose Charvet, is author of the international bestseller *Words That Change Minds: Mastering the Language of Influence*. This book describes the below-conscious motivation triggers that drive people's behaviour, based on the applied NLP model called the Language and Behaviour Profile.

1264 Lemonville Road, Burlington, ON, Canada L7R 3X5
Telephone: +1 (905) 639 6468, Fax: +1 (905) 639 4220
Email: info@successstrategies.com, Website: www.successstrategies.com

INDIA

Shinota, founded by S. Ashok in 2001, is one of the premier training institutes in India, spearheading the spread of NLP in the country. The main objective of this institution is to support people in their journey from "Shinota," and to serve as a resource centre, for those who crave to unleash the infinite power from within.

Our mission is to improve the quality of life of people by aiding them to rediscover themselves. Our vision is to make a significant and constructive difference in the lives of at least 1,000,000 people.

We hold introductory lectures and Business Practitioner training, Master Practitioner Training, Trainer Training and Masterclasses in various states in India, most especially in Kerala and the Himalayas, supported and contributed to by Sue Knight. We also run short lectures every week on selected NLP topics. These are open to the public. We cater to students and the staff of leading educational institutions and colleges on an invitation basis. Business consultancy to corporates based on NLP and TQM concepts for building sustainable change is our speciality area, where we attempt some new models for excellence, on a research basis for selective companies.

Shinota Consulting, 10A New Co-operative Colony, Krishnagiri-635001, Tamil Nadu, India
Telephone: (+91) 4343 233333, Fax (+91) 4343 233363, Cell phone: +91 94484 55556
Email: office@shinota.com, Website: www.shinota.com

USA

NLP University was founded by Todd Epstein and Robert Dilts and is now run by Robert Dilts, Judith Delozier and Teresa Epstein.

We at NLPU like to offer a comprehensive education in NLP, including a sense of the history and development of the discipline, as well as the most recent developments.

NLP University is dedicated to presenting the best possible NLP seminars to the international NLP community and we are proud of our legacy as the home of NLP and a catalyst where people gather to research and develop the future of NLP. We are committed to bringing the best trainers in the world to NLP University, each year, to teach the latest and most comprehensive range of NLP seminars available. NLPU is the place where the latest developments, generative applications and creative activity in the field of NLP are most focused. Above all, NLPU is a place to live the NLP presuppositions with a group of peers – in other words, to create a real-life reference experience for an NLP community.

NLP University, P. O. Box 1112, Ben Lomond, CA 95005, USA
Phone: +1 (831) 336-3457, Fax: +1 (831) 336-5854
Email: teresanlp@aol.com, Website: www.nlpu.com